Public Television in the Digital Era

Also by Petros Iosifidis

EUROPEAN TELEVISION INDUSTRIES
(*with J. Steemers and M. Wheeler*)

Public Television in the Digital Era

Technological Challenges and New Strategies for Europe

Petros Iosifidis
City University, London

© Petros Iosifidis 2007
Softcover reprint of the hardcover 1st edition 2007 978-1-4039-8961-1

All rights reserved. No reproduction, copy or transmission of this publication may be made without written permission.

No paragraph of this publication may be reproduced, copied or transmitted save with written permission or in accordance with the provisions of the Copyright, Designs and Patents Act 1988, or under the terms of any licence permitting limited copying issued by the copyright Licensing Agency, 90 Tottenham Court Road, London W1T 4LP.

Any person who does any unauthorised act in relation to this publication may be liable to criminal prosecution and civil claims for damages.

The author has asserted his right to be identified as the author of this work in accordance with the Copyright, Designs and Patents Act 1988.

First published 2007 by
PALGRAVE MACMILLAN
Houndmills, Basingstoke, Hampshire RG21 6XS and
175 Fifth Avenue, New York, N.Y. 10010
Companies and representatives throughout the world

PALGRAVE MACMILLAN is the global academic imprint of the Palgrave Macmillan division of St. Martin's Press, LLC and of Palgrave Macmillan Ltd. Macmillan® is a registered trademark in the United States, United Kingdom and other countries. Palgrave is a registered trademark in the European Union and other countries.

ISBN 978-1-349-54218-5   ISBN 978-0-230-59286-5 (eBook)
DOI 10.1007/978-0-230-59286-5

This book is printed on paper suitable for recycling and made from fully managed and sustained forest sources.

A catalogue record for this book is available from the British Library.

Library of Congress Cataloging-in-Publication Data
Iosifidis, Petros.
   Public television in the digital era : technological challenges and new strategies in Europe / Petros Iosifidis.
     p. cm.
   Includes bibliographical references and index.

   1. Public television—Europe. 2. Public broadcasting—Technological innovations—Europe. I. Title.

HE8700.79.E85I67 2007
384.55'4094—dc22   2007017069

10 9 8 7 6 5 4 3 2 1
16 15 14 13 12 11 10 09 08 07

Transferred to Digital Printing 2011

To my daughter Eftihia who always inspires me

Contents

List of Tables xii

Preface xv

Acknowledgements xvii

Part I   General Overview 1

1 Introduction, Aims and Methodology 3
   Significance of the TV industry 3
   Public television 5
      The US model 5
      The European model 6
      The mission of public television 8
   Public TV in a competitive market 8
      Political and economic developments 9
      Technological changes 9
      Socio-cultural shifts 10
      Regulatory changes 10
      Market concentration 11
   Dilemmas 12
      Competition and programming strategies 12
      Funding method 13
      Investment in new technologies 14
      Organisational reform 15
   National strategies 16
   Aim of the book 17
   Methodology 18
      Limitations 20
   Sources 21
   Structure of the book 21

2 Factors Affecting the Development of Public Television 22
   Technological factors 22
      Cable and satellite delivery methods 22

The Internet	23
Company investments	25
Changing consumer habits?	25
Third Generation (3G) mobile telephony	26
Digital television	27
DTV adoption	28
Strategic alliances between DTV consortia	30
Regulating digital TV services	31
Political and economic factors	33
Deregulation and liberalisation	33
Critique	35
Can the free market deliver programme diversity?	36
Globalisation and media concentration	36
Regulation and media concentration	39
Social changes	41
Consequences on public television	42
3 Competition and Dilemmas	**47**
Competition	47
National markets	48
Effects of competition on public channels	51
Slight increase in TV viewing time	54
Internet users spend less time in front of television	55
Funding model	56
The licence fee	58
Commercial revenue	60
State funding	61
Programming strategies	62
Towards programming convergence?	63
Publicly funded PTV broadcasters' output	64
The SVT case	66
Programming of the PTV broadcasters that depend on advertising revenues	66
The ERT case	67
The TVE case	68
The German and Italian cases	68
Distinctive PTV broadcasters	69
Involvement in new technologies	70
The BBC case	72

The case of France Télévisions	73
The RTE case	74
Strategic alliances	74
Organisational restructuring	76
The case of France Télévisions	77
The BBC case	78
Conclusion	79

Part II National Cases — 81

4 Britain — 83
- General characteristics of the TV market — 83
- The regulatory framework — 85
- Public television — 88
  - Funding — 88
  - Audience shares — 89
- Multi-channel development — 89
- Programming — 90
- Governance reform — 93
- Investment in new media — 94
  - Criticism on BBC's new services — 95
  - BBC's new services and the licence fee — 96
- Commercial activities — 98
- Restructuring — 100
- Prospects for the BBC — 101

5 France — 105
- General characteristics of the TV market — 105
- The regulatory framework — 107
- Public television — 109
  - Funding — 110
- Programming policy — 111
- Thematic portfolio — 114
- Digital initiatives — 115
  - Development of DTT — 115
- Prospects for France Télévisions — 116

6 Spain — 120
- General characteristics of the TV market — 120

The regulatory framework	122
Public television	124
Audience shares	124
Funding	125
Programming strategy	126
Digital initiatives	129
Restructuring attempts	130
Prospects for TVE	133
7 The Republic of Ireland	**136**
General characteristics of the TV market	136
The regulatory framework	138
Public television	139
Audience shares	140
Funding	141
Programming policy	142
Independent production	145
Organisational development	145
Involvement in new technologies	147
Digital terrestrial television	147
Multimedia services	149
Thematic channels	149
Prospects for RTÉ	149
8 Sweden	**152**
General characteristics of the TV market	152
The regulatory framework	154
Public television	155
Funding	155
Audience shares	156
Reorganisation	156
New services	158
Programming strategy	158
Prospects for SVT	160
9 Greece	**163**
General characteristics of the TV market	163
The regulatory framework	165
Public television	166

Audience shares	166
ERT's income	167
Restructuring efforts	168
The implementation of the early retirement programme	170
Next phase of ERT's modernisation	171
Programming strategy	172
Criticism	174
Digital initiatives	175
Prospects for ERT	176
10 Discussion and Conclusion	178
Notes	*185*
Bibliography	*191*
Index	*201*

List of Tables

2.1	DTV Household Adoption in Europe (June 2005)	29
2.2	Development of the Western European sports rights market (1992–2005, US$m)	45
3.1	Television liberalisation in the six European markets under study	52
3.2	Cable, satellite and multi-channel penetration in the six European countries under study (%, 2004)	52
3.3	Impact of new channels on audience share in Britain	53
3.4	Viewing time per individual (in minutes, 2003)	54
3.5	Evolution of the public channels' average daily viewing shares (1997–2005)	55
3.6	Funding models of PTV broadcasters in the counties under study (%, 2005)	57
3.7	Annual TV licence fees in the countries studied (in 2005, Euros)	58
3.8	Level of advertising revenue for public and private channels in Europe (1990–95, US$m)	60
3.9	Programming genres of public channels in selected countries (%, 2004)	65
4.1	BBC revenues (2005, £m)	88
4.2	Annual % shares of viewing (individuals) (1985–2005)	89
4.3	Multi-channel development 1992–2006 (homes 000s)	90
4.4	BBC One and BBC Two hours of output by genre (2004–2005)	91
4.5	Allocation of cost of the BBC's TV services (1999, 2002, £m)	95
5.1	Audience shares of the national terrestrial TV channels in France (1995–2005)	109
5.2	Annual output of the national terrestrial TV channels in France – breakdown by genre (%, 2002)	112
6.1	Audience shares of the Spanish TV channels (1999–2005)	125
6.2	Revenues for free-to-air TV in Spain (2004, Euros m)	126

6.3	Public channels in Spain: share of transmissions by genre (%, 2004)	127
7.1	National individual all day and peak-time channel shares in Ireland (%, 2005)	140
7.2	RTÉ's income sources (1998–2005, Euros m)	141
7.3	Top 10 TV programmes in Ireland in 2005	143
7.4	Indigenous hours of content on RTÉ's in peak-times by genre (2004)	144
8.1	Breakdown of income for Swedish SVT (1998, 2000)	156
8.2	Audience shares of television channels in Sweden (%, 2001, 2005)	157
8.3	SVT programming genres (%, 1991–2004)	160
9.1	Annual % audience shares of the Greek TV channels (1992–2005)	167
9.2	ERT's income (in million Euros, 1997–2005)	167
9.3	Advertising expenditure of TV channels in Greece (million Euros 2000, 2003)	168
9.4	ERT's programming mix by genre (1998–99 and 2004–2005)	173
9.5	Programming mix by genre – ERT, MEGA, ANT1 (2004–2005)	173
9.6	Top 10 TV programmes in Greece (2005)	174

Preface

The European television industry is undergoing profound technological, economic, socio-cultural and regulatory changes. These changes open up new opportunities for businesses to expand and converge and offer viewers a vast array of TV offerings at a national or even international level. However, these developments present a formidable challenge for public television (PTV) broadcasters, who for a number of decades enjoyed a monopoly status and were tasked to preserve the national culture, language and identity.

The aim of this book is twofold. First, it examines the way technological developments and the internationalisation of the television industry affects these guardians of the public interest. Secondly, it focuses on the policies pursued by PTV broadcasters in selected European countries in response to the challenges that confront them in the era of digital convergence. The changes in the European television landscape force public channels to rethink their position toward new digital technologies, organisational structures, and programming policy and scheduling. In order to illustrate the difficulties but also the opportunities that arise during this period of change, the book analyses specific activities and strategies undertaken by public channels in the main areas examined (reorganisation, programming and technology) in three large and three small European countries (Britain, France, Spain, Sweden, Ireland and Greece). Information has been gathered partly from secondary, but mainly from primary sources (interviews).

This volume intends to fill a growing need for research that would address contemporary developments in television and the public service institutions that operate within the sector from a European perspective. The international nature of developments in the field of television has made it necessary to develop a comparative approach among national situations with local variations and use this experience to arrive at workable suggestions concerning the role of public channels. The discussion of public television across Europe moves from the more general and theoretical Part I to the more specific and empirical Part II, which includes six case studies. The text is addressed to scholars and students in Sociology and Media and Communications Departments across Europe and intends to develop discussion and stimulate thinking in the field.

Acknowledgements

This volume would not be written without the generous support and funding from the Department of Sociology, City University. I would like to express my gratitude to Nicholas Nicoli, PhD candidate at City University, London, who undertook some of the interviews for the purposes of this research as well as his valuable feedback. My special thanks are due to those who agreed to be interviewed for this volume and very generously provided insight information. I am also very grateful to Jeremy Tunstsall, Emeritus Professor at City University and Jeanette Steemers, Professor at the University of Westminster, for their welcomed comments and suggestions at the beginning of this effort. Thanks also to Jill Lake at Palgrave Macmillan for helpful advice.

Every effort has been made to trace all copyright holders, but if any have been inadvertently overlooked, the publisher will be pleased to make the necessary arrangements at the first opportunity.

Part I
General Overview

1
Introduction, Aims and Methodology

Significance of the TV industry

Europe – with its 731 million inhabitants (460 million in the EU 25, plus 271 million in the rest of Europe) – represents the largest audiovisual market in the world. The continent has a thriving audiovisual sector that in 2004 was worth more than 100 billion Euros and employed more than a million people. The economic significance of the sector is further revealed by the fact that it accounts for 5 per cent of Europe's Gross Domestic Product (GDP), 20 per cent of growth and 40 per cent of productivity (Reding, 2004).

Television represents the largest segment of the European audiovisual sector and in 2005 there were nearly 4000 TV channels which constituted the primary source of information for most people. The remarkable development of analogue television during the second half of the twentieth century led to widespread penetration and today nearly 99 per cent of the 176 million European households in the EU 25 own at least one TV set. Digital television is also developing at a steady pace. In the end of 2004 there were more than two thousand digital channels, up from eight hundred in the end of 2000 (EAO, 2005). In June 2005 the take-up of digital services in the 25 European Union member states was 23.7 per cent, with digital satellite the market leader, but digital terrestrial gaining momentum (Dataxis, 2006). Digital TV penetration is expected to accelerate following national and Europe-wide policies to fix a date for switching off the analogue frequency (Iosifidis, 2006a).

In terms of finances, the European Audiovisual Observatory informs us that revenue of TV organisations in the EU25 rose by 10 billion Euros between 1999 and 2003, reaching 64.5 billion Euros in 2003, an average annual increase of 4.4 per cent. Over 90 per cent of this revenue came from three main sources: licence fees, advertising and subscription. However, the report also mentions that growth rates vary across Europe (in 2003 Britain was by far the country with the largest television organisation revenue at 17.3 billion Euros, compared to 13.6 billion Euros in Germany and 10.5 billion Euros in France) (EAO, 2005). In 2005 television had the lion's share of advertising expenditure at 37.1 per cent and despite the rise of online and broadband advertising, this is forecasted to remain at the same level for both 2006 and 2007 (Zenith/ Optimedia, 2005).

The European Union has acknowledged television's strategic role and has set up support programmes to strengthen audiovisual production. In particular, Media Plus (2001–2006) aims to create a powerful and competitive audiovisual industry to safeguard Europe's multiculturalism. Media Plus has a budget of 453.6 million Euros (an additional 59.4 million Euros allocated for media training)[1] and has replaced Media II (1996–2000), which had a smaller budget of 205 million Euros. Media Plus is intended to strengthen the competitiveness of Europe's audiovisual industry with a series of support measures dealing with training of professionals, development of production projects, distribution and promotion of cinematographic works and audiovisual programmes. It is estimated that Media Plus will both contribute to the competitiveness of Europe's audiovisual industry and also safeguard the cultural diversity that lies at the heart of Europe. The proposal for a new programme to support the European audiovisual sector (Media 2007) was adopted by the Commission on 14 July 2004 and passed to the European Parliament and the Council of Ministers for approval.

In terms of regulation, the 'Television Without Frontiers' (TWF) Directive (89/552/EEC), adopted on 3 October 1989 by the Council and amended on 30 June 1997 by the European Parliament and the Council Directive 97/36/EC, provides a sound legal framework within which broadcasters can pursue their activities in the European Union. The TWF's core element is the 'country of origin principle', which allows companies to provide services across the EU as long as they adhere to the regulations of their home state. The Directive established the legal framework for the free movement of television broadcasting services throughout the Union to promote the development of a European market in broadcasting and related activities such as television advertising and production. The basic point of departure for any EC regulatory activities is the main role which the media – especially television – play in society, namely to develop and disseminate social values. In this context the Directive governs the protection of minors, content quotas, human dignity and the right to reply. In 2006 the TWF Directive was under further review to address issues relating to 'new media' and interactive services. The Commission on 29 March 2007 adapted an amended proposal of the modernised TWF Directive, to be renamed Audiovisual Media Services Directive (COM (2007) 170 final).

Public television

Public television can play an essential role in safeguarding a pluralist society and meeting its cultural and social needs and it is therefore at the centre of the democratic systems. Through its mass reach and influence public broadcasting has the capacity both to enrich people's lives as individuals and improve the quality of life in society. In Europe public TV occupies an important part of the television sector. However, in the USA its role and influence is minimal.

The US model

The United States present a unique case in that commercial broadcasting was permitted before the development of public broadcasting. When public television was launched in 1967, following a recommendation by the Carnegie Commission (1967), a small number of commercial networks (Disney, Viacom, General Electric, Time Warner and Fox) controlled most of the programming in the USA. The American market-oriented, highly commercialised TV system never actually embraced a 'public service' notion of television. The public sector was intended to compensate for the limitations of commercially-driven media and offer alternative programming that 'would enhance citizenship and public service'. In the language of the Carnegie Commission, public broadcasting was to serve as a 'forum for debate and controversy', providing a 'voice for groups in the community that may otherwise be unheard' so that we could 'see America whole, in all its diversity' (Starr, 2004). In its early years public TV was indeed an observably critical social perspective, providing the audience with a healthy alternative media diet to the fast food of commercial networks. It was thought-provoking by offering cultural programmes, documentaries, children's programmes and so forth of a kind that are rarely found on US commercial channels (Nissen, 2006). However, many observers suggest that it has become increasingly integrated into the commercial broadcasting industry. Hoynes (1994) argues that the public TV system has turned mainly to business, talk, news and wildlife formats in its programme offerings, owing to an inadequate funding structure.

Today US public TV stations are independent and serve community needs. However, all public TV organisations are linked on a national level through three organisations: the Corporation for Public Broadcasting (CPB), created by Congress in 1967 to channel Federal government funding to stations and independent producers. The CPB does not produce or distribute programmes; the Public Broadcasting Service (PBS), formed in 1969, responsible for distributing programming to about 348 public TV stations across the country. The PBS is a private, non-profit enterprise owned and operated by the member stations; and the Association of Public Television Stations (APTS) which assists member public TV stations with research and planning. In addition to these public TV stations there are numerous non-commercial stations run by Christian Evangelistic ministries, supported by donations from viewers and churches.

The overall impact of public television on cultural, social and political life is negligible and in 2005 it claimed less than 3 per cent of the average daily audience share. As a McKinsey & Company (1999) report mentioned, with such a small share US public television is hardly a significant rival to commercial operators and cannot meaningfully shape national programming strategies. It follows therefore that US public TV is consigned to a position of a 'niche' broadcaster, out of reach for the vast majority of Americans. On the contrary, public TV is Europe has an obligation of reach and being in touch with its audience. According to the McKinsey & Company report European public broadcasters have influenced the overall development of television by inducing their commercial competitors to offer equally distinctive programmes.

The European model

In Europe television is not considered merely an economic activity, as it is in the USA, but rather a social and political tool, accessible to all and contributing to pluralism, diversity and democratic expression. In the USA, television developed in an intensely competitive environment from its very inception and public service media have minimal impact in cultural, social and political terms. In stark contrast, the European model has been characterised by state intervention and occupies an important part of the whole TV industry. Historically, monopolies in television (and radio) were justified on technical grounds (spectrum scarcity), but a raft of political and social arguments were added to these technical reasons, as it was believed that broadcast media could exert powerful influence and had to therefore be heavily regulated (Humphreys, 1996, pp. 112–13; Iosifidis *et al.*, 2005, p. 9). With the notable exception of Luxembourg, which never experienced state control in the sector, as well as Britain, Belgium (Wallonia) and Finland, where private television was introduced in the 1950s, public television (PTV) broadcasters in Europe functioned under a monopoly regime until the 1980s and constituted the sole source of information and entertainment.

A single European model?

However, the organisation and functioning of public channels are not the same across Europe, for they vary in the way they are funded and structured, their political independence, and so on. For example, revenues of the British PTV broadcaster BBC and Swedish SVT derive almost exclusively from the licence fee, but the income of the Spanish TVE comes mainly from advertising and state grants. Greece's national public broadcaster ERT is funded by a surcharge on electricity bills. In the Netherlands the Parliament decided in 2004 to replace the licence fee by a special levy as a supplement to income tax. Apart from differences in funding, PTV broadcasters differ among themselves in structural terms. For instance, while TVE in Spain is characterised by an integrated structure, controlling every area of TV activity, local governments oversee the autonomous regional public TV stations across the country. Also some countries (France, Spain and Greece) witnessed the emergence of state rather than public broadcasting. The difference between public and state television lies in the degree of its independence from political power. While state television promotes the interest of the state, that is the government, public television enjoys autonomy and editorial independence.[2] In France, Spain, Italy and Greece, conditions variously defined as 'political clientelism' or 'state paternalism', have prevented the full emancipation of public television from direct political control (Council of Europe, 2004). In France and Italy state broadcasters began to be transformed into public service broadcasters in the 1970s, whereas in Spain and Greece the dictatorships of Franco and the Colonels respectively delayed the transformation processes.

But even the flagship of independent broadcasters, the BBC, was attacked by the British government over its coverage of the Falklands war in the 1980s as well as the 2003 war in Iraq. Furthermore, some large PTV broadcasters have expanded internationally (the BBC and the Spanish TVE) or embarked on cross-border cooperation (the Swedish SVT with other Nordic broadcasters), but others have focused on the domestic market due to small size and language barriers (the Irish RTE and the Greek ERT).

The mission of public television

The large variations among the broadcasting systems stem from the different traditions, political cultures as well as regulatory systems that exist across Europe. It follows therefore that it is difficult to identify a single public television model and/or accurately define public television. In general terms, however, there are some common obligations bestowed upon public TV by society which define the remit of its activities. These obligations can be summarised as follows:

- Universality of content and access.
- Provision of programmes which contribute to social cohesion and democratic process.
- Setting of high quality[3] standards in the areas of entertainment, education and information.
- Contribution to political pluralism and cultural diversity.
- Enriching the lives of individuals through history, the arts and science.
- Preservation and promotion of national culture and heritage.
- Editorial independence and accountability.
- Serving the needs of an increasingly multi-cultural society (new obligation).

Public TV in a competitive market

Since the mid-1980s the European television market has undergone significant upheaval. The rapid development of new communication technologies alongside with the relaxation of strict ownership and content rules have allowed new players to enter the sector, changed the dynamics of the market and led to privatisation and commercialisation. The gradual convergence of different communication sectors, combined with the development of the Internet and online services, has led to the creation of new market structures, as well as new roles for the owners of communications companies. This has resulted in concentration of capital and control of information flow in an ever smaller number of multinational conglomerates. These factors – political, economic, technological, socio-cultural and regulatory – have all had a great influence on the development of public television. Let us summarise them briefly (a more thorough discussion is provided in Chapter 2):

Political and economic developments

Political and economic factors have affected the structure and functioning of television in Europe. During the past three decades the TV sector has been characterised by a trend towards de/re-regulation, privatisation and commercialisation. The process, as well as the speed, of these developments was not uniform in all European countries. In some places a regime of complete and unregulated liberalisation of the television sector prevailed. Elsewhere a fundamental, regulatory framework was applied in a carefully pre-determined way, with built-in transitional stages. Despite these differences, the impact on public television was decisive, as it moved out of a protected environment into a competitive one. TV liberalisation has intensified over recent years, coinciding with the globalisation of communications and the impending technological convergence of audiovisual media, telecommunications and information technology. All these multifaceted pressures have affected the status and influential position previously enjoyed by public television.

Technological changes

The introduction of new technologies – more specifically the development of cable and satellite transmission systems in the 1980s, as well as the introduction of digital technology and the rapid development of the Internet in the 1990s – has resulted in an unprecedented proliferation of commercially driven channels and intensified competition between public and private media. Digitalisation of information has multiplied the means of communication and prompted the appearance of thematic channels that focus on specific issues. There has been a ten-fold increase in the number of television channels since 1990. A total of 1100 channels operated in Europe by the end of 2003, up from 103 in 1990. Also in 2003 multi-channel penetration was as high as 99 per cent, 98 per cent, 90 per cent and 80 per cent in Belgium, the

Netherlands, Germany and Sweden respectively. The relevant figure in Ireland was 60 per cent, in Britain 40 per cent, France 30 per cent, while at the other end Spain and Greece had a 22 per cent and 6 per cent multi-channel penetration respectively (EAO, 2005). Although the stages of technological development may differ from country to country (for example the adoption of digital television and the use of the Internet are more widely spread in the countries of northern Europe, in comparison with Europe's southern countries), inevitably digital technology will penetrate our lives and the Internet will offer an alternative way of accessing audiovisual material. This change will erode further the market share currently held by mainstream channels, including traditional PTV broadcasters.

Socio-cultural shifts

Parallel to these politico-economic and technological factors, a wide spectrum of social and cultural changes is shaping the role and influencing the status of public television. At the individual level, citizens are increasingly becoming customers motivated in their choice and behaviour more by individual needs and preferences than by their civic role in the community (Nissen, 2006, p. 22). Globalisation, the free movement of capital, goods and services, and migration from other continents on a hitherto unseen scale, are all forces that have disrupted integration and eroded social cohesion. Increasing individualism and radical change in western lifestyles have combined with a more general climate of discontent with public service broadcasting, by definition no longer able to reach out to satisfy all viewers. Deregulation has offered the benefits of many more sources of information, empowering citizen-consumers, enabling them to select services to satisfy their increasingly varied demands. This has left PTV broadcasters with the difficult task of trying to reverse these trends by re-establishing the lost societal and cultural commons.

Regulatory changes

Many European countries have introduced new regulatory regimes which aim to abolish previous restrictions on business development. For example, with the Communications Act of 2003, British broadcasting saw the introduction of new legislation which liberated media markets and extended 'light touch' regulation. In particular, the Act abolished many complex ownership regulations, enabled further

Introduction, Aims and Methodology 11

consolidation of ITV ownership, and allowed non-European companies to buy British companies (The Communications Act 2003). Also, changes in French law during the 1990s, in particular the raising of maximum holdings in television channels, were followed by higher levels of concentrated ownership in the television sector. Other large European countries, such as Spain, Germany and Italy, but also the smaller territories of Ireland, Sweden and Greece, have followed the same route towards relaxing television ownership rules observed in France and Britain (Iosifidis *et al.*, 2005, pp. 71–5).

Furthermore, the European Commission has developed a 'light-touch' approach towards industry consolidation over the years, as evidenced by the introduction of the new regulatory framework for electronic communications adopted in 2002 and applied in July 2003.[4] The very essence of this framework lay in the principle that regulation must not separate markets, but instead allow for their convergence; and that only minimum regulation should apply to media and telecommunications markets. Also, the EC competition authorities have allowed many more media mergers in recent years, as evidenced by the approvals of the $135 billion, all-stock AOL/Time Warner deal in 2000 and the 2004 merger of Sony and BMG's respective music units,[5] which have resulted in market imbalances in the form of anticompetitive practices and dominant positions. The established relationship between communications networks and owners of content, along with the increased complexity of mergers in the age of digital convergence, has reduced the effectiveness of the EC competition policy to tackle consolidation trends (Iosifidis, 2005a).

Market concentration

The powerful economies of scale and scope generated by new digital technology leads to mergers, acquisitions and other business alliances between previously separated media companies. Corporate development in the European market has been facilitated by the introduction of the new liberal regulatory regimes and has inevitably resulted in higher levels of concentration which can endanger media diversity (Iosifidis, 1999). The market has witnessed the emergence of large companies with a trans-national orientation, which cannot easily be monitored at national or even European levels. Important phenomena are horizontal concentration across the value chains of different parts of the media industry and vertical integration of the media value chain from the development and creation of concepts and formats and content production to channel management, distribution and consumption (Nissen, 2006, p. 10). There were just seven major companies operating in the continent in 2004:

- Germany's media conglomerate Bertelsmann – a powerhouse of integrated communication, media and entertainment in numerous countries.
- Italy's Fininvest – owned by the Berlusconi family.
- France's Lagardere Media.
- John Malone's Liberty Media – controlling United Pan-Europe Communications (UPC, Europe's largest cable operator).
- Murdoch's News Corporation – its media holdings extending to the USA, Europe, Australia, Latin America and Asia.
- Luxembourg's SBS Broadcasting.
- NBC-Universal – owner of television network NBC and Universal Studios, acquired from French company Vivendi in 2003 (Kevin et al., 2004, pp. 242–3).

Competition policy is an important instrument to address the structural tendency towards monopoly or oligopoly in television. The imposition of media ownership rules can also limit concentration of ownership and enhance plurality. However, as will be shown later, the role of PTV broadcasting is paramount because it can act as a counterweight to monopoly power.

Dilemmas

These developments have cast into doubt, not only the way public television is financed, but also its very *raison d'être*. Inevitably European public channels face a series of dilemmas which fall into four main areas.

Competition and programming strategies

The abolition of state monopolies and the introduction of competition in the audiovisual sector have put public television stations in an inferior position *vis-à-vis* commercial channels. Although PTV broadcasters make efforts to respond to these new conditions, these efforts are limited by the fact that they have a social mission to fulfill, namely defending the public interest.[6] Carrying out this mission means that public channels have to offer quality (therefore high-cost) informative, educational and entertainment services, not normally provided in the free market. The obligation of public television to preserve the nation's culture, offer educational services and cater for minorities does not make it easy to compete directly with private broadcasters. However, failure to deliver popular programmes that attract large audiences may result in a competitive disadvantage. One senses a disturbing contradiction between the necessity for PTV broadcasters to be aggressive in the market-place and their public service obligations (Padovani and Tracey, 2003, p. 133). Therefore the dilemma posed is the following: should public television stations continue to act in compliance with their statutory remit, or should they adopt competitive tactics similar to those of private channels? In other words, should they take part in the battle for ratings and therefore offer services similar to the private sector (where at times profit prevails to the detriment of programme quality)? Or should they focus on services that the private sector by definition does not cover? But if they choose the latter scenario, they may not be in a position to maintain audience shares at a reasonable level (around 20 per cent), so as to defend their position as servants of the public interest. As we shall see, public channels are already in a ratings battle and have adopted a more mainstream programming approach to address the competitive challenge.

Funding method

The licence fee constitutes the main source of revenue for public television in Europe. Additional revenues come from advertising, sales of programmes and television magazines, government subsidies, and subscription income. In the days of monopoly, it was much easier to justify the licence fee, but this collective funding system has come under intensive pressure owing to technological developments which have allowed many more channels in the market. The fact that advertising and other commercial revenues constitute only supplementary resources for the majority of public television channels, combined with the unwillingness of most governments to increase the licence fee to the required level of inflation, has caused economic difficulties for public broadcasters. In addition, discussions have for some time been taking place at a European level about how to reduce public television's dependency on the licence fee and find more efficient and rational methods of funding it in the digital multi-channel era.

The choice of the funding scheme can influence the activities of public channels, and in particular the content of their programme offerings. As will be shown in Chapter 3 funding by the licence fee reduces dependence on advertising, avoids direct competition with commercial broadcasters and allows public channels to formulate a programming strategy that includes distinctive, innovative and risky programmes. Still, private broadcasters often accuse public ones of using public money for commercial activities and populist programmes offered by the free market anyway, therefore resulting in market distortion and unfair competition. Despite numerous complaints lodged with the European Commission relating to financing systems, the EC rejected practically all of them and declared the use of the licence fee compatible with the Treaty. Still, such developments have caused confusion and created uncertainty about future revenue levels for public channels, thus putting a brake on investment, and pushing up operational costs.

Investment in new technologies

The question initially posed regarding the rapid development of new communications technologies is whether public television stations should take advantage of alternative ways of transmitting their programmes. Should they be allowed to provide thematic channels, or services on the Internet, for example? It is worth noting that across the EU25 only in Britain and Spain it is explicitly stated in the public broadcaster's remit that they should embark on digital activities. One argument in favour is that investment in new communication technologies allows public channels to re-acquire their competitive advantage and therefore play a leading role in the new era. Another is that public television should be present on all platforms and ensure that digital content is accessible to all citizens in order to fulfill the universality principle. This can be achieved by offering a free-to-air package and by promoting a common, open standard for the broadcasting of digital television signals that would address the problem of closed, proprietary technical standards. This way guarantees participation and promotes wide-spread take-up of digital technologies. As we will see in Chapter 3, most public broadcasters have launched, or participate in, free-to-view digital consortia.

Also, some large public broadcasters have already invested in areas such as the Internet and multimedia, whereas PTV broadcasters in some of the smaller countries are still in the planning stage. The dilemma however has to do as much with the means of funding these initiatives as with the access of viewers to new services. In fact, the method of funding such activities determines the level of access citizen-consumers can enjoy. For example, if the new services are funded by subscriptions, then they will be accessible only to those who can afford the subscription, thereby sacrificing the universality principle. If on the other hand they are funded by the licence fee, then they are accessible to all. This scenario, however, logically presupposes increasing the licence fee at regular intervals to cover this investment, something which national governments are on the whole unwilling to implement because of the political fall-out.

Organisational reform

Long-term operational and organisational strategies for PTV broadcasters are essential to address commercial changes, shifts in audience preferences, as well as technological advancements. The search for new content, but also for new centres of production and organisational units able to meet new demands, presupposes the creation of a modern and rational organisational model elaborated and designed by specialist advisers, external managers and consultants, who can clarify priorities and look for specific objectives, rather than vague principles. As Coppens and Saeys (2006) argue, the pre-eminent instrument for a more specific definition of tasks is the public service contract. While laws and/or decrees continue to lay down a number of principles, the specific tasks themselves are defined in the contracts. A growing number of countries, including Britain, France, Ireland and Sweden have specified the mission of their PTV broadcasters in contracts, while the television systems of the remaining two countries under scrutiny in this book (Spain and Greece) have no contracts as yet. Most contracts urge the PTV broadcaster to adopt a more modern human-resources policy, spend public money efficiently and justify their financial resources, increase revenue from self-help activities such as overheads reduction and job redundancies. As a result the mission of PTV broadcasters is increasingly defined in terms of specific and measurable targets.

The merit of a new administrative system for PTV broadcasters, in which the public service contract is a basic element, is that it urges the public corporations to be held more answerable to the community that they serve. However, the new administrative system may place too tight restrictions on the broadcaster's autonomy, for the assessment of the broadcaster's performance can be submitted to the relevant political authorities who will appraise it from their own perspective and perhaps impose sanctions (ibid.). Another drawback of encouraging a more management-oriented approach is that the public sector may operate openly on the basis of commercial criteria and no longer as a public service. Moreover, a Council of Europe report (2004, p. 15) points out that it has been proved difficult to develop a managerial culture required to downsize the organizations, reduce staffing, cut costs and promote cost-effectiveness and efficiency because labour laws generally prevent easy dismissal of personnel and in any case most attempts to carry through reform have become bogged down in political conflicts. Even though the broadcasters' attempts to re-organise are necessary for survival, it is evident that these attempts are often troubled.

All the above constitute only a small part of the complex web of dilemmas that emerge in the new television order, characterised by the development of new communications technologies, the prevalence of market forces, the liberalisation and the internationalisation of television markets, as well as the convergence of technologies. Despite the existence of different public broadcasting systems, the dilemmas and the problems that public channels face today are common among European PTV broadcasters.

National strategies

Most public channels are in the process of developing strategies to adapt to the new television order. However, these organisations are not entirely free to decide their own fate, for each public broadcaster exists and operates within a specific environment, in which room for manoeuvre and initiative-taking depends on many factors, both external and internal. Internal factors include the readiness of public channels to respond to the demands of the competitive digital era, which in turn depends on organisational reform, programming policy, and involvement in new technologies. External factors (the specific conditions that prevail in each country) include past history, traditions, language and culture, the political climate, the level of economic development, the size of the market, the technological infrastructure, and the regulatory framework. These factors can hinder potential strategies and at times limit the public sector's room for manoeuvre.

This explains to some extent the important differences observed in the initiatives undertaken by different public channels.

As will be shown in Part II, a group of PTV broadcasters from mainly larger European countries (the BBC in Britain, France Télévisions in France and TVE in Spain), but also smaller countries of Northern Europe (SVT in Sweden), have been active by investing in online services and creating interactive web sites (BBC, SVT, France Télévisions), launching 'niche' channels (BBC, France Télévisions, TVE) and reaching agreements with other public and even commercial channels for the joint production and promotion of new services (BBC). In the majority of cases, these initiatives were combined with attempts to reorganise internally (especially on the part of the BBC, France Télévisions and SVT), but also to save resources, at times requiring unpopular measures (dismissing superfluous personnel). In these countries, public television managed to defend its principles, justify its public service mission and cope with competition from private channels.

A second group of PTV broadcasters coming mainly from smaller countries (Ireland, Greece) find themselves still at the review and planning stage. Activity in new technologies is limited and important steps toward internal reform have only recently commenced. Undoubtedly market size and the social and political context embedded in these smaller countries play a defining role in the decision to enter new, unfamiliar and commercially risky activities. For example, in Greece television took its first steps under a dictatorship regime and was openly used for propaganda purposes. The restoration of democracy found the medium wounded, lacking vision and not trusted by the Greek public. This explains to some extent the Greek broadcaster ERT's limited involvement in new technologies and the late adoption of organisational reform strategies.

Aim of the book

This book presents the essential aspects of these developments in communications and puts under the microscope the factors that cause such multifaceted pressures on PTV broadcasting. It defines the mission and role of public television in Europe, outlines the interrelated political, economic, social, cultural, legal and technological factors influencing its development, and looks at the strategies employed by different PTV broadcasters to adapt to the new era. In doing so it examines the position of public television in a range of European countries and intends to ensure a comparative approach across the countries monitored. Although the European PTV broadcasters are barely comparable due to differing national regulations as well as politico-economic and socio-cultural circumstances, it is of some interest to provide a cross-national overall picture of the situation in different national contexts. The close observation of national strategies will help in identifying the prospects and the future role of public TV in Europe.

Each national case study provides a picture of the general characteristics of the television market and the regulatory framework. It then reports the state of public television and focuses on the following three main areas:

- The technological, economic, political, regulatory and socio-cultural factors influencing the development of PTV in each country
- The dilemmas that PTV broadcasters face in the era of digital convergence
- The initiatives and strategies that are developing to face competitive pressures in the fields of new technologies, organisational reform and programming policy/scheduling.

Methodology

To achieve these aims, research is focussed on the six European countries of Britain, France, Spain, Sweden, Ireland and Greece. These have been selected on the basis of the following criteria:

- They present a combination of large and small European states, from across Europe.[7] This is important because it takes into account the relative sizes of the internal markets, and thus defines in business terms PTV broadcasters' room for manoeuvre. The size of the market usually defines the relative strength of a country in the television sector and thus the influence it can exert or is exerted on it by neighbouring countries. For small countries such as Ireland, for example, influenced as it is by a powerful neighbour (Britain), it is more difficult to develop an independent television system.
- The range of countries represented here is very broad, both in terms of traditions, history and culture, and in economic terms – a situation

that in itself reflects different stages of development of public television. This allows us to identify problems common to public television stations in all European countries as they face more or less common challenges in order to survive in the new television ecology, but at the same time it reflects differences that derive from the various cultural, structural, political factors which characterise each country. In Britain, for example, the Thatcher administration was ideologically opposed to public enterprises, but with a few exceptions the BBC has always enjoyed independence from political power. In France, by contrast, the government considered it necessary to intervene in the television sector to safeguard and promote national culture and identity. In France (as in Spain and Greece) one can find some degree of political subordination of public television by the government. The television system in Spain is characterised on the one hand by the absence of a regulatory authority responsible for overseeing the television sector, and on the other by the operation of powerful public television stations in the autonomous regions. Television in Ireland operates within the framework of strict morals and tradition. In Sweden PTV broadcasting is characterised by the presence of a mixed public-private system, offering a balanced programme output. In Greece, intense competition after 1990 resulted in the shrinking of the public sector and the marginalisation of ERT, which was seen as a mouthpiece of the government. Greece, along with Spain, represents a model closer to the East European situation, where deregulation of television emerged in an unstable political and social environment.

The countries selected illustrate different levels of competition in the field of communications more generally, and more specifically in television. The marked differences can be attributed partly to the size of a national market, partly to its regulatory framework, and partly to the political and economic climate. Observing national experiences gives us a picture of the way in which external factors (for example the level of competition in television or the effectiveness of the regulatory framework) influence the ability of public broadcasters to compete with the private sector. The examination of the areas that are more directly controlled by public channels (internal reorganisation, programming policy and digital initiatives) highlights the readiness of the public sector to adapt to the digital age.

Limitations

The limited number of countries selected for the purposes of this book may be problematic in drawing general conclusions about the policies and strategies employed by public channels. Nevertheless, the thorough analysis of the national case studies, along with the careful initial selection of countries and the in-depth semi-structured interviews undertaken with experts ensures that our research into public television in each country is based on reliable and comparative data and thus constitutes a firm basis on which to identify future prospects for public television at the pan-European level.

The book largely concentrates on Western European countries and in particular the EU15, and has therefore excluded post-Communist countries that entered the EU in 2004.[8] The reason is that the introduction of public service broadcasting in these countries of East and Central Europe was established in a completely different historical time and in altogether different social, political, cultural and technological circumstances. As a Council of Europe report explains, there is a lack of social embeddedness of public service broadcasting in post-Communist countries, depriving it from its natural social habitat and cultural context (Council of Europe, 2004). Freedom of the press and deregulation of television in these countries emerged in an unstable political and social environment, in societies yet searching for an identity and a normative system to replace the old Communist one (Mungiu-Pippidi, 1999). Of course some degree of political subordination of public television by governments can be found in Western European countries (France, Italy) and models emerged in Spain, Portugal and Greece are closer to the East European situation. These second-wave democracies were, however, authoritarian and not totalitarian regimes, in the sense that they had merely accepted the official ideology (and not internalised it) and also permitted and even encouraged a degree of escapism (ibid.). The investigation of public television in former Communist countries requires a substantially different approach and therefore falls outside the scope of this research.

Another issue worth pointing out is that in every national market the focus is on the main public television channels offering general content. Certain countries have introduced extra channels that in one way or another can be characterised as public service broadcasting. In Britain, for example, Channel Four was founded in 1982 with the main purpose of providing distinctive output and programming content that is innovative and experimental. In France, the Franco-German Arte, a trans-national public channel launched in May 1992 specialises in cultural output. Channels of this nature do contribute to plurality of viewpoint, but do not have wide appeal. The importance of these channels is less compared to PTV broadcasters offering general content and this is why they are not investigated thoroughly in this work.

Sources

The main sources used to collect and process relevant information and data were as follows:

- In-depth semi-structured interviews (personal, via telephone, fax or email) with experts from the media industry, regulatory bodies and the academia in the countries examined.
- Author's participation in international conferences.
- PTV broadcasters' annual reports.
- Published documents by the European Commission and the Council of Europe, as well as bodies such as the European Broadcasting Union and the European Audiovisual Observatory.
- Books and articles in relevant journals and newspapers.
- Information available on the Web.

Structure of the book

This book is divided into two parts. Apart from the introduction and methodology, Part I consists of two additional chapters. The second chapter examines the factors that have affected the development of public television in Europe, while the third develops an understanding of the dilemmas that public television stations face in today's era of digitalisation, technological convergence and deregulation. Part II of the book consists of six chapters, each looking at the strategies that public channels in the countries under scrutiny (Britain, France, Spain, Sweden, Ireland and Greece) adopt to cope with the intense competition and digital challenge. The tenth and final chapter presents the general conclusions of the research and attempts an overall evaluation of the future role of public television in Europe.

2
Factors Affecting the Development of Public Television

There are many factors shaping the development of public television broadcasting – technological, political, socio-cultural, economic, and legislative. Although these factors differ in importance between countries, the role they have played in changing Europe's television ecology is crucial. This chapter attempts to document these changes.

Technological factors

The appearance of new communication technologies has completely transformed the European television scene. The development of cable and satellite transmission systems in the 1980s has significantly increased the number of sources available to the public for information, education and entertainment. The rapid development of the Internet at the beginning of the 1990s, the speed with which 'electronic' information increased its share of the market, combined with the digitalisation of information have led to the creation of integrated networks of data transmission as well as the introduction of interactivity between broadcasters and consumers. There follows a description of these new technologies.

Cable and satellite delivery methods

The introduction of alternative delivery methods in the 1980s, such as cable and satellite systems, enabled many more channels to enter the European television market. In 2004 TV reception modes in the EU15 were as follows: terrestrial only 42.6 per cent; cable 31.1 per cent; satellite 26.20 per cent. The new 10 members' group affected slightly the whole EU TV reception market by increasing the proportion of cable TV penetration. TV reception modes in EU25 in 2004 were 42.5 per cent for terrestrial only, 32.5 per cent for cable and 25 per cent for satellite (IDATE, 2004).

However, the advent and advancement of new distribution technologies was not uniform across Europe. Cable, in particular, developed rapidly in the Netherlands and Belgium, where cable connections became almost universal from as early as 1990, whereas penetration rates of satellite dishes have been particularly high in Austria and Denmark. However, in Britain and France, cable and satellite developed at a slower rate than predicted. In 2004, only 17 per cent of British households and about 15 per cent of French homes were connected to cable. In the Mediterranean countries of Italy and Greece, cable and satellite technologies have been underdeveloped, mainly because of the availability of numerous free-to-air terrestrial channels.

These technological developments have, nevertheless, influenced the traditional structure, regulatory framework and dynamics of the television industry. While in the past television services were largely confined to domestic markets, new cable and satellite transmission networks have brought television into the trans-national arena. This is particularly evidenced by the advent of satellite television, capable of crossing borders by beaming signals to different territories. This made it difficult to rely on national legislation alone to cover the sector. Also the introduction of these new delivery methods led to an unprecedented proliferation of channels, undermining the spectrum scarcity argument for regulation. Whereas in the past frequency scarcity prevented the accommodation of many competing services, the new delivery systems of cable and satellite have challenged the traditional technical arguments for the regulation of television broadcasting. This has become more apparent in recent years with the development of digital television, permitting the simultaneous existence of many more channels (see below). The result has been erosion of the market share of traditional terrestrial channels, including public television stations.

The Internet

The Internet is a global network of interconnected computers, communicating through a common Transmission Control Protocol/ Internet Protocol. The Internet is the successor of Arpanet, a network founded in 1969 by the Advanced Research Projects Agency Network (Arpanet) – a service of the American Department of Defence. Arpanet was initially designed to connect the computers of various universities with those of American Defence Department employees for the exchange of data. Thus until the end of 1980 it was used mainly for communication between scientists and researchers. In the 1990s it expanded beyond the academic and scientific community, and included private companies as well as individual users, connected via Internet Service Providers (ISPs) (Leiner, 2000).

A fast-developing sector of the Internet is the World Wide Web (WWW), which in essence is a network of ISPs using the same transmission control protocol. This protocol was designed by Tim Berners-Lee, headquartered in CERN, the European physics laboratory in Geneva. The WWW facilitates the exchange of information and knowledge between all computer users with an ISP contract. It also enables anyone to create home pages on the Internet, with the assignation of a universal resource locator (url) and an Internet address. In fact, all large media and communications companies have their own websites and in recent years, individual users have also started to create personal web pages. Apart from information exchange and knowledge-sharing, the Internet is also the lead player in the communications sector. Via hypertext transport protocol (http) users can send messages to each other or attach texts via email.

The number of Internet users has increased significantly over recent years. According to the Internet World Stats (2006), by the end of March 2005 there were about 216 million Internet users in the EU25, representing a 46.9 per cent adoption (131.6 per cent growth in the period 2000–2005). The rest of Europe, with some 44 million Internet users, had a 16.2 per cent penetration in March 2005, representing growth of 341.9 per cent since the year 2000 (ibid.). A milestone in the wide-spread use of the Internet was reached when technology made it possible to transmit audiovisual content via a PC. The limited capacity of traditional telephone networks – through which users usually had access to the Internet – can inhibit access to multimedia as well as to audiovisual content. However, technological advances such as Integrated Services Digital Networks (ISDN) and Asymmetrical Digital Subscriber Lines (ADSL) led to an increase in bandwidth which enabled the transmission of high quality audiovisual content and moving images.

Company investments

These technological developments have prompted an interest in the new media and an increasing number of telecommunications firms and internet service providers are examining the delivery of TV over the Internet in the development of their customer offerings. This interest is triggered by the vision of convergence between telecommunications, the Internet and media industries (Iosifidis, 2002). Technological convergence is hardly a new concept, for it used to be a buzzword associated with all the hype in the late 1990s. However, the 2005 renewed company interest is backed up by technology that works and by huge investments (Odell and Edgecliffe-Johnson, 2005, p. 23). Indeed, companies as diverse as semiconductor maker Intel, consumer-electronics firm Sony, computer-makers Hewlett-Packard and Apple, telecommunication giants Verison, BT or SBC, cable companies such as Comcast and NTL, broadcasters like BSkyB, Internet firms such as Yahoo! – all try to play a leading role in the digital converged era. British Telecommunications, for example, once a traditional telecommunications company, is offering a version of television which allows broadband customers to download films from a back-catalogue on demand via their phone-line and to watch and rewind the movie as they please for a certain amount of time.

Changing consumer habits?

The market is going through an evolutionary change and the major companies are quick to respond to have good chance of playing a key role. However, an important area of consideration will be whether consumers will be equally quick to respond to these changes too. For example, will they want to view TV over their PCs? Evidence suggests that browsing the net may affect TV viewing. The EIAA European Media Consumption Study II (2004) found that one third (35 per cent) of those surveyed in 2004 were watching less TV because of the web. Along these lines, reports by Jupiter Research said that 27 per cent of web users in Europe were spending less time in front of their televisions and were instead surfing the web in 2004, up from 17 per cent in 2001. The reports covered Britain, France, Spain, Germany, Italy and Sweden and found that in the first three territories the Internet was having the greatest negative impact on TV consumption. In these markets (Britain, France, Spain) higher broadband penetration was the key driver of this trend as broadband users tend to spend more time online compared with dial-up users. The ability to browse web pages at high speed, download files such as music or films and play online games is changing what people do in their spare time, the reports found. They concluded that TV companies face a major long term threat over the next five years, with broadband predicted to grow from 15 per cent to about 37 per cent of households by 2009 (Jupiter Research, 2004a, b). A March 2006 research conducted in Britain by TNS and sponsored by Google goes even further to suggest that the Internet has actually overtaken watching TV as Britain's favourite activity. According to the research, a typical user spends 164 minutes a day online, compared with 148 minutes spent watching television (Johnson, 2006).

The message from the above surveys is clear: with broadband connections improving and Internet usage rising, the share of TV viewing is likely to drop. With increased bandwidth and better compression techniques more and more people are choosing to download programmes and films onto laptops and PCs. But it is also clear that watching TV on a PC has its limitations. Despite the increases in bandwidth, the wholesale product required to deliver TV on the web (4Mb+) was not available in 2005. Also in its current format consumers actively and laboriously have to search out and download content using a keyboard and a small computer screen (Deloitte and Touche, 2005). Despite this, it is evident that the increased use of the Internet and the ability to transmit images will eventually lead to some loss of viewer ratings among traditional television stations, including public channels. So far the general public uses television for entertainment and the computer for information, but this will change as technology develops further and new generation of users becomes familiar with new technologies and multimedia.

Third Generation (3G) mobile telephony

The European mobile telephony markets are approaching saturation – in 2005 there was a 96 per cent and 94 per cent population penetration in EU15 and EU25 respectively. However, it is the advancement of 3G mobile telephony which can affect the development of traditional terrestrial broadcasters, for it offers the potential to a full portfolio of mobile video services comprising telephone, messaging and content. In 2004 there was limited demand for video services among end users because 3G handset penetration had not reached a satisfactory level. However, by 2007 3G telephony will flourish and the mobile video market in Western Europe will be worth almost 4 billion Euros, up from just 0.5 million Euros in 2004 (Yankee Group, 2004). Already broadcasting channels are taking steps in the move towards mobile viewing. In Britain, the main commercial channel ITV1, public broadcaster BBC One and niche channel E4 are to be broadcast to mobile phone as part of the TV Movio mobile TV service, which was expected to be launched by British Telecommunications in late 2006.

Third Generation mobile telephony, along with the development of the Internet, can drive the development of specific programming genres, such as feature films and major sport events, and bring them even closer to consumers. Sport, in particular, can contribute to the roll-out of most new technologies – digital platforms, pay-per-view TV, broadband, new Internet and mobile telephony services – as access to sports images constitutes a key incentive for the use of these media (Reding, 2004). In an ever more competitive environment, broadcasters need to strengthen their position *vis-à-vis* their competitors through premium content. This is especially true for pay-TV operators who have to provide exclusive programming to show that they offer value for money. In this competitive market place and with budget constraints, public broadcasters find it increasingly difficult to acquire the rights to broadcast premium programming. Despite the compromise reached to watch major events on free-to-air television (see below), the market position of free-to-view TV broadcasters, including public broadcasters, is expected to deteriorate as new technologies develop and competition intensifies.

Digital television

Digital television (DTV) is essentially an advanced form of television allowing new applications and services, such as interactive television and video on demand (VOD) and as such it offers multiple possibilities for consumer use. The capabilities of DTV can be compared with those of the personal computer. In digital transmission, sound and images are subjected to electronic processing and are converted into 'bits', which are nothing but a series of codes. These codes are then transmitted in groups, and reconverted through appropriate decoders into programmes on screen. Moreover, video compression allows the broadcaster to transmit selected elements from a wide range of stored data, omitting superfluous information. Thus a large number of programmes and services, broadcast digitally, can 'fit' into the same frequency. In fact one of the main advantages of moving into the digital era is the possibility to offer more television channels on the same frequency than is technologically feasible in the analogue era. Alongside these quantitative advantages, DTV allows the transmission of picture and sound without jamming or interference, exactly as they are produced in the studio. It also speeds up the broadcast of data and services and makes interactivity possible between the broadcaster and the viewer.

DTV has largely developed as pay television and has introduced new methods of financing such as pay-per-view and Near Video on Demand (NVOD), the forerunner of VOD. Subscription revenue allows television firms to raise revenues directly from the viewers thus freeing the industry from its traditional dependence on advertising (Papathanassopoulos, 2002, p. 38). DTV also comes with the promise to lower entry costs for new broadcasters, creating an ideal scenario in which it is possible to imagine a proliferation of channels with the entry of new, small and talented broadcasters creating fresh ideas contributing to innovation, choice and diversity. DTV can also offer full Internet access and bring broadband to a large number of potentially excluded households. Viewers can also access an array of interactive services based on the television set, including e-mail, news on demand, television shopping, betting, access to Internet sites, and other enhanced services, such as the ability to follow individual football players and look at different camera angles or statistics during a football match (Iosifidis *et al.*, 2005, pp. 118–20).

DTV adoption

Digital television in Europe has taken a rapid development path and from the beginning of the twenty-first century, all citizens of the EU's 25 Member States without exception have had access to some form of digital television services. However, penetration rates vary greatly between EU countries. Dataxis (2006) found that DTV adoption in June 2005 was particularly high in Britain (63.5 per cent), Ireland (38.1 per cent), Sweden (28.9 per cent) and Finland (28.6 per cent). DTV adoption in the other large territories of Italy and France was 26.9 per cent and 25.3 per cent respectively. However, in large countries like Germany and Spain the viewings were just above 17 per cent, while DTV adoption was particularly low in the smaller territories of Belgium (3.7 per cent), Greece (5.6 per cent) and the Netherlands (12.4 per cent). Most of the eastern and central European countries which joined the EU in 2004 had negligible DTV penetration rates. DTV penetration across the EU 25 was around 23.7 per cent of households (see Table 2.1).

However, the availability of digital terrestrial television (DTT), along with the Member States' plans to switch off the analogue transmission in the next decade, may accelerate the take-up of DTV services. Until 2003 the economic model for DTV had been largely based on pay television services offered by private consortia. These consortia have acquired exclusive popular programming and require

Table 2.1 DTV household adoption in Europe (June 2005)

Countries	Subscribers (000)	Penetration (%)
Austria	288	8.8
Belgium	159	3.7
Cyprus	16	6.5
Czech Rep.	90	2.2
Denmark	477	19.2
Estonia	9	1.5
Finland	693	28.6
France	6,664	25.3
Germany	6,678	17.1
Greece	218	5.6
Hungary	154	3.9
Ireland	533	38.1
Italy	6,039	26.9
Latvia	18	2.0
Lithuania	8	0.6
Luxembourg	1	0.6
Malta	2	1.5
Netherlands	873	12.4
Poland	1,275	9.3
Portugal	769	15.1
Slovakia	15	0.8
Slovenia	7	1.0
Spain	2,498	17.3
Sweden	1,300	28.9
U.K.	15,713	63.5
Total EU 25	44,497	23.7

Source: Dataxis (2006).
Note: includes the four DTV platforms – satellite, terrestrial, cable and Internet Protocol Television (IPTV).

subscribers to buy a set-top box (and, in the case of satellite, a dish) to access it. While pay television has driven the initial uptake of DTV in Europe, saturation of the pay television market in terms of penetration may be occurring. Already the market may have arrived at a situation in which those consumers prepared to sign-up to digital pay television services have already done so. In Britain, the re-direction of DTT towards a primarily free-to-air system has already proved compelling to many households which are negative about pay television (Iosifidis et al., 2005, pp. 124–6). This is evidenced by the success of Freeview, the BBC-led free-to-air service which in just four years after its launch in September 2002 signed up more than 7 million customers.[1] Freeview replaced the bankrupt pay digital terrestrial consortium ITV Digital, jointly owned by Carlton and Granada groups, which closed down in April 2002 owing to overbidding for football rights and bad management. Other European countries, such as Italy, Spain and France, also launched successful free-to-air DTT platforms.

Another driver for DTV take-up could be the setting of a firm date for analogue terrestrial switch-off. So far a few European countries have committed to a prompt date for analogue switch-off. The Netherlands is the first territory to convert to digital in the end of 2006. Finland and Sweden have asserted that they expect to switch-off the analogue frequency as early as 2008. In some of the other large European countries, such as Germany, Britain, France, Italy and Spain, the phasing out of analogue terrestrial transmission is expected to occur between 2010 and 2012, while in some of the southern and Balkan European territories national government support for digital switchover has not resulted in the fixing of a final date as yet.[2] At an EU level, the European Commission's priority is to work with EU member states to ensure a smooth and rapid switchover to DTV. The EC intends to play a key role in setting out a guide on how best to migrate from analogue to digital broadcasting in a consumer-friendly fashion. The Commission's active role in the area verified with the publication of a 2005 Communication (EC, 2005), which builds on a 2003 Communication (EC, 2003), and proposes a deadline of 2012 for the switch off of analogue terrestrial broadcasting across the EU (Iosifidis, 2005b, 2006a).

Strategic alliances between DTV consortia

In some EU countries DTV consortia have been involved in alliances and mergers to limit revenue losses and cope with competition. This strategy has helped firms to avoid bankruptcy but it has resulted in high levels of concentration of the market in pay digital television services. In May 2002 in Spain, the two main satellite DTV bouquets Canal Satellite Digital (which was controlled by the media company Sogecable), and Via Digital (whose main shareholder was the Spanish telecommunications giant Telefonica) merged with the aim of reducing their huge deficits. The main shareholders considered that the Spanish market is too small to support competing digital pay television services. The fact is that at the end of 2001, the total number of subscribers on both platforms barely reached 2 million, in a 37 million Spanish market. If one considers the closure of the DTT consortium Quiero TV in 2002, as well as the low digital cable adoption, it is not difficult to conclude that the market has monopolistic tendencies.

In Italy in October 2002, Rupert Murdoch's News Corporation group, then owner of the digital satellite channel Stream, acquired rival digital satellite bouquet Telepiu (which belonged to the French multinational company Vivendi) in an 870 million Euro deal. Murdoch renamed the digital channel Sky Italia, and similarly to Britain he is now the sole provider of satellite pay digital services in the country. The take-up of DTV services is relatively good and in 2005 Sky Italia managed to sign up 2.3 million subscribers. In Greece, the 2002 bankruptcy of Alpha Digital Synthesis meant that satellite digital bouquet Nova maintained the monopoly status for digital TV services. The European experience shows that only a single platform for digital pay television services has enough margin to survive in any one national market. Acquisitions and mergers will be a daily occurrence, and similar monopolistic trends are expected to prevail in other countries as well. This makes it of paramount importance to control concentration of ownership and to prohibit a single company from acquiring a dominant position in any national market.

Regulating digital TV services

The creation of dominant market positions[3] in the DTV industry can potentially reduce plurality of viewpoint and as such should be prevented. Areas that need attention include:

- Exclusive agreements for the broadcast of popular content such as major sporting events and feature films. In 1998 there was intense discussion at the European level about whether some categories of sporting events should be accessible to the total citizenry. This is possible only where universally accessible channels, either public or private, own TV broadcast rights. Denmark and Britain were the first countries that drew up lists of national sports events of public interest that had to be accessible to all citizens. Their example of drawing List Events has been followed by other EU member states (see below).

- The formation of monopolies in conditional access systems, or decoders, necessary for the reception of programmes and other services by households. Decoders are a necessary tool for the reception of digitally transmitted programmes and so the danger of monopoly in this area is clear, as evidenced by the proprietary systems developed by large DTV operators. Private operators are not prepared to use a common conditional access interface system in their set-top receiver because they want to control access to the viewer with proprietary hardware. Measures must be taken to eradicate the danger of creating a closed market for DTV receivers by encouraging technical interoperability (that is making different systems of decoders compatible). At the European level, the Digital Video Broadcasting Project developed the Multimedia Home Platform (MHP) as the only standardised specification for an Application Program Interface (API). However, MHP came into the market late, in 2005, so that proprietary APIs were already operational. As the Digital Strategy Group of the European Broadcasting Union acknowledges, there is a pressing need for cooperation in this field, and public broadcasters should collaborate[4] to promote open standards (DSG, 2002).
- The misuse of Electronic Programme Guides (EPGs). The EPG is an on-screen display of channels and programme data, which helps viewers navigate through the many channels available in digital television. EPGs are especially useful on platforms that offer a large number of channels. The design and operation of the EPG system will influence both the presentation and the provision of programmes. When, for example, a specific private channel, programme or service is promoted by the EPG to the detriment of others, this may lead to unfair competition. Publicly funded channels should be in a prominent position within EPGs because the public, who are obliged by law to pay the annual fee, must be entitled to have easy access to their content. The EC does not propose any specific action and tends to reduce this issue to the level of general competition

rules. However, most national regulatory frameworks have laid down procedures to allocate new frequencies to PTV broadcasters (the so-called 'multiplexes'), wherever DTT is introduced.

Political and economic factors

In the previous section we presented how new communications technologies contributed to the emergence of a new television order. At this point it should be emphasised that the change to a new communications environment did not come exclusively from technological developments, but also from profound economic, ideological and political shifts. More specifically, since the 1980s, the main trends in European television have been those of globalisation, deregulation, privatisation and commercialisation. Undoubtedly these trends add dynamism to the market, facilitate the spread of new technologies, and occasionally result in enhanced consumer choice. On the other hand, however, TV market liberalisation may lead to higher levels of concentration of ownership. Taken together, these developments constitute a threat to public television organisations which in the past operated under a monopoly regime. This section examines these trends in some more depth.

Deregulation and liberalisation

The perception of television as a public service has today significantly lost much of its appeal, as the process of deregulation is rapid. Deregulation (or liberalisation, or restructuring) of television refers to the design and introduction of looser and more flexible legislation applying to the medium. In other words it means the abolition of some regulations.[5] This idea stems from a change of political preference from left to right and the prevalence of a neo-liberal ideology in many European territories since the beginning of the 1980s. The wave of liberalisation of European markets and the opening up of state monopolies was profoundly influenced by the American political climate, especially during the Reagan presidency (1980-88), which together with the Thatcher government in Britain attempted to diminish the welfare state, discipline the working classes and allocate regulatory power to the market. A central characteristic of the liberal ideology is reliance on market mechanisms to deliver the optimum level of media pluralism and diversity. Proponents of liberalisation put much emphasis on competition to achieve important economic and social objectives, such as the more efficient provision of products and services to satisfy the increasingly diverse needs of the consumers-citizens.

In very simplified terms, the followers of this neo-liberal ideology argue that a competitive environment promotes the unhindered operation of channels, favours business enterprise, encourages necessary investment in new technologies, and protects freedom of expression. The neo-liberal ideology also asserts that a competitive environment guarantees independence from paternalistic state control. In fact, the change of political preference from left to right was partly the result of extreme state intervention in the media in some countries and the restriction of choice under a monopoly regime. Liberals argue for the removal of any form of state control in the media. The view advocated by supporters of a conservative political colour, but also by left-leaning scholars,[6] was that television channels would have to adopt impartiality when covering events, as well as show political neutrality, something that can only be achieved by independence from state control and coercion.

In one way or another all EU countries have embarked upon a process of regulatory adjustment. However, this process as well as the speed of deregulation and liberalisation was not uniform in all European countries. While in some places (Italy and Greece) a regime of uncontrolled liberalisation of the television sector prevailed, in other markets (Britain, the Nordic countries and Germany) the process was carefully planned, with the implementation of a basic regulatory framework and transitional phases. Despite this, the immediate result of deregulation was a rapid increase in the number of private television channels. It is basically these advancements in new media technologies that gave the followers of neo-liberalism the much needed justification for the argument that a competitive market-place best safeguards the public interest. Reliance on the market allows communication channels to multiply, which can in turn enhance plurality of viewpoint.

The development of cable and satellite delivery systems, in conjunction with new digital technologies and online services, have increased consumers' choice and allowed them to watch programmes of their choice at will. The development of specialised thematic channels has led to the appearance of so-called 'personal media', which enable users to choose services tuned exactly to their needs. The emergence of these new media, alongside market fragmentation, can increase consumer choice and programme diversity and therefore contribute to 'external pluralism'. The model of external pluralism can be achieved only under conditions of competition between different media outlets. Its main characteristic is the production and transmission of a wide variety of services satisfying different social strata, through a large number of communication channels. This is in contrast to the model of 'internal pluralism', where a wide spectrum of ideas and views is provided to the public through just one communication organisation, usually a universally accessible, collectively funded, public television channel.

Critique

Undoubtedly the model of external pluralism facilitates the development of numerous media (on condition, naturally, that the national television market is large and mature enough to support them), where each offers specific services to satisfy different needs. However, there are several problems with this model. First of all, the existence of many channels in the market does not necessarily lead to the production and dissemination of a wide spectrum of cultural ideas and social trends. According to media scholar Garnham (1986), within the model of external pluralism, where market forces prevail, the individual is perceived as producer and consumer, exerting his/her individual rights through his/her consumer power in the pursuit of personal interests. However, within the model of internal pluralism, the individual is characterised as a citizen[7] exercising his/her inalienable rights to critical social and political dialogue. The context within which this dialogue is carried out is the 'public sphere', a concept developed by German scholar Habermas (1979, 1989), which takes shape only with the availability of general interest, free-to-view channels, aiming to serve all citizens. From this viewpoint, the existence of profit-motivated private channels does not necessarily promote critical political and social dialogue.

This argument is reinforced by referring to the audiovisual sector in the USA, the country where commercialisation and competition 'reign', and where public control of the mass media is limited. According to Bagdikian (1992) and Aufterheide (1992, 1999), private channels adopt a risk-averse policy by offering a daily diet of mass appeal programming such as game and talk shows and neglect other genres that are unlikely to generate large audiences. This results in limited programme diversity and innovation, as well as under-provision of minorities, as evidenced by a comparative study conducted by Ishikawa (1996). Naturally, this contributes little to critical political dialogue.

Can the free market deliver programme diversity?

The reason that market forces do not necessarily lead to political and cultural programme diversity is two-fold. Firstly the production cost of quality home-grown programmes such as drama series is extremely high. This has led television channels, especially from smaller European countries, to the solution of importing cheap mass appeal programmes to 'fill' their schedules, especially at the initial stage of their operation. It is the norm for the majority of private channels to broadcast American soap operas and talk shows when they first appear in the market, but when their ratings and commercial income increase the channels usually invest in their own productions. Secondly, the high cost of production of quality programmes has led commercial channels to adopt the strategy of constant re-purposing of programmes. Here we mean that a successful cinema film can be reworked into a television programme; this in its turn can become a newspaper article, later to constitute the basis for a musical piece, and so on. This process, called 'economies of scope', does not increase public choice, since the theme of the product is basically the same, but made available in a different form (Garnham and Locksley, 1991).

Television channels have also been found to ally with other communications organisations to share both the high production costs and the risk of being involved in new unfamiliar digital technologies. While the economic advantages of this process are undeniable, it nevertheless carries the danger of an increased level of concentrated ownership in the field. Basically it is here that the greatest problem with the model of external pluralism lies since, as we will see below, high levels of concentration of ownership in the media may result in market domination and endanger pluralism. Media concentration has intensified over recent years and, in combination with the trend towards globalisation and the impending technological convergence of audiovisual media with telecommunications and IT, has accelerated media market integration.

Globalisation and media concentration

The liberalisation of the television industry is closely connected with the process of globalisation of communications. The cross-border broadcasting transmission via cable and satellite, together with the development of the Internet, has rapidly facilitated the worldwide dissemination of programmes and services. This has in turn abolished much of the rationale for applying strict regulatory controls in the media industry and has therefore reinforced the idea of deregulation. The convergence of technologies has constituted one more factor leading to the loosening of regulatory controls, allowing large telecommunications and Internet companies to enter the television sector and vice versa. Encouraged by this new favourable regulatory regime a number of players in the field of IT and telecommunications are looking to invest in the audiovisual sector, and are forming alliances with other companies to share the cost and business risk. These players have sought the abolition of all regulatory intervention that may hinder the operation of the free market, so as to expand freely in different communications sectors.

A typical phenomenon arising from this market restructuring is that of concentration of media ownership. The communications industry has been marked by a big wave of mergers and acquisitions, mainly due to technological convergence, which has opened up opportunities for new investment in different areas. These mergers and acquisitions can be classified into two categories: those that include companies that operate in traditional markets (television, radio and the press), and more complex mergers in the context of the new economy (for example, mergers of Internet companies with television networks). The most typical example of the first category is the merger between Luxembourg CLT and the German UFA in 1997. This resulted in the creation of the largest organisation by turnover in the European audiovisual industry (in 1997 the turnover of the new merged company was 21 billion Euros). The merged company (CLT–UFA) was controlled by the German group Bertelsmann AG, and by the Belgian company Audiofina, which belongs to the powerful Belgian Groupe Bruxelles Lambert. In June 2000 CLT–UFA strengthened its market position by acquiring the production department of the British group Pearson TV and reporting a consolidated net profit of 67 million Euros. In 2002 the consortium renamed RTL Group S.A. (a Bertelsmann subsidiary) and following the acquisition and sole control of terrestrial channel Five in Britain (cleared by the EC on 29 August 2005 under the simplified merger review procedure) is Europe's largest broadcasting group specialising in free-to-air TV, the sale of advertising space and the commissioning and acquisition of television rights in Britain.

In the context of the new economy, the gigantic acquisition of Time Warner by American Online (AOL) in the beginning of 2000 for the astronomical sum of $135 billion stands out as an example of the second category of corporate alliances. This signalled the dawn of a new era of acquisitions. Time Warner owns the CNN network, the Time, People and Fortune magazines, and entertainment businesses ranging from motion pictures and television programmes such as Warner Bros Films, to music and information, such as Warner Music. AOL is the top-ranking Internet enterprise in the world. The dynamic synergy of AOL/Time Warner lies in its combination of different businesses – music productions with television, telecommunications with cinema, and especially television with a new generation of Internet products. With these new possibilities, the content that the merged company has available (TV programmes and films, music and information) can be delivered to an ever wider audience that includes AOL Internet subscribers.[8] The acquisition received the go-ahead from the European regulatory authorities at the end of 2000 on condition that AOL/Time Warner would cut its links with Britain's EMI. EC competition officials were concerned that the tie-up between EMI and Time Warner's music subsidiary could have placed Europe's recorded music business in the hands of just four global giants – Vivendi's Universal Music, Bertelsmann's BMG Entertainment and Sony Music were the three other main players. In fact, AOL/Time Warner and EMI withdrew their intention to merge after it became clear that the EC would block the $20 billion deal. EMI's withdrawal meant that the EC could clear the much bigger merger between the Internet company AOL and giant entertainment conglomerate Time Warner.

A further example of mergers in the context of the new economy is General Electric's acquisition of the French multinational company Vivendi, owner of the largest European pay-TV channel Canal Plus, America's Universal Studios, and the Vizzavi portal. More specifically, in October 2003 Vivendi agreed to merge Vivendi Universal Entertainment with the US television network NBC (a unit of General Electric), in a 43 billion Euro transaction, to create a new giant in the entertainment industry. The deal brought together assets including Vivendi's Universal Pictures with NBC's broadcast network and cable channels CNBC and Bravo. General Electric now owns 80 per cent of the merged company and Vivendi holds 20 per cent.

It can be seen that for some time now the convergence of technologies, especially the marriage between content and transmission networks, has drawn the attention of large organisations operating in the wider field of communications and information. Acquiring contents enables distribution companies both to ensure priority in access to programmes and gain monopolistic advantages through the creation of a barrier to entry. By operating in the value chain from the production of content such as films, pay-TV programming, and music, to its delivery via pay-TV channels or Internet portals, large incumbent operators can retain strong or even dominant positions in the media industry. This logic was behind the acquisitions of Time Warner by AOL and that of Vivendi by General Electric. The trend of vertical integration is hardly new in the media industry,[9] but has intensified as we entered the digital age, for digital television channels need content to be able to fulfil the programming schedule of hundreds of available services. Those therefore that control content find themselves in an advantageous position. For example, Australian tycoon Rupert Murdoch is in a position to supply programmes to his satellite digital channels BskyB in Britain and newly acquired Sky Italia in Italy, through the American Fox network, which he also controls.

Regulation and media concentration

Most national governments have applied sector-specific structural regulation to limit concentration of media ownership, but at an EU level media concentration is subject to competition rules only. The European Union's competition policy framework lies in Articles 81 and 82 of the Treaty. Competition policy is concerned firstly with preventing agreements between undertakings which reduce the effectiveness of the competitive process, secondly with controlling mergers which increase the probability of exercising excessive market power, and thirdly with anti-competitive behavior which enables firms either to acquire excessive market power or to increase barriers to entry for newcomers. The main objectives of competition rules are first to foster technological innovation and price competition, and second to guarantee consumer choice. Competition rules apply equally to all parts of the economy, but intervention in the media and telecommunications cases has in recent years become more frequent than in other sectors. This is both due to the size of the transactions and because the media and telecommunications companies have developed a complex network of commercial interrelationships and agreements with partners that require investigation.

In addition to competition rules, a Regulation on the Control of Concentrations between Undertakings was adopted by the Council of the European Economic Community in 1989 and became effective on 21 September 1990. The Merger Regulation (Council Regulation (EEC) No. 4064/89) was intended to complement the European Commission's anti-trust powers conferred by Articles 81 and 82 (then Articles 85 and 86 of the Rome Treaty) and also give the Commission pre-emptive powers to deal with mergers.[10] Under the Merger Regulation, the EC has exclusive jurisdiction for mergers between firms with an aggregate turnover of at least 5 billion Euros and a turnover within the European Economic Area of more than 250 million Euros each. It becomes clear that the Regulation covers only large mergers, which affect competition in the market in question and, as a consequence, has allowed many mergers to proceed as they fell outside its scope (Iosifidis, 2005a). In fact, the Merger Regulation has vetted over 2300 cases since September 1990 and cleared the vast majority of them (over 90 per cent) after a routine one-month investigation. It has prohibited just 18 mergers in total, while a further 14 have been withdrawn when it became clear that regulators would veto them. Six of those cases were in the wider media and telecommunications sectors.

The process of industry convergence, resulting in numerous strategic alliances between previously separated companies, is seen quite favourably by the European Commission as this will lead to the creation of strong European companies capable of competing globally. Such activity was once looked upon with alarm by the Commission. Companies which have control of numerous assets also have the power to seize out any potential competitors with the result of distorting the economy with monopolistic controls over prices. But over the years the EC has developed a more light-handed approach towards industry consolidation as demonstrated by the merger cases cleared. This is also evidenced by the introduction of the new regulatory framework for electronic communications, which was adopted in 2002 and applied in July 2003. The very essence of the framework is that regulation must not separate markets, but must allow for their convergence; and that only minimum regulation should apply to the media and telecommunications markets to encourage investment. As a result concentration of media ownership in Europe has increased over recent years, and is approaching levels observed in the US. As mentioned in Chapter 1, in 2004 there were just seven major companies operating in the continent.

Social changes

The previous sections showed that television deregulation can be understood both as a consequence of technological changes and as a part of a shift in the political and ideological climate. However, larger social developments have also contributed to the radical structural change of the European television industry. Shifting the focus away from the political process and digital challenge and towards broader social trends, this brief section looks at how social change is likely to affect viewers' consumption of television, and public television in particular.

Over the past decades, Western societies have shown a tendency towards differentiation and constant social change – often leading to individualism and a multiplicity of lifestyles. Important developments include the growing affluence of individuals, the fragmentation of the traditional family unit, the growing diversity of the society, and changing attitudes towards membership of communities and other social networks. As Nissen (2006, p. 22) argued, citizens are increasingly becoming customers motivated in their choice and behaviour more by individual needs and preferences than by their civic role in the community. This is reinforced by a change in the relationship between the state and the citizen. Today one can observe a shift of responsibilities from the former to the latter and therefore an emphasis both on self-regulation and private initiative. The importance of the 'state as provider', caring for its citizens, tends to be replaced by an affluent relationship, where citizens are largely regarded as consumers. This so-called 'cultural differentiation' partly relates to the large immigrant populations in many Western European countries that have given these societies a more pluralistic composition (Dalhgren, 2000, p. 27). As a result new subcultures are emerging – each one with its own characteristics, its own cultural identity and traditions – all of which, however, coexist in a single society.

Multi-channel and time-shift technologies have changed the way television is consumed and added to the cultural and social uncertainties. Although it is yet unclear how extensive are these changes and what their final form will be, they impact on established mainstream channels, including PTV networks, in two principal ways. First, viewers want different types of television and watch it in ways different to the mid-1980s. Second, these changes in society are affecting the way people think about what public television should be. Ongoing changes in the way people consume media and watch television make it difficult to ensure the maintenance of public service in European television. For example, the various thematic channels, specialising in sport, music or news, serve the needs of different social groups and mirror increased differentiation in social behaviour and preferences. This is so because these 'niche' channels can delve more deeply into specific matters than general content channels. In short, this means that thematic channels can satisfy the emerging diverse consumer needs better than traditional terrestrial networks, a practice that gives them a 'competitive advantage'. General interest channels, including those public TV broadcasters unable to raise the required funds to develop new services and launch thematic services, often remain spectators in these kinds of activities. This trend is expected to intensify in the coming years as the appearance of new means of communication (notably 3G mobile telephony as a means of mobile broadcasting[11]) will result in further social fragmentation that will reduce the cultural homogeneity that prevailed under a limited-channel system.

Consequences on public television

The above-mentioned technological, political, economic, regulatory and social shifts have reshaped the European television landscape and had a profound effect on the citizens' perception of public television. Public channels have found it difficult to respond to new technological advancements, regulatory changes and ideological shifts and therefore face an unclear future. Let us summarise the trends observed throughout this chapter and briefly outline their repercussions for the public sector.

First, the liberalisation of television was accompanied by the increase in the number of frequencies available, due mainly to the development of cable and satellite delivery methods in the mid-1980s and the introduction of digital television in the late-1990s. The proliferation of television channels, effectively abolishing spectrum scarcity, made strict regulation redundant and left state television's monopoly of airwaves unjustified. This has led to an open debate as to whether it is desirable to support the existence of public television broadcasters funded exclusively or partly by the public (who may not wish to watch), at a time when viewers now have the luxury of choosing (and paying exclusively for) only what interests them.

Second, public television channels have come under scrutiny by the EC competition authorities for unfair competition as most of them are recipients of both the licence fee and commercial revenue (usually advertising). This issue is raised frequently by private broadcasters, who ask the EC Competition Directorate to carry out checks to assess whether public channels operate within the framework of 'fair and open competition', and whether they enjoy privileged treatment from national governments. Since 1992, commercial channels in various European countries have filed 11 formal complaints against a PTV broadcaster.[12] These complaints are largely based around State Aid issues[13] and in particular public broadcasters' dual forms of funding (licence fees and advertising) which they claim give them an unfair advantage.

The European Commission, which is sympathetic to the introduction of competition in the television sector, has nevertheless acknowledged the importance of maintaining a strong and healthy public broadcasting sector. Several EU documents stress the vital role of public service broadcasting in society. For example, the 1997 Protocol of the Amsterdam Treaty was designed to rectify any unfairness between competitive advantage and the maintenance of diverse and pluralistic services through public service television. It stipulated that national governments were free to determine both the method of funding and the remit of public corporations in their respective territories. However, the Protocol made clear that the EU would continue to allow PTV broadcasters' access to public funds only when they did not distort the commercial market. The EU recommends that there should be separation between the high costs of public interest services (minority or educational programming), where state funding is justified, and other programming genres, which should be funded only by commercial revenues (Council of the European Union, 1997).[14]

Third, it has been put forward that deregulation would offer more sources of information, that citizen-consumers would be in control, and that they would be able to select services to satisfy their specific needs. In this era of deregulation and intense competition, consumers are the centre of attention, having at their disposal a wide range of television services, while technology makes it possible to access, and naturally to pay only for, those services of specific interest. This has resulted in a much more critical stance towards mass appeal programming offered by public channels. As the appearance of thematic channels that delve into specialised topics can satisfy specific consumer preferences, traditional public television channels that are legally required to cover topics of a general nature, may be disadvantaged and led to marginalisation.

Fourth, liberalisation coincided with a wave of mergers and acquisitions in the media field that has brought about large media conglomerates. This trend towards horizontal and vertical concentration meant that public channels had to compete, not only with their private counterparts operating within national borders, but also with multinational enterprises with large financial resources. These companies have the financial clout to outbid competitors to secure popular programming (notably films and sports events) thus gaining a competitive advantage in the digital age. Moreover, public broadcasters operate under more restrictive rules than the private sector, with the result that their room for manoeuvre is much reduced in planning schedules and taking business initiatives.

Fifth, the cost of digitalising public channels is greater than that of their private counterparts. This is because public broadcasters are legally bound to broadcast both in analogue and digital form – the so-called 'simulcasting' – until the final termination of analogue frequencies (in most EU countries this is loosely set somewhere between 2010 and 2015). Public broadcasters are required by their statue to offer universal service and therefore not to exclude anybody, especially poorer households, from receiving television services. Households with limited financial means may not afford to buy the equipment required to receive digital television (that is, an integrated TV set or a digital set-top box).

It follows that public channels are not likely to be in the position to take early advantage of the significantly lower cost of digital broadcasting. On the contrary, private pay-TV consortia do not face this problem, as they can convert to digital transmission at any time. In Britain, for example, the satellite monopoly provider BSkyB launched its digital bouquet as early as October 1998 with an initial high cost, escalated by its strategy to offer free decoders to new digital subscribers. However it balanced these losses against attracting more subscribers (just over 8 million in early 2006). It is indicative that since the beginning of 1999 BSkyB has accepted only subscribers registering for its digital platform, and at the end of 2000 it ceased broadcasting in analogue form. However, the analogue frequency in Britain will terminate in 2012 and until then public broadcaster BBC is obliged to broadcast in both frequencies.

Sixth, public broadcasters' financial burden becomes more striking if one considers the increasing cost of acquiring premium programming, such as sports and film rights. For example, the cost of acquiring broadcast rights for major sporting events increased significantly during the 1990s, owing mainly to competition and the intense bidding wars between private channels. Table 2.2 shows that there has been a more than 120 per cent increase in the cost of acquiring these rights in the period 1992–98. This trend continued in more recent years and the cost of rights almost doubled from 1998 to 2005.

This increase in the cost of broadcast rights for sports events is mostly due to an escalation of the cost of acquiring the rights for live football matches, brought about by the intense competition between new digital consortia which challenged established operators. This is evidenced by the following examples. In Germany in 1999 the ISL/Kirch group offered FIFA (the international football federation) the astronomical sum of $2.34 billion for the rights to broadcast the football World Cup in 2002 and 2006. In Britain, Murdoch's satellite broadcaster BSkyB paid the sum of £1.024 billion in 2004 for the rights to broadcast live the English Premiership for three years. However, France holds top position for the purchase of football rights, for in December 2004 the

Table 2.2 Development of the Western European sports rights market (1992–2005, $USm)

Year	Value
1992	1,479
1995	2,083
1998	3,304
2001	5,475
2005	6,335

Source: Kagan World Media, 1999; http://europa.eu.int/comm/avpolicy/stat/2005 (accessed May 2006).

pay-TV channel Canal Plus signed a 3-year agreement (for the period 2005–2007) under which French football teams will receive 1.8 billion Euros.

Article 3a of the Television Without Frontiers Directive allows Member States to take 'national measures' to protect events regarded as being of major importance to society. The goal behind these measures is to ensure that these events can be accessed freely by the general public. Many European countries, such as Italy, Germany, Britain, Austria, Ireland, Belgium and France, had, by the end of 2005, taken measures in relation to article 3a of the TWF Directive. The regulation is widely perceived as a reasonable compromise between the public's interest to watch major events on free-to-air television, and the interest of rights holders and operators in the economic exploitation of these events.

Despite this compromise, it is becoming evident that public broadcasters, especially those with limited financial power, cannot cope with such competition to acquire broadcast rights to broadcast sports events and in particular live football matches. However, public broadcasters have managed to hold on to rights to cover some important events, through the European Broadcasting Union – EBU. More specifically, the EBU gained the collective right to cover the 2004 European Football Championship in Portugal, as well as the 2006 World Cup in Germany. In addition, the International Olympic Committee has sold the EBU the rights to cover all the Olympic Games up to the year 2008. In effect, this means that viewers will have the opportunity to watch the games for free, without having to pay a subscription.

3
Competition and Dilemmas

The previous chapter outlined developments in the wider field of communications that have threatened not only the financial viability of traditional public television broadcasters, but also their very existence. Public channels face a series of dilemmas in the way they confront these challenges. This study has identified a number of dilemmas relating to the following areas:

- Funding model.
- Programming policy.
- Technological upgrade.
- Organisational restructure.

The following section outlines the competitive situation in the six countries covered in the book and its impact on the public channels, while the next deals with the dilemmas faced by these channels.

Competition

With the exception of Britain, Luxemburg, Belgium (Wallonia) and Finland, public television channels in the rest of Europe operated under a monopoly regime until the mid-1980s and were solely responsible for television broadcasts in their national markets. As pointed out in Chapter 2, the arrival of terrestrial commercial stations, cable and satellite broadcast systems, and more recently digital services, radically changed the status quo. Today, PTV broadcasters have to operate in a completely different media environment, where the following actors interact:

- Consumer-citizens, who demand a wide range of programmes in the entertainment, education and information spheres.
- PTV broadcasters, who have a statutory obligation to provide high quality and therefore high cost programmes and services (which the private sector may not cover) that are accessible to all citizens.
- Profit-oriented private television channels of general or specific interest which aim to increase market share and advertising/subscription income. At times profit dominates to the detriment of programme quality.
- Advertising companies, which normally target population segments with high spending power.
- National governments and regulatory bodies which set licensing rules, technical standards, content and structural rules.
- Programme makers and television production companies, including independent producers.

These actors coexist in a new television ecology, characterised by intense competition both for viewers and revenues. Let us now turn to the competitive TV environments in the six European countries under study.

National markets

In Britain, the television sector is one of the largest and most 'mature' in Europe. ITV, the main private Independent Television station (renamed ITV1 in 2004), has been a licensed operator and in competition with the BBC from as early as 1954. ITV1 (as indeed the BBC for that matter) has always been subject to strict regulation, especially regarding the content and the requirement to cover local and regional events. A unique characteristic of the British TV market is that all terrestrial channels have public service obligations, with the exception of cable and satellite TV operators. The duopoly between ITV1 and the BBC ended in 1982 with the launch of Channel Four, primarily covering minority interests, while one additional private channel, Channel 5 (renamed Five in 2004), was licensed in 1997. The television scene in Britain is also characterised by the presence of cable channels, the most important being NTL and Telewest (merged in 2005 and renamed Virgin Media), as well as the predominance of a monopoly in satellite broadcasting by Rupert Murdoch's BSkyB. The roll-out of digital TV services is the highest in Europe (see Chapter 2). In this intensely competitive market, the publicly funded BBC has maintained a significant audience share, managed largely to retain its impartial editorial policy, and is actively investing in new technologies.

The French TV system, on the other hand, has traditionally been associated with politics and during the 1960s successive governments exerted tight control over television. The rise of Francois Mitterand to the Presidency in 1981 became the catalyst for change in the structure and organisation of French television. Essentially the Socialists, with the 1982 Law on Audiovisual Communication (also known as the Fillioud law) abolished the state television monopoly and liberalised the market (Kuhn and Stanyer, 2001, p. 4). This new government policy of deregulation (Loi Leotard, ratified in 1986 and amended several times since) allowed the entry of many new private channels and formed a system in which the remaining public stations of France 2 and France 3 (formerly public channel TF-1 was privatised in 1986) were competing openly with the powerful private channels TF-1, Canal Plus and M6. The privatisation of TF-1 indicated that commercialisation and a deregulatory philosophy prevailed in the television market. Since the change of its status TF-1 has retained a dominant market position. In sum, PTV channels France 2, France 3 and France 5 (launched in 2001) compete with a small number of powerful private channels with substantial financial resources. But similarly to the BBC, France Télévisions (the company under which all public broadcasters operate) has managed to retain satisfactory levels of audience share.

The picture is rather different in Spain, where the PTV broadcaster TVE has to compete, not only with national private channels such as Antena 3, Tele 5 and Canal Plus but also with powerful stations in the autonomous regions. The entry of private channels in the early 1990s adversely affected the public broadcaster, driving down its audience and advertising shares. The arrival of the digital satellite consortia Canalsatelite Digital and Via Digital in 1997 (now merged), as well as numerous cable TV networks, affected TVE's market position and in 2004 the flagship TVE-1 lost the leadership in ratings to a private rival for the first time. The Spanish public TV system is unique because TVE is not funded by the licence fee; its income derives from advertising and state grants. Parent company RTVE's (Radio y Television Espanola) budget has run a large deficit over the last few years. In 2004 its consolidated debt escalated to 8 billion Euros, and in summer 2005 the government was planning to introduce legislation establishing an independent board of directors to oversee the heavily-indebted RTVE.

Commercial TV is relatively new in Sweden, with competition for Sveriges Television (SVT) commencing only in 1987 with the launch of satellite channel TV3. Commercial satellite free-to-air channel Kanal 5 was introduced two years later in 1989. The first terrestrial commercial competitor to SVT, TV4, launched as late as 1991, but it now commands the highest audience share. Sweden was the second country in Europe to launch digital terrestrial television in 1999 and because of the relatively high DTV adoption the government aims to complete the digitalisation of TV broadcasting by 2008. About one third of households is connected to cable or satellite TV and can choose from among dozens of channels. Publicly funded SVT ranks high as the most trusted medium and enjoys good support from the Swedish audience. The Swedish public TV system is in many respects modeled after the British one, and SVT shares many traits with its British counterpart, the BBC – both are funded exclusively by the licence fee and share similar public service obligations.

Television in Ireland has been dominated by the public broadcaster Radio Telifis Eireann (RTE), which is still the major player in Ireland's television scene. Competition comes mainly from the British main terrestrial channels easily accessible to most Irish viewers since the 1950s, as well as BSkyB which at the end of 2005 had more than 1.5 million Irish subscribers. The only indigenous competition to RTE comes from private channel TV-3, which entered the market in November 1998. TV-3 is owned jointly by Canadian TV firm CanWest Global Communications and the British ITV plc, whose strong financial backing ensures the channel's survival in a small country with a population of just over 3.6 million. The programming of TV-3 is entertainment-led and its strategy of targeting the high-spending 15–45 age group has seen its advertising revenues grow substantially in 2003, a year in which other broadcasters saw a fall-off in revenues. This has affected RTE adversely, as its income derives as much from advertising as from the licence fee. Indicative of RTE's financial difficulties is the fact that in1999 it failed to raise the 100 million Euros necessary to develop a terrestrial digital platform. In 2003 RTE had a 71 million Euros deficit, but in 2004 it recovered and earned a net surplus of 6.8 million Euros, following a successful restructuring programme (see Chapter 7).

TV broadcasting in Greece was developed in the late 1960s during a military junta which ruled the country between 1967 and 1974. Throughout the 1980s, as Greece began to reform and modernise, audiences demanded a wider choice of their viewing options than those offered by the Greek public broadcaster ERT. In the late 1980s private TV broadcasters MEGA and ANT1 took advantage of loopholes in the existing legislation and began broadcasting programming mainly consisting of variety shows, American films and tabloid news broadcasts. ERT was forced, completely unprepared, into a regime of unregulated liberalisation where competition was expanding explosively. ERT's bureaucratic organisation and the frequent changes in administration, all made its programming and the efficient exploitation of its resources difficult.[1] The absence, furthermore, of any strategic planning in the company, which should have responded to social and technological shifts during the critical phase of abolition of state monopoly and the appearance of private television, marginalised ERT's development, and alienated it from the public. The arrival of advertising funded private channels resulted in an unprecedented reduction in ERT's audience share to below 10 per cent, as well as the loss of 80 per cent of its advertising revenue in the 10-year period 1989–99. As will be shown in Chapter 9, important steps have been taken in the last few years to reform ERT so as to move it on to the next phase of its modernisation. Today the TV market consists of numerous free-to-air commercial channels (which broadcast in a quasi-legal state as the Greek government has yet to issue official licenses) and the digital subscription service Nova, launched in 1998 by Multichoice Hellas. Cable TV is virtually non-existent.

Effects of competition on public channels

Television liberalisation in the six European markets under examination did not take place uniformly over the same period and differed in pace. Table 3.1 shows that the television markets in France, Spain and Greece were liberalised in the mid or late 1980s, whereas Sweden followed at the beginning of the 1990s. Satellite and cable television services were introduced in France in 1984 and in Sweden in 1987, while Spanish citizens have only had access to these technologies since 1993. Conversely, Britain's BBC had a competitor long before the 1980s, while on the other extreme television in Ireland was liberalised in 1998,

Table 3.1 Television liberalisation in the six European markets under study

Country	Entry of terrestrial private channels	Entry of cable and satellite TV broadcasting
Britain	1954	1983
France	1984	1984
Spain	1989	1993
Sweden	1991	1987
Ireland	1998	1990*
Greece	1989	1990**

Source: Zenith Media 1999; Television Business International 1999.
Notes: * Since 1990 the Irish households have had access to satellite BSkyB; ** ERT re-broadcasts satellite channels such as CNN to the Greek public.

Table 3.2 Cable, satellite and multi-channel penetration in the six European countries under study (%, 2004)

Country	Cable TV penetration	Satellite TV penetration	Multi-channel penetration
Britain	17	28	54
France	15	20	37
Spain	11	29	30
Sweden	67	21	83
Ireland	54	28	78
Greece	1	7	8

Source: World Screen (2006).

much later compared to other countries. Today, however, without exception, all public channels in the countries under study operate in an intensely competitive (and occasionally inhospitable) TV environment, in which terrestrial channels compete for audiences and revenues with cable and/or satellite operators.

Table 3.2 portrays the degree of competition coming from cable, satellite and multi-channel TV in the six EU countries under scrutiny. In 2004 cable TV penetration was particularly high in Sweden and Ireland, while at the other end the Mediterranean countries of Spain and Greece had low rates due mainly to the availability of numerous terrestrial free-to-air channels, which inhibits the development of cable and satellite pay services. With the notable exception of Greece,

Table 3.3 Impact of new channels on audience share in Britain

All households		Multi-channel households	
Channel	Share (%)	Channel	Share (%)
BBC One	26.9	BBC1	19.5
BBC Two	11.1	BBC2	8.9
ITV1	26.8	ITV1	20.6
Channel Four	10.0	Channel 4	7.8
Five	5.7	Five	4.5
Other	19.7	Sky One, UK Gold, Sky Sports 1, Sky Premier, Carlton Network, Nickelodeon, BBC Choice (total share)	64
		Living, UK Style, Sky Sports 2, Sky Moviemax, Disney, Discovery, E4, Granada Plus, S4C Wales, Sky News, Sci-Fiction (total share)	3.8
		Other	28.5

Source: BARB (2001); Tunstall (2003).

satellite TV adoption does not present great differences among the countries and ranges between 20 and 29 per cent. However, multi-channel penetration in 2004 was advancing at high rates in Sweden and Ireland, was moderate in Britain, France and Spain and very low in Greece.

The number of new channels is multiplying and their share continues to grow at the expense of terrestrial channels, as the British case demonstrates. British households with access to cable and satellite channels spend less time watching programmes broadcast by traditional channels than households with only the terrestrial channels of BBC One, BBC Two, ITV1, Channel Four and Five. More specifically, as shown in Table 3.3, in 2001 the share of the BBC One in multi-channel households was on average about 7 percentage points lower, compared to all households (from 26.9 per cent to 19.5 per cent). Private broadcasters experienced similar losses, with ITV1's share dropping to 20.6 per cent in multi-channel households from 26.8 per cent in all households.

Multi-channel share continued to grow in more recent years at the expense of the traditional channels. In December 2005 multi-channel share in multi-channel homes was 42.4 per cent and had over twice the share of the biggest terrestrial public channel BBC One (Ofcom, 2006).

Slight increase in TV viewing time

Despite the availability of many more channels, there has been no proportionate increase in television viewing time. This resulted in a further reduction in the shares of traditional television channels, including PTV broadcasters. Looking at European TV consumption, Kirsch's 2004 report showed a marginal increase in the average time viewers spend in front of television. In Western Europe the average viewing time for adults increased from 196 minutes in 1995 to 217 minutes in 2003. A slightly higher increase of the average daily viewing time has occurred in Eastern Europe – from 208 minutes in 2000, the average figure rose up to 228 minutes in 2003. In Western Europe, the countries with the highest viewing time are mainly located in the south, with Greece reporting 243 minutes and Spain 222 minutes. British and French households are also fond of their TV set, averaging 239 and 213 minutes per day respectively. Northern European countries tend to be below the European average with 162 minutes in Sweden, for example. Ireland also scores low, with 184 minutes viewing time per individual (see Table 3.4). In 2003, the average daily time per person across Europe remained stable at 3.5 hours, much lower than in the USA at 4.5 hours.

Table 3.4 Viewing time per individual (in minutes, 2003)

Country	Target group	2003 (Mon.–Sun.)
Britain	16+	239
France	15+	213
Spain	16+	222
Sweden	15+	162
Ireland	15+	184
Greece	15+	243

Source: Kirsch (2004).

Internet users spend less time in front of television

Research suggests that in recent years there has been an increasing trend in the use of the Internet, with a consequent reduction in the total time spent watching television. TV has certainly not lost its mass appeal yet, as evidenced by the high daily viewing time figures listed above. On the contrary, in 2004 TV remained the most widely used medium controlling a third of all media consumed, despite gloomy forecasts from some social scientists who foresaw the end of TV due to the rapid rise of the Internet. As showed in Chapter 2, however, there are signs that this trend may be reversed. An EIAA study (2004) involving 7,000 random telephone interviews in selected European countries, found that one third of those surveyed are watching less TV because of the web. The argument that the Internet is causing Europeans to spend less time watching TV has also been supported by a December 2004 Jupiter Research report.

These changes resulted in a further reduction of market shares enjoyed by established TV networks in Europe. The ability to browse web pages at high speed, download files such as sport, music or films and play online games is changing what people do in their spare time and this has big implications for traditional television networks. The rapid increase of digital thematic channels is another factor contributing to the decline of shares for the established channels. Table 3.5 shows the declining trend of market shares held by public channels in the countries

Table 3.5 Evolution of the public channels' average daily viewing shares (1997–2005)

Channel	Share (%, 1997)	Share (%, 2000)	Share (%, 2005)
BBC One	32.0	28.4	23.3
BBC Two	10.0	9.6	9.4
FRANCE 2	22.5	22.0	20.8
FRANCE 3	18.3	18.2	17.0
TVE1	26.5	23.8	19.6
La2	7.5	7.6	5.8
SVT1	29.2	27.8	24.3
SVT2	20.0	19.2	13.7
RTE1	32.1	30.2	25.8
RTE2	20.9	20.8	12.5
ET1	5.4	5.6	4.2
NET	3.2	5.1	8.7

Source: Annual reports of channels.

under study over the last decade. While up to 2000 the public television sector typically captured audience shares close to 40 per cent, in more recent years there has been a significant decrease in the shares. BBC One and BBC Two recorded sharp ratings declines and in 2005 their combined share stands at 32.7 per cent – down from 38 per cent in 2000. Mainstream TVE1 in Spain saw its share dropping below 20 per cent for the first time in 2005, but even in Sweden and Ireland the strong position of the respective national broadcasters is threatened as their share is now below 40 per cent. Greek public broadcaster ERT, which had seen its ratings reaching bottom levels in previous years, is the only one which has seen signs of improvement due to organisational and programming changes.

Funding model

Having established the level of competition in the six national television markets and identified the major trends affecting the development of PTV broadcasters, we now turn to the dilemmas faced by the public channels operating in these markets. The choice of the funding scheme constitutes one of the main factors defining PTV broadcasters' ability to remain distinctive and competitive in the multimedia environment. The reason is twofold. First, the funding model influences investment decisions – it determines the financial capability of public channels to expand in new directions, launch new products and services, and so on. Second, the funding method is seen as an important way of influencing the programming of the public organisations. Empirical evidence suggests that funding by the licence fee allows the broadcasting of a wide range of programming genres, including content for minorities, and therefore best contributes to achieving public service objectives (McKinsey & Company, 1999). In short, the ideal system of funding will have to:

- Provide sufficient income for public channels to compete on equal terms with their private counterparts.
- Be able to withstand political, commercial or other pressures.
- Be stable and predictable, at least in the short to medium terms, so as to encourage business investment.
- Grow at the same or faster pace than operating costs (ibid.).

Traditionally there has been no single funding model for all European public broadcasters. This does not come as a surprise given the noticeable historical, political, cultural and regulatory differences between countries. In more recent years, the 1997 Amsterdam Protocol gave the freedom for each state to set up, organise and define the remit of the public broadcasting system, and to provide for its funding, including mixed funding (Council of the European Union, 1997). As a result funding systems for public television continue to show a high level of heterogeneity across Europe. Table 3.6 enables us to identify three clusters of broadcasters in terms of funding: RTE in Ireland and France Télévisions fit within a cluster of broadcasters where licence fee income accounts, roughly, for between a half and two thirds of revenue; the British Broadcasting Corporation, the Swedish SVT and the Greek ERT have much higher percentages of revenue derived from licence fees; Television Espanola stands in stark contrast to its publicly-funded peers across the continent, for its financing comes from commercial activities (chiefly advertising) and state subsidies.

One can thus infer that the pattern of public (and commercial) funding across the six countries is very diverse. The choice of the funding system is correlated with the national historical, cultural and regulatory circumstances and not with population. The larger-population member states (Britain, France and Spain) differ substantially in their approach to funding their national public broadcasters. Conversely, Ireland's percentage of public funding is different to that of other

Table 3.6 Funding models of PTV broadcasters in the counties under study (%, 2005)

Country/channel	Licence fee	Government grants	Commercial income	Other income
Britain (BBC)	97	3	–	–
France (France Télévisions)	68	2	30	–
Spain (TVE)	–	48	50	2
Ireland (RTE)	40	–	58	2
Sweden (SVT)	91	2	6	1
Greece (ERT)	88	2	10	–

Source: annual reports of the public channels.
Notes: The Greek households pay a levy on their electricity bills to finance public broadcaster ERT.

smaller-population countries such as Sweden and Greece, where the licence fee constitutes the main source of revenue.

The licence fee

Which funding model, however, can ensure wide viewer accessibility and promote programming distinctiveness, while at the same time securing adequate income for the long-term survival and development of public broadcasters? It is a fact that public funding (the licence fee – a tax linked to TV set ownership) is the most widespread form of funding for public broadcasting in Europe. In the past few years public channels have opened up to other forms of funding – more reliance on advertising; creation of new subscription services; or the setting up of wholly commercial activities to finance their core services. Despite these developments most PTV broadcasters are still recipients of the licence fee. The level of the licence fee revenues for the public channels differs from country to country. The highest rate can be found in Sweden and the lowest in Greece (see Table 3.7).

But is the licence fee the most appropriate source of income? Research conducted in 1999 by McKinsey & Company showed that the licence fee constitutes a more stable, predictable (though many countries have to deal with growing evasion rates) and less volatile funding model for public channels than other systems (commercial income and government grants). Alongside ensuring their survival, this robust source of financing enables public channels to meet their public service obligations, take certain risks and devise more distinctive forms of programming. However, the research acknowledges that such revenue is also static because TV-set ownership has reached saturation, with a

Table 3.7 Annual TV licence fees in the countries studied (in 2005, Euros)

Country and channel	Licence fee
Britain (BBC)	179
France (France Télévisions)	116.5
Sweden (SVT)	214
Ireland (RTE)	155
Greece (ERT)	50.9

Source: Annual reports of the public channels.
Note: The Spanish TVE is not funded by the licence fee.

limited potential for growth. A study contacted by the European Publishers Council found that public revenue for Western European broadcasters only increased by 4.7 per cent in the ten-year period from 1995 to 2004 (EPC, 2004, p. 14).[2] A Council of Europe report lists a number of additional potential drawbacks with this system: increases in the level of the licence fee may be unpopular and politically difficult to implement; the need to adapt fees periodically may create dependency on state institutions; State-Aid rules of the European Union may result in complication and uncertainty; political and social acceptance of the broadcasting fees may decrease over time. However, the report emphasises that funding by the licence fee involves considerable independence of PTV broadcasters, rooted in tradition in Britain and Germany, and extended to other Western European countries, including particularly Scandinavian ones (Council of Europe, 2004).

In a 1998 report on public broadcasting, the French regulator CSA distinguished two main broadcasting models, the 'Anglo-Saxon' (Britain, Germany) and the 'Latin' model (France, Spain, Italy). The report argued that in Britain and Germany public broadcasters have long received sufficient funding that allowed them to avoid being drawn into direct competition with their private counterparts. On the contrary, the public sector in France, Spain and Italy has suffered chronic under-financing, resulting in destabilisation of public channels (CSA, 1998), as evidenced by TVE's accumulated debt of about 8 billion Euros. The 'Anglo-Saxon' model could be extended to other Western European countries, including particularly the Scandinavian region. In turn, the 'Latin' model could be extended to Greece and Portugal (Council of Europe, 2004).

A closer look at national cases verifies that the licence fee can be a predictable and reliable income stream against a backdrop of increasing competition and escalating rights costs. Britain's BBC and Sweden's SVT – both deriving their main income from the annual fee – have not in fact experienced significant fluctuations in the level of licence fee income in the period from 1992 to 2000. The same applies also to France Télévisions and Ireland's RTE, which depend significantly but not exclusively on the fee (68 per cent and 40 per cent respectively) (see Table 3.6). However, Spain's TVE, funded from advertising and government grants, showed a dramatic reduction (46 per cent) in advertising revenue during the same period. The declining trend continued in more recent years. Whereas in 2000 TVE accounted for over

30 per cent of total TV advertising, in 2005 TVE's share of advertising as a percentage of the total TV advertising fell to below 25 per cent. Greece's ERT is a special case, having experienced a precipitate fall in advertising revenue over the last years, and therefore being more dependent on the licence fee (paid by all households through their electricity bill).

Commercial revenue

The output television market includes viewers and advertisers who are hotly contested because the former allocate limited time to media among the various options available. In dual funded markets, both public and private operators aggressively compete in the advertising market, each selling their ability to deliver the viewers to advertisers (EPC, 2004, p. 20). Advertising experienced major growth after the liberalisation of television in the 1980 and 1990s. Table 3.8 provides a picture of the situation that prevailed at the beginning of the 1990s when competition increased, indicating that the private sector emerged the winner. The level of advertising revenue for European private channels in the period from 1990 to 1995 almost doubled, while at the same time advertising revenue for public channels declined. A European Publishers Council report shows that advertising revenue continued to grow in more recent years, albeit at much slower rates. There was a reported growth of only 2.9 per cent from 1995 up to 2004, owing to the world recession that led to a crisis in the advertising market during the period 1999–2003 (EPC, 2004, p. 14). However, this growth was not sufficient to support the arrival of numerous new private channels.[3] Meanwhile, public broadcasters, where advertising revenue constitutes the main or additional revenue, have been unable to maintain a healthy income.

Revenue from advertising (and sponsorship) is highly volatile – it depends not only on the general economic climate (which is subject

Table 3.8 Level of advertising revenue for public and private channels in Europe (1990–95, US$m)

	1990	1991	1992	1993	1994	1995
Public	4,614	4,451	4,869	4,323	4,379	3,997
Private	6,936	8,109	10,134	11,636	13,456	14,835

Source: Screen Digest, April 1996.

to fluctuation), but also on competitive pressures. This does not encourage long-term programme and organisational planning. The more competition intensifies for a share of the advertising spend, the more urgent the need for sophisticated, flexible advertising techniques. This however requires specialised and therefore highly-paid staff, who can sell advertising time more efficiently. The public sector rarely demonstrates such financial ability.

Furthermore, public channels that depend on advertising revenue suffer an identity crisis as they strive to combine their public service obligations with chasing ratings. These channels have a mission to deliver a wide range of programming in order to address society as a whole. By definition, however, the provision of cultural, educational or other programmes addressed to minorities do not necessarily attract advertising revenue. If public channels concede to advertisers' demands and show a greater proportion of mainstream programming, they will not be able to meet the above social expectations. On the other hand, however, if they do not invest in programming that meets advertisers' needs, PTV broadcasters may not be able to maintain ratings sufficiently high (say, 20 per cent and over) to allow them to set quality standards in culture, education, entertainment and information. As we shall see below, PTV broadcasters have increased the overall quantity of entertainment programmes in a bid to remain competitive, but this trend is more noticeable among public channels which have a high advertising figure as a proportion of total revenues.

State funding

The Spanish example demonstrates that levels of income are insufficient in countries where public broadcasters depend to some degree on state grants. TVE is partly funded through state subsidies, rather than the licence fee, which was abolished in 1965. This reliance on state-guaranteed loans has proved insufficient to cover the broadcaster's operating costs as demonstrated by the accumulation of debt of around 8 billion Euros in 2004. Similarly to commercial revenues, levels of state funding usually go down in periods of economic recession (as it was the case in the late 1990s) and this can reduce the public channels' income. On a more serious note such dependence on state grants may bring the public channel too close to politicians and therefore jeopardise its independence and editorial freedom. PTV broadcasters who depend on government funding may be subject to political intervention when it comes to news and current affairs, thus resulting in subjective coverage of events. Traditionally the Spanish governments have adopted a more interventionist approach of interfering with the programming of the public corporation than it is the case in the other countries under study.[4] This has signalled significant concerns over a culture of political interference at TVE's programming. In sum, PTV broadcasters' funding by state grants runs the risk of achieving neither their own objectives, nor the ambitions of their sponsors, that is, the government in power.

Programming strategies

The PTV broadcasters' role is to provide content with the following characteristics:

- High quality of programmes and services, extending from the tested and familiar to original, challenging and risky content that could enhance the audience's taste and knowledge.
- Universality of content, including a basic supply of mass-appeal entertainment programming, as well as services tailored for specific audience segments. Universality of content can be achieved through both wide geographical coverage and participation in all relevant media platforms (DSG, 2002; Council of Europe, 2004).

Despite this core of widely accepted common features, in practice programming strategies show wide variations between countries. Theoretically, PTV broadcasters' programming should satisfy their main objectives (making quality programmes, supplying accurate and reliable information and involving viewers in a democratic culture), but what prevails in practice is the dilemma of ratings versus quality. Two issues need to be addressed at this stage: First, have PTV broadcasters become more commercial in recent years? Empirical research suggests that certain public channels have indeed become more mainstream in the multi-channel era. Second, is there any correlation between the programming policy and the funding model? Some studies show that there is a close relationship between the different funding bases (particularly licence fee revenue versus advertising) and programming output.

Towards programming convergence?

Empirical programme studies demonstrate that in the past two decades there has been a tendency of excessive similarity of programme choices between public and private channels, but in many cases PTV still offers more news, information and cultural content than commercial channels. A study carried out by Leon (2004) compares prime-time programming of public and commercial television in all the member states of the EU15 in 2003, except Luxembourg, and attempts to analyse differences in four aspects: level of information; level of entertainment; relationship of programming to advertising income; and diversity of programming. The study, which was part of the GLOBAPLUR project, undertaken at the University of Navarra in Spain during 2003, concluded that in general, European prime-time programming shows a strong orientation towards entertainment, although information also plays an important role. On the contrary, educational programming is scarce. The study found that the commercial sector is more oriented to entertainment, whereas the public sector tends to present a more balanced proportion of information and entertainment. In the overall picture, the diversity of genres is slightly higher in the public sector but the difference is relatively small, and the study notes that in five countries (out of 14) diversity was higher among the commercial channels. Overall, the study concluded that the public television sector does maintain some differences from the commercial sector which can constitute a solid basis for its legitimisation. However, the fact that the difference of content diversity is not very significant can be seen as a signal of convergence with the private sector. Earlier studies, conducted by McQuail (1998) and de Bens and de Smaele (2001), have established that PTV broadcasters still offer more distinctive news, information, current affairs and cultural programmes than commercial channels.

Some studies have examined more closely the relationship between programming and dependency on commercial revenues. The Leon research mentioned above concluded that public channels with higher advertising income are more oriented to entertainment, suggesting that there is a relationship between programming and type of income. However, the study found some relevant exceptions, suggesting that the need for wide audiences and the particular situation in some countries play an important role in the social legitimisation of the public sector. In a report for the BBC, McKinsey & Company (1999) found that public broadcasters whose main source of income is the licence fee have a higher level of information and cultural programming than those depending more on commercial means like advertising. As competition intensifies the high dependency on commercial income results in a loss of mixed schedules, as well as lower consumption of news, factual and educational output. McKinsey & Company's analysis concluded that the public sector's reliance on advertising income leads to programming which is relatively indistinctive from commercial television.

Undeniably the entry of commercial competitors into the TV market has forced certain incumbent PTV broadcasters to abandon their original programming profile and employ a strategy of subtle imitation in order to defend their market share. The convergence argument is supported by economic theory on programme choices which suggests that competitive environments produce strong market incentives for programming similarity. However, Meijer (2005) argues that the theory does not take into account the relevance of programme costs and different institutional environments of broadcasting organisations. By focusing on the German market, Meijer's work shows that the distinctiveness of the German PTV broadcaster can be mainly explained through the organisational self-interest of the corporation. This self-imposed regulation to maintain the informational functions of public broadcasting, the argument goes, has been chosen because of strong market incentives to offer this kind of programme profile.

Publicly funded PTV broadcasters' output

Earlier on we mentioned that three groups of PTV broadcasters can be identified in relation to programming output. In the first category are those public organisations that maintain a balance between entertainment, information and education. Britain's BBC and Sweden's SVT, whose income comes mainly from the licence fee, maintain audience loyalty through a balanced output of programmes that give equal importance to education and information as entertainment and children's programmes (see Table 3.9). The Irish RTE as well as France Télévisions, where licence fee revenue makes up a significant part of total income, also offer a good mix of information and fiction. For example, France Télévisions has steered clear of many of the reality TV formats taken up by commercial channels and has instead given a greater focus on regional and local fare, news and current affairs magazines, high-quality fiction and documentaries. France 3, in particular,

Table 3.9 Programming genres of public channels in selected countries (%, 2004)

Country/channel	Culture/arts	Children/education	Information/news	Sport	Entertainment	Other
Britain						
BBC One	4	28	28	10	28	2
BBC Two	15	32	25	8	18	2
France						
France 2	1	3	35	8	49	4
France 3	2	6	36	6	40	10
Spain						
TVE-1	2	3	26	10	58	1
TVE-2	18	10	30	12	28	2
Sweden						
SVT-1	5	9	40	10	32	3
SVT-2	24	12	47	6	10	1
Ireland						
RTE One	8	9	50	5	25	3
RTE Two	29	18	22	8	12	11
Greece						
ET-1	5.7	11.8	35.5	10.9	31.1	5
NET	11.3	0.3	76.7	2.7	8.3	0.3
Germany						
ARD	5	8	43	4	39	1
ZDF	4	8	42	7	38	1
Italy						
RAI	3	9	33	8	47	–

Source: Annual Reports of the public channels.

has several regional programming 'windows' during the day (see IsICult/Screen Digest Report, 2004). Naturally, certain differences are observed, as SVT provides strictly non-commercial programming, the BBC excels greatly in children's and educational programmes, while France Télévisions' output clearly puts more emphasis on entertainment than either SVT or the BBC. Irrespective of these differences, however, the majority of these channels have brought viewers knowledge and insight, encouraged participation in the democratic process and instilled a sense of inclusion.

The SVT case

Sweden provides a good example of how the choice of the funding scheme influences the programming policies of PTV organisations. Commercial television is relatively new in Sweden as TV-4, the first terrestrial private competitor to public broadcaster SVT, launched in 1991 (satellite channels TV-3 and Kanal 5 started transmissions in 1987 and 1989 respectively). TV-4, which is still the only major commercial terrestrial channel, quickly gained significant audience share and since 1995 it has been leading the ratings. This did not affect SVT's level of income, however, as the public broadcaster is funded almost exclusively from the licence fee. This funding model allowed the channel to maintain relatively high, stable revenues in a competitive environment (McKinsey & Company, 1999).

Undeniably, SVT had to take steps to improve its programme planning to cope with competition. For example, in a major reorganisation in 1987 the management moved entertainment programmes to the beginning of peak viewing times. Also the year 2000 saw the reorganisation of the news desks (launch of a new channel plus two regional services), while in 2001 new programme schedules were introduced, which made SVT-1 the broader mainstream channel and SVT-2 the more narrow channel (see Chapter 8). All these changes made the public broadcaster more efficient and competitive, but had minimal impact on the overall programming output. As Table 3.9 shows, SVT maintained a balance between entertainment, education and information, mainly because there has been no major financial pressure. SVT has long received sufficient funding that enabled it to avoid being drawn into direct competition with commercial broadcasters. This allowed the public organisation not only to maintain high ratings (the peak time level being around 46 per cent), but also to retain its distinctiveness and remain the point of reference in the television landscape by achieving programme quality and promoting national culture, identity and indigenous production (in the past five years domestic production covers double the hours of programming as against overseas-sourced programmes).

Programming of the PTV broadcasters that depend on advertising revenues

While the above group of PTV broadcasters largely managed to maintain a diverse programme schedule with the help of an adequate level of public funding, another category of public channels, partly funded by commercial revenues, have left their followers with a much narrower range of programmes. The cyclical nature of advertising affected certain PTV broadcasters' ability to commit to funding high-cost, high quality but risky genres. Owing to commercial pressures to increase market share, public organisations such as Spain's TVE and Greece's ERT have been left with little choice but to become consumer-oriented services and improve their performance by transmitting more mainstream programming. Whereas in Britain and Sweden and to some extent in Ireland and France the respective public channels managed to survive keeping intact their identity despite important programme adjustments, financial considerations led the Spanish TVE and the Greek ERT to adopt a more commercial strategy. Following TV liberalisation in these markets, public channels focused on entertainment at the expense of education, and on viewer numbers often to the detriment of quality, making their programming output virtually the same as their private competitors. Maintaining this 'convergent' programming policy over the long term prevents these channels from providing output with any significant social value, and exposes them to negative criticism.

The ERT case

The case of the Greek PTV broadcaster ERT strengthens this assertion. The 1989 TV market liberalisation resulted in a sharp fall in the public broadcaster ERT's share to about 10 per cent, the lowest in Europe. Private TV stations soon gained a significant audience share as well as a large portion of the total advertising spend. In 1990, the first full year of their operation, the two largest private terrestrial channels, MEGA and ANT1, topped the audience charts and shared between them 55.5 per cent of the total advertising spend. The commercial channels achieved this by focusing on demographic groups attractive to advertisers, notably higher socio-economic groups and younger audiences, and by adopting a light entertainment programming strategy, that is, broadcasting of soaps, game-shows, films and serials, which were mainly of foreign origin in the first years of operation but later Greek, especially at peak times. In the years that followed liberalisation, public broadcaster ERT tried to improve its ratings and advertising income by offering commercial programmes similar to those of its private counterparts. This tactic did not work, not least because Greek citizens had lost faith in the public channel and preferred to follow the new and fresh commercial stations. It was only in the late 1990s that ERT started to win back some of its followers thanks to the introduction of a reorganisation plan, under which the first channel ET-1 would remain pre-eminently a general interest family channel, with an output that appeals to a wide spectrum of Greek society, while the second channel NET would operate as a news and information channel. As Table 3.9 shows, more than 70 per cent of NET's output is devoted to news and current affairs, while a significant amount is devoted to arts and culture, language and children's programmes, education, classical music, scientific documentaries, programmes for people with special needs, and programmes reflecting regional culture. Although it is still early days to assess the impact of this well-received programming reorganisation, it has nevertheless helped the public organisation to regain part of its distinctiveness and adapt to the evolving environment (see Chapter 9).

The TVE case

In Spain, commercial TV broadcasting began in 1989 with the launch of private terrestrial channels Tele 5 and Antena 3, which put an end to TVE's monopoly. The consequences for public TVE, whose income derives mainly from advertising but also from government grants, was the loss of 55 per cent of advertising revenues during the 1990s. TVE has struggled with commercial competition and was forced to emulate private rivals and therefore adopt a more commercial programming strategy to stem advertising losses. Table 3.9 shows that about 58 per cent of the TVEs' programming output is entertainment-oriented, thus making it difficult to distinguish it from the programming of its private competitors. Proof of TVEs' commercial orientation is the airing of a number of soap operas, game and reality shows, such as Operacion Triunfo, the Spanish version of Fame Academy, with an averaged 44 per cent audience share (the screening of this format was to compete with Gran Hermano, the Spanish edition of Big Brother, shown by commercial channel Tele 5.[5]

The German and Italian cases

In this context public broadcasters that depend more on commercial revenues offer less distinctive programming, compared with public channels that depend exclusively or to a great degree on the annual fee. Thus a perceptible trend is emerging that shows a correlation between the funding model and final programme output. To confirm this claim we focused on PTV broadcasters in two additional countries not covered in this study, Germany and Italy. The main German public channels ARD and ZDF, with a 36.5 per cent total share, are primarily funded via a licence fee (to the significant levels of 82 per cent and 73 per cent respectively). These channels offer programming types very similar to the BBC in Britain and SVT in Sweden, both funded via a licence fee. In Italy on the contrary, the high 47 per cent audience share enjoyed by the public channel RAI, whose income derives mainly from advertising and secondarily from the annual fee, is due mainly to an emphasis on sports and light entertainment such as game-shows and sitcoms (see Table 3.9).

Distinctive PTV broadcasters

A third category of public channels not fully covered in this study, such as the French Arte and France 5, as well as the British Channel 4, focus on cultural, educational or art programmes, or programmes for minorities. These channels do not normally compete closely with commercial channels and are not driven by commercial or ratings considerations. However, there are some important differences between these channels. For example, Channel 4 is an advertising-funded, non-profit making organisation with a general obligation to provide something different from the other broadcasters and to act in the public interest. Although Channel 4 today competes with the other channels both for audience share and advertising revenues, it has largely retained its unique programming remit. The channel's licence renewal in 1998 required an increased commitment to innovation and experiment, educational and multicultural programming, and to training and regional production (Born, 2003, p. 3).

France 5 was set up in December 1994 under the name La Cinquieme and was renamed France 5 in 2002. It is an educational channel devoted on 'education, training and employment' by airing educational and cultural programmes as well as documentaries – 80 per cent of its schedule is devoted to documentaries and current affairs magazines (IsICult/Screen Digest Report, 2004). France 5 aims to appeal primarily to schools and young people. It shares the same frequency with Arte, which enjoys a special position in the public broadcasting system. The channel has a bi-national status because it was established by the

Franco-German Treaty of 2 October 1990. It offers high-quality cultural programmes, with news programmes and 'thematic' evenings hosting films, documentaries and talk-shows on the same topic (EUMAP, 2005, pp. 667–8). It follows that France 5/Arte's content is very distinctive, not only from that of commercial broadcasters, but also from the rest of public channels.

Involvement in new technologies

Rapid developments in new communication technologies force PTV broadcasters to re-think, not only their programming policies, but also the way they operate, their technical set-ups and their involvement in new digital media. As the delivery systems for electronic media evolved from a 'limited channel flow' world to the 'multi-channel flow' world and lately to the stage of 'on-demand services' (DSG, 2002, pp. 7–10), public broadcasters have the opportunity to fulfil their mission in new ways, by for example upgrading their production processes, making their programming available in additional platforms, and therefore adding more value to society. In fact, if universality is to be maintained as a fundamental principle of public television in the digital age, then public service content must be available on all media and delivery networks at affordable prices (analogue or digital terrestrial, cable and satellite, the Internet, Digital Subscriber Lines, and so on). PTV broadcasters must also launch web sites which can be used as methods to 'expand' their services, or merely as 'attractors' to the television service, and also experiment with interactive multimedia services. The introduction of Digital Video Broadcasting (DVB), along with the broadband internet, gave broadcasters the potential, but also the obligation, to develop new interactive, on-demand and 'individualised' services to meet changing viewer preferences and audience fragmentation. Investment in these advanced technologies both enables PTV to regain a competitive advantage and play a leading role in the new era, and come closer to maintaining the universality objective (ibid.).

However, critics argue that PTV broadcasters should stick to traditional broadcasting and stay out of new media activities, including developing new thematic channels or Internet sites. As the Internet becomes an increasingly important distribution channel for media content certain public channels have invested in Internet offerings.

This activity, however, is seen with alarm by commercial rivals who argue that the well-known brand of the public sector helps it to attain market leading positions and therefore bolsters the position of their own Internet services. Similar arguments are put forward in the case of the launch of new channels of a 'thematic' nature – narrowly focused in terms of subject area or target audience. The availability of channels specialising in certain subject areas (cultural activities, sport or education) allow public channels to delve more deeply into specific subject areas and therefore contribute to knowledge and understanding. While commercial arms on behalf of the PTV broadcasters have largely been established as separate entities – as required under the EC's Transparency Directive (EC, 2004) – there has been criticism that there is still interaction between the 'public' organisation and the commercial production of new services (EPC, 2004, pp. 23–5). Commercial activities must trade fairly in the markets in which they operate and be subject to the full requirements of competition law. Any cross-subsidisation between the public and commercial activities of public channels may lead to market distortion, endanger the balance of the public/private European media system, and as such should be avoided, the European Publishers Council argue.

As a general rule commercial activities should be allowed so long as they trade fairly and be consistent with the PTV broadcasters' purpose as public service broadcasters. But the dilemma of being involved in new services has to do as much with the means of funding these initiatives, as with viewer access to these new services. In fact, the way such activities are funded also determines the level of user access to them. For example, in the case of new services funded by subscription, these are accessible only to those who wish and can afford to pay the monthly subscription (but this jeopardises the universality principle). If such services are funded by advertising, then they may be universally accessible but their content may be subject to commercial pressures. The licence fee system best fits the principles and values of the public sector, but its extension to new services presupposes a significant annual increase in order to cover business expenses, something that politicians are in general reluctant to approve fearing the political cost. It also requires a high level of consumer adoption of digital services and as explained in the previous chapter this is not the case in some European countries. It may be difficult to justify the launch of new publicly funded services that are not universally available.

But how PTV broadcasters are reacting to this exciting technological challenge? Not surprisingly, it is mainly broadcasters from larger countries who have invested in areas such as the Internet, DTV and multimedia, as evidenced by the following case studies.[6]

The BBC case

The British Broadcasting Corporation sees the take-up of digital services as offering real, tangible benefits to its audiences. The two previous BBC Director-Generals (DGs), Lord John Birt (1992–2000) and Gregory Dyke (2000–2004), and indeed their successor Mark Thompson, have repeatedly pointed out in their public speeches that the BBC should take advantage of new broadcast methods such as digital television and the Internet. In the early 1990s Birt began the reorganisation of the BBC to enable it to respond to digital opportunities by employing management consultants. Dyke has followed a pragmatic, streamlined strategy in response to particular conditions in the areas of broadcast and production (Born, 2003, p. 9). Current DG Thompson continues aspects of this and pays significant emphasis on digital expansion and audience satisfaction.

The BBC has general obligations to promote DTV, notably, to develop the market for consumers who want DTV but do not want to subscribe to pay-TV services. It is required to provide an attractive free-to-view package, appealing enough to motivate consumers to invest in the necessary receivers. For this purpose in September 2001 it proposed and obtained approval for a new set of digital services, including Cbeebies (a service for children under 6), CBBC (another service for children aged 6–13), BBC Four (aiming at 'anyone interested in culture, arts and ideas'), alongside BBC News 24 and BBC Parliament. In 2002 approval was also given to a new digital television service for young adults, dubbed BBC Three. A great deal of market research was carried out under DG Dyke on the industry impact of the new services (macro-level), as well as on content and audiences (micro-level). These services are available through the main satellite and cable digital consortia, as well as the BBC-led free-to-air digital terrestrial platform Freeview (Iosifidis, 2005b).

The BBC has also kept pace with technological developments in the areas of interactive TV (BBCi) and the Internet. The public broadcaster has been offering interactive services on all digital platforms (satellite, cable and terrestrial) since 2001. These are made up of information services in text and video as well as interactive TV broadcasts such as Wimbledon, Glastonbury and election coverage. According to BBC (2005b, p. 26), BBCi in 2005 was viewed by an estimated 11 million digital viewers per month. Another service is the website Action Network (previously BBC iCan), which is basically a community space online where users can find others with whom they share a concern. It offers citizens a database of resources on approximately 1200 civic issues (ibid.).

The case of France Télévisions

In contrast to Britain, digital terrestrial television in France started as late as March 2005 and at the end of the year it was only available to just over 60 per cent of the population. The DTT platform, known as TV numerique terrestre (TNT), is a joint venture between public broadcaster France Télévisions and a handful of cable and satellite operators. It offers more than a dozen free-to-view channels, including the free new services France 4, BFM (business/economy channel), Gulliver (children's entertainment), IMCM (music) and I-Tele (information channel), as well as a handful of pay-TV niche channels, such as Canal J (children's entertainment), Canal + (cinema), Canal + Sport (sports) and Planete (documentaries). In December 2005 the entry level set-top boxes were selling at around 60 Euros and approximately 1.3 million French households were equipped to receive the DTT services (this figure includes the 75,000 TV sets with integrated adapters). However, success depends as much on boosting the signal (the coverage of the French territory was forecasted to reach two thirds of the French population by the end of 2006), as on extending the programming offer to attract more customers.

France Télévisions has not ignored expansion into thematic TV with channels like Euronews, Festival, Ma Planete, Planete Thalassa and the music service Mezzo. In more particular, since 1993 France Televisions has introduced (in collaboration with 20 other European public TV organisations) the news channel Euronews, with a share of 47.4 per cent in TV5, specialising in both international news, and entertainment. Euronews is France Télévisions' jewel and Festival, in which the public broadcaster has a shareholding of 56 per cent, was founded in 1996 and shows fictional programmes. A year later Histoire, specialising in documentaries, was founded, but the service has now been acquired by the TF1 Group. In 1998 licences were granted to the music channel Mezzo and Regions, the core of which is entertainment and documentaries. All the above subscription services are accessible through the main satellite operators CanalSatelite (Canal Plus group) and TPS (TF-1/M6) and cable networks.

France Télévisions has also introduced interactive services, accessible both via the Internet and television and for this purpose in 2001 it initially invested 7.2 million Euros, while a further 30 million Euros have become available during the 4-year period 2002–2006. Subsidiary company France Télévisions Interactive has been set up to manage these interactive services. There is a specific reason behind the launch of interactive services as well as additional thematic channels. In 2003–2004 France Télévisions' President, Marc Tessier, was facing a challenging time, being criticised for not airing enough culturally diverse material to reflect France's immigrant communities. Tessier has since promised to do more to reflect France's ethnic makeup and the expansion of thematic channels together with the launch of interactive services were part of this strategy.

The RTE case

Not all plans by PTV broadcasters to launch new services have been successful, for national governments are sometimes unwilling to increase the licence fee to meet the broadcasters' costs for embarking on digital initiatives. For example, in Ireland in November 2002, RTE asked the government for a generous increase in the licence fee from 43 Euros, to reach almost 150 Euros. Following intense lobbying, eventually in 2003 the Irish government accepted the RTE's arguments and approved a fee increase (see Table 3.7), but this was not enough for the deployment of a terrestrial digital platform, something that RTE has been aiming for since 1998. Despite the fact that intense planning took place over several years, involving RTE and the government, political inertia and long delays combined to freeze out the development of DTT and open the way for cable and satellite platforms to seize new opportunities at the expense of the public broadcaster (Corcoran, 2002). However, a DTT pilot is the build phase and its second phase was expected to be operational by March 2007.

Strategic alliances

The above analysis showed that there are divergent opinions relating to the involvement of PTV broadcasters in new technologies. A further issue that causes dispute is whether or not to enter into alliances or business collaboration with commercial operators. Such corporate strategies, mainly in the development of digital and online services, are considered essential both to cover the high costs involved, and to share the business risk. Joint ventures and partnerships for investment in new products such as interactive websites and interactive digital television, offer public channels access and know-how to advanced technologies and therefore help them to prepare better for the digital world. Public channels from mainly larger countries have been developing cooperation with private companies for many years. The BBC has entered into a long-term partnership with Flextech plc, the US broadcaster Discovery Communications Inc (since 1998), and in 2002 it joined forces with satellite operator BSkyB to develop the terrestrial digital platform Freeview.

From the strategic planning viewpoint, one cannot deny that such alliances offer public broadcasters invaluable benefit. Joining forces with commercial partners enables PTV broadcasters to establish new business models which may improve performance and enhance returns. However, it has been put forward that the cost of being involved in such activities may be against the public channels' social mission in so far as they neglect their core services and are unable to provide a balanced output satisfying all interests in the society. As will be shown in Chapter 4, the BBC has attempted to address this issue by guaranteeing that a large volume of cash generated via commercial partnerships is returned to public service programming. Another concern is how accessible are these services to the public. For example, the involvement of France Télévisions in one of the three digital consortia of the country has provoked intense debate regarding the identity of the public service broadcaster. More specifically, France Télévisions took an 8.5 per cent share in the digital satellite platform TPS, where, naturally, its programmes were broadcast encrypted to subscribers. Many argued that public programmes should be broadcast free and be accessible to all. Eventually in 2001, in the context of restructuring and reduction of operating costs (see Chapter 5) France Télévisions sold its share for 66.3 million Euros.

While strategic public/private alliances are considered necessary for the public sector in order to keep in contact with new products and ideas, it is equally important to ensure that these partnerships do not adversely affect the public channels' ability to undertake activities of clear public value, particularly in the areas of news and information (for example, coverage of regional events, provision of impartial and reliable news and quality political discussions). This aim may be achieved through a clear separation between commercial activities (which can be a product of collaboration, funded by commercial means, and can be broadcast encrypted) and activities of a public nature, which must be free and accessible to all. Responding to this challenge, public corporations such as the BBC have developed a strong portfolio of businesses operating in the commercial market-place, all funded completely separately from the licence fee: BBC Worldwide, BBC Ventures, and BBC World (see Chapter 4).

Organisational restructuring

As already argued, PTV broadcasters are faced with financial difficulties for many reasons: pressures regarding the level of the licence fee; cost increases in acquiring exclusive rights to premium content; increases in pay for staff specialising in programme planning and marketing. Given the licence fee's static income as well as the fact that advertising revenue is subject to market fluctuations, it is imperative for public channels to generate revenues from other activities, such as modernising their operations, and improving the efficiency of various departments to reduce operating expenses. The very fact that most PTV broadcasters use public funds makes it more important for them to be cost-effective. This objective requires organisational and technological restructuring. The search for new content, but also for new centres of production and organisational units capable of meeting these new demands, presuppose that a modern and rational organisational model must be designed and implemented by specialist advisors. The above aims can be achieved by means of the following:

- Initiating activities in new technologies and familiarising senior and middle management and the employees with this process. Providing internal human resources with new skills and new attitudes will ensure smooth entry to the multimedia environment and result in better planning.
- Increasing staff productivity through motivation.
- Advanced marketing.
- A more efficient system of programme production, for example with the optimum use of external collaborators.

The case of France Télévisions

Once again, a few public channels, mainly from larger countries, have adopted such practices. In France, the re-organisation of public television has been debated since the mid-1990s. In 1997 the idea first conceived of setting up France Télévisions, aiming to combine the strengths of all public channels. This re-configuration was designed to improve the organisational and operational structure of the company. In 1998 the French government presented a draft plan under which France Télévisions would form the axis around which public channels France 2, France 3, Arte (cultural) and La Cinquieme (educational) (renamed France 5 in 2002 and shares the same frequency with Arte) would revolve. In October 1999 the President of France Télévisions, Marc Tessier, announced his intention of making it a joint stock company, including all the above channels, in order to make better use of programming and personnel. Eventually, the Law on Freedom of Communication 2000 established France Télévisions which would unify all public channels under single management, reinforce their coordination and generate economies of scale. Whereas before 2000 the public channels were operated by autonomous public companies, the new Law provided that they would have limited autonomy and function as subsidiary companies under the umbrella of France Télévisions.

In 2001, AT Kearney, the consultancy company, presented the 'Plan Synergy', with the aim of improving the financial efficiency of France Télévisions. More specifically, the plan aimed to reduce expenses by 50 million Euros per annum over a period of 5 years. Essentially, this amounts to a 5 per cent reduction in the operating costs of the company. France Télévisions has so far moved towards the following steps to achieve this aim:

- It has sold its share in the digital satellite platform TPS for the sum of 66.3 million Euros.
- Proceeded to make excess staff redundant. In 2002 France 2 and France 3 had 1,600 and 500 employees respectively (of which 340 were journalists), but this number still considered high compared with the 1,330 staff (among whom 195 were journalists) employed by the largest commercial channel TF-1 (L'Express, 2002).
- Reduced its public relations budget.
- Moved towards a centralised provision of programmes, as in the past the channels operated separately, with consequent higher costs.

As a result the public broadcaster managed to pay off the deficit of 245 million Euros it declared in 1999 and in 2002 it presented a small surplus in its budget for the first time.

The BBC case

France Télévisions is not the only broadcaster which undertook internal restructuring. The BBC has benefited significantly from the internal restructuring plan that its ex DG Lord Birt introduced. Initially, during the period 1992–96, the organisation made financial savings by a mass exit of personnel (the BBC lost 4,000 posts). The coming into effect of the Broadcasting Act 1996 was equally important, in that it approved the immediate privatisation of the BBC's network transmission infrastructure. The sale of this network was completed in February 1997 and netted the organisation £244 million. With this agreement, all assets as well as staff involved were transferred to the buyer, Castle Transmission Services.

Another important restructuring step was the launch of the 'Producer Choice' scheme in 1992. This essentially revised the BBC's working relationship with external collaborators and independent producers, and secured their best possible use. The philosophy of Producer Choice lies in the separation of commissioning departments from programme production. The programmes are either produced by the BBC itself, or supplied by external collaborators or independent producers. The advantages gained are the following:

- Cost reduction. Competition between the in-house production department and independent producers improved productivity and contributed to cost reductions. During the period 1992–96 the BBC saved £300 million, of which £233 million was reinvested in programmes.
- Knowledge transfer. Collaboration with other production companies produced a priceless windfall to the BBC in experience gained regarding new production techniques. Moreover the BBC now has access to the most talented producers (outside the organisation).
- A more powerful team of independent producers. Increased demand for programmes by the BBC gives more power and influence to this team, resulting in higher quality programme standards.

From the mid-1990s there has been a change in the government policy requiring the BBC to increase its commercial operations, expand in foreign markets and establish its presence in the international multimedia industry. More recently, the BBC was tasked with accelerating the take-up of digital television services and leading to an 'all-digital' Britain. In February 2000 the government agreed a 7-year, £200 rise in licence fee income to fund the BBC's digital expansion, but ruled that the corporation should generate additional funds for the development of new digital and online services through efficiency savings and growing commercial income. The BBC has responded by launching a new portfolio of digital services, by developing an online service, and by being at the leading edge of interactive television. The total spend on digital services increased from £185 million in 1999 (9 per cent of the total BBC spend), to £436 million in 2003 (16 per cent of the total BBC spend) (BBC, 2005a, p. 93; Levy, 2005). In order to finance its digital expansion the BBC had to complement licence fee revenues with generating additional income from organisational changes – for example, moving certain facilities to different locations, staff cuts, and so on.

Conclusion

All the above constitutes but a small part of the complex web of dilemmas that have arisen in the field of television today, characterised by the development of new communication technologies, prevalence of market forces, liberalisation and privatisation of television markets, as well as technological convergence. Of course, the establishment, shape, organisation, also the way public television is funded, are not similar in all European countries. However the problems and dilemmas faced by public broadcasters today are more or less common. The next chapter analyses in more detail the technological, programming and organisational strategies that public channels in six European countries have adopted in order to address these concerns and adjust to the digital era.

Part II
National Cases

Part I of the book demonstrated that the challenges faced by PTV broadcasters are common to all countries under study; significant differences, however, can be observed in the way in which public channels attempt to cope with these pressures. This Part examines the status of public television in six European countries – Britain, France, Spain, Sweden, Ireland and Greece. These country reports concentrate on the digital and online initiatives taken by PTV broadcasters to face the digital challenge, the pressures to change programming and scheduling to face intense competition, and the steps for internal restructuring to make public channels more efficient and cost-effective. The case studies also provide an overview of the national television markets, report on the regulatory frameworks and evaluate prospects for public channels. The developments and prospects for the public channels are largely determined by the following factors:

- The political climate. In some countries public channels are regarded positively by the political leadership, while in others they lack support and adequate levels of funding to launch new products and services.
- The regulatory framework. Initiatives by the public sector are facilitated in countries where a suitable regulatory framework has been established, adapted to the contemporary technological, economic and political ecology.
- Size of the market. Prospects for the development of PTV are better in larger than in smaller countries. Public revenues in smaller markets do not allow activities – especially in the field of new

technology – on the same scale as those undertaken by broadcasters in larger countries.
- Infrastructure. In countries where the deployment of new technologies have reached a satisfactory level, more favourable conditions for PTV to flourish have been created than in countries with only a medium level of infrastructure.
- Language and culture. The development of the public sector depends to a great degree on cultural factors, but also on language. For example, in countries where English is used extensively, citizens have easy access to new technologies such as the Internet, and can exchange cultural products relatively easily.

4
Britain

> Population: 60.2 million
> Monetary unit: Sterling (£) (1.34 Euros)
> GNI per capita: £19,000 (World Bank, 2006)
> TV households: 24.15 million
> Average daily TV viewing : 234 minutes
> Penetration of cable TV: 18%
> Penetration of satellite TV: 29%
> Number of pay-TV subscribers: 10.6 million
> Number of digital viewers: 18.1 million (Sky 8.1 m; Freeview, 7 m; cable: 3 m)
> Households with computers: 50%
> Households with Internet access: 40%
> Supervisory body: Office of Communications (Ofcom)

General characteristics of the TV market

The British public has been well served by the mixed economy of a public broadcaster, a regulated private sector and the arrival of satellite and cable broadcasters. The television market is among the most mature and dynamic in Europe. It consists of two public (BBC One, BBC Two) and three commercial terrestrial channels (ITV1, Channel 4, Five), which together accounted for about 70 per cent of television viewing in 2005. British households also have access to the Welsh

Fourth Channel S4C. All these terrestrial television broadcasters have public service obligations, that is, to offer high quality and diverse programmes that are universally accessible. In Britain there has traditionally been a political consensus on the positive contribution of television to society and this has resulted in an unprecedented support for the concept of public service in television. Despite the progressive move away from a highly regulated commercial sector towards market deregulation (reflected in the 2003 Communications Act which seeks to liberalise), there is a determination to retain the public service principles that have shaped the TV market. This is evidenced by the setting up of a Content Board, a committee of the main Ofcom Board, which serves as Ofcom's primary forum for the regulation of content-related aspects of the broadcasting industry, particularly quality and standards. It is also evidenced by the government's endorsement and support for the British Broadcasting Corporation (BBC) in an increasingly crowded market place (see below). However, critics argue that technological and regulatory changes have affected the emphasis and character of the programming of both public and private terrestrial channels which now provide less pluralistic, less distinctive and less diverse output.

Satellite and cable television channels are also widely available but are not subject to public service obligations. British Sky Broadcasting (BSkyB), set up in 1990, dominates the satellite TV market with 8.1 million subscribers in June 2006. The cable TV market developed in the late 1980s with the entry of numerous networks, but in 2006 only two providers prevailed, NTL and Telewest, which are now merged into a single company (Virgh Media). Britain is a leader in the rollout of digital television services. Following the collapse of pay digital terrestrial consortium ITV Digital in April 2002, a BBC-led terrestrial digital television consortium launched in late 2002 and in a course of just four years has attracted more than seven million households by offering free-to-air digital services. The BBC-backed Freeview is set to overtake Sky by the end of 2007 as Britain's biggest digital television provider. In June 2006 digital cable TV had about three million subscribers. Overall, digital households exceeded the 18 million (about 70 per cent of British households) in mid-2006. Over the same period, the reach of multi-channel TV grew to 60.1 per cent. The BBC continued to take the biggest broadcaster share in multi-channel homes, with a 30.8 per cent share for all BBC channels in December 2005, compared with 22.6 per cent for the ITV channels and 9.8 per cent for all Sky channels (Ofcom, 2006).

The years 2005 and 2006 were a defining period for the television market. Commercial broadcasters, faced with fragmentation in audience share and diminishing advertising revenues, began to experiment with new funding models and portfolio expansion (ibid.). For example, in October 2005 Channel 4 launched More4 which offers factual programmes, drama and comedy to over 35s, while in November 2005 ITV launched ITV4 targeted at men and showing US acquired material, sports and movies (in 2004 it had introduced ITV3). In autumn 2006 terrestrial commercial channel Five launched two new digital services – Five Life, providing pre-school shows, popular factual and lifestyle shows aimed at women, as well as drama, films and soaps; and Five US, offering drama, films, sport, comedy and youth programming from across the Atlantic. Meanwhile, broadcasters have developed mobile services, with ITV signing a content deal with mobile operator 3 (I'm a Celebrity Get Me Out of Here! was the first in a range of programmes to be made available on mobile platforms), and Channel 4 announcing the launch of a mobile TV channel for 3G subscribers with Vodafone and Orange. Media consolidation continued with the October 2005 £5.5 billion merger between NTL and Telewest, a move that paved the way towards the creation of a larger player capable of competing with BSkyB and British Telecommunications. BT's 2006 launch of the new broadband television service TV Movio (formerly known as BT Livetime) represents a major shift in strategic direction which brings the company into direct competition with cable and satellite TV consortia. TV Movio is a converged triple play service, supporting phone calls, Internet and television.

The regulatory framework

The Communications Act 2003, which received Royal Ascent on 17 July 2003, is the main piece of legislation governing the media and communications sectors in Britain. The Act has been the joint responsibility of the Department of Culture Media and Sport and the Department of Trade and Industry. It delivers significant changes to the regulatory structure and claims to strike the right balance between protecting the interests of consumers and citizens and keeping burdens on industry to a minimum. The key principles behind the Act are to ensure access to a choice of high quality services, ensure that public service principles remain at the heart of British broadcasting, deregulate to promote competitiveness and investment, and impose self-regulation whenever appropriate. The key points of the Act are:

(a) Transferral of functions to a single powerful regulator – the Office of Communications (Ofcom) – replacing the existing five regulatory agencies (the Independent Television Commission, Radio Authority, Office of Telecommunications, Broadcasting Standards Commission, Radio-communications Agency).
(b) Reform of the rules on media ownership. The Act freed up the communications industry far more than was expected, removing most of the ownership regulations that characterised British broadcasting as it was thought these deprived companies of the economies of scale and scope required to expand into foreign markets. This provided for the removal of rules preventing:
- joint ownership of television and radio stations,
- large newspaper groups (for example Rupert Murdoch's News Corporation) from acquiring the minor commercial terrestrial broadcaster Five,
- non-European ownership of broadcasting assets, effectively clearing the field for take-overs by the world's corporate media giants like Viacom and Disney,
- single ownership of the main commercial terrestrial broadcaster ITV, opening the way for the creation of a single ITV company, which allowed Carlton and Granada to merge and form ITV plc.

In terms of content, the Act proposes that broadcasting services should meet 'universal minimum standards' which will be ensured by a Content Board (within Ofcom) responsible for formulating and implementing content codes applicable to all broadcasters. These 'universal minimum standards' of content regulation are largely 'negative' (prohibiting broadcasters from showing certain programmes that could invade privacy, harm or offend), but also 'positive' (for example, standards for news services, quotas for independent television production and a requirement for all broadcasters to subtitle programmes). 'Positive' content regulation applies to all broadcasters with public service requirements, notably BBC One, BBC Two, ITV1, Channel 4 and Five. These channels are subject to a general public service broadcasting remit (the 'first tier' remit), which requires diversity in programming, accuracy and impartiality in news, reflection of national concerns, and regional production. The content regulatory regime is applied with greater stringency to free-to-view terrestrial services than to cable and satellite services.

Ofcom has only limited jurisdiction over the British Broadcasting Corporation, which continues to be predominantly self-regulated. In more particular, the BBC is subject to Ofcom oversight in: (a) the application of Ofcom's codes coveting harm, offence, privacy and fair treatment in programmes; and (b) the application of statutory quotas, particularly the independent television production quota. Also Ofcom licences and manages the BBC's use of radio spectrum and, together with the Office of Fair Trading, policies the BBC's compliance with the competition law, which applies equally to the BBC as to other broadcasters. It can be seen that Ofcom was not given a wider role of oversight or scrutiny in relation to the BBC as a whole as many predicted. For example, Ofcom does not have the power to approve strategies and objectives for the delivery of the BBC's public purposes, or ensure accuracy and impartiality in programmes. These matters are subject to the oversight of a dedicated governance structure focused on the public interest in meeting the BBC's remit. However, the regulator is responsible for providing the 'market impact assessment' whenever the BBC Trust (the unique organisation that runs the BBC) carries out a 'public value test' of a proposed new service.

In short, the Act integrated Britain's principle electronic communications regulators into a single agency. It liberated media markets, extended 'light touch' regulation and allowed further consolidation of ITV ownership in order to match the changing structures of the sector arising from convergence of electronic communications technologies. The probable future scenario of unrestricted foreign ownership, a combined ITV (which is now the case) and the creation of vertically integrated media giants has raised concerns about both sustaining healthy competition and safeguarding the public interest. Precisely because of these concerns, the Act (with a final amendment in summer 2003) stated that any merger or acquisition must pass a 'public interest plurality test', meaning that it will have to show that the proposed consolidation will add to the plurality of voices. By agreeing to a plurality test, the British government acknowledged the concerns of those who fear for pluralism and free speech in an era dominated by global media conglomerates (see Iosifidis *et al.*, 2005, pp. 72–3).

88 *National Cases*

Public television

Since 1927, when the British Broadcasting Corporation was set up under Lord John Reith, the BBC has utterly dominated the British media. It controls two of the country's five terrestrial broadcast channels (BBC One and BBC Two) and a plethora of regional/local services. The BBC is run and held to account by a Trust (which in January 2007 replaced the Board of Governors) and an entirely separate, formally constituted Executive Board is now responsible for delivering the BBC's services (see below). The BBC's Royal Charter, which is renewed every ten years, effectively makes it an autonomous organisation, nominally free from state intervention, not subject to political influence, and answerable only to its viewers.

Funding

The corporation is primarily funded by an annual licence fee paid by all households with a TV set, although there is also a significant sum raised through commercial activities such as sale of merchandise and programming. In 2005–2006 the annual cost of the licence fee, which is set by the government, was £126.50 for a colour TV (£42 for a black-and-white TV)[1] and resulted in total revenues of £2.9 billion. Since 2000 the licence fee has risen in real terms by over 1.5 per cent per year in order to finance the expansion of BBC's digital services. Income from commercial enterprises as well as overseas sales of programmes has substantially increased over recent years totalling £624.3 million in 2005. World Service, primarily funded by the Foreign and Commonwealth Office contributed some £247.2 million, while a further £23.5 million were raised from providing content to overseas broadcasters and concert ticker sales (see Table 4.1).

Table 4.1 BBC revenues (2005, £m)

Licence fee	2,940.3
Commercial activities	624.3
World Service	247.2
Other Income	23.5

Source: BBC Annual Report 2005–2006.

Audience shares

About half of the BBC's revenues are allocated to television production and programming, and in particular to the flagship channels BBC One and BBC Two, which among them accounted for 32.7 per cent of television viewing in 2005. Although the public broadcaster has held up well in a competitive environment, it is noticeable that its share of total television viewing has been falling steadily. Table 4.2 shows that in the past two decades the BBC's main TV networks lost about 15 per cent of their audience share. Meanwhile the main commercial channel ITV1 has seen its audience share fall by more than 24 per cent since 1985, while Channel 4 and Five (launched in 1982 and 1997 respectively) were the only terrestrial networks not to see their share decline sharply.

Multi-channel development

Such drops in the shares of the terrestrial networks can be explained by the intense competition as the number of the analogue and digital terrestrial, cable and satellite channels grows rapidly. Table 4.3 shows the multi-channel development from 1992 to 2006 and reflects a strengthening multi-channel line-up on DTT (notably the BBC-led Freeview). The collective share of the digital-only channels exceeded that of any one of the five main channels for the first time in 2005 by reaching 30 per cent. Ratings for most of the BBC's digital services (BBC Three,

Table 4.2 Annual % shares of viewing (individuals) (1985–2005)

Year	BBC One	BBC Two	ITV (incl GMTV)	Channel 4	Five	Others
1985	36	11	46	7	–	–
1990	37	10	44	9	–	–
1995	32	11	37	11	–	9
2000	27.2	10.8	29.3	10.5	5.7	16.6
2001	26.9	11.1	26.7	10.0	5.8	19.6
2002	26.2	11.4	24.1	10.0	6.3	22.1
2003	25.6	11.0	23.7	9.6	6.5	23.6
2004	24.7	10.0	22.8	9.7	6.6	26.2
2005	23.3	9.4	21.5	9.7	6.4	29.6

Source: BARB, 2006
Note: Shares before 1996 have been rounded to nearest whole number.

Table 4.3 Multi-channel development 1992–2006 (homes 000s)

Year	Month	Satellite	Cable	DTT	Total
1992	January	1,893	409	–	2,302
1996	January	3,542	1,399	–	4,941
2000	January	3,963	3,352	303	7,618
2001	January	4,991	3,490	529	9,010
2002	January	5,732	3,794	794	10,320
2003	January	6,409	3,440	873	10,600
2004	January	6,946	3,272	2,075	12,036
2005	January	7,277	3,363	4,216	14,327
2006	January	7,932	3,297	6,363	16,815

Source: BARB, 2006
Note: From 2002 figures include homes with two or more reception capabilities. Satellite and cable figures include homes on both analogue and digital platform

BBC Four, CBeebies, CBBC, BBC News 24 and BBC Parliament) continued to grow and in 2005 had just under 3 per cent of total viewing, compared with 2.3 per cent in 2004. The audience share for all the BBC channels for 2005 stand at 35.2 per cent.

Programming

The BBC Royal Charter states the objectives and promises for the corporation's services and programmes and monitors the extent to which it has met these objectives. In 2005–2006 there was a wide-ranging debate about the future of the broadcasting industry and especially the role of the BBC in the run up to the renewal of its Charter in the end of 2006. In terms of the services that the BBC should provide, the Charter states that the objectives of the corporation are to offer programmes of information, education and entertainment for all British citizens. The corporation is also charged with providing a range of new services on digital television platforms. The BBC has delivered many of the public policy objectives and consistently produced a broad range of programmes that, as will be shown below, audiences value and enjoy.

BBC One is more mainstream than its sister channel BBC Two. It aims to offer a broad range of quality programmes that widen the appeal of all genres to a broad audience. It is committed to covering national events and offering news across the day, current affairs and debates (the most popular current affairs programme, running since 1953, has

Table 4.4 BBC One and BBC Two hours of output by genre (2004–2005)

Programme genres	BBC One 2005–2006	BBC One 2004–2005	BBC Two 2005–2006	BBC Two 2004–2005
Factual/Learning	1,880	1,748	1,438	1,343
Education/formal	–	–	1,579	1,567
News/Weather	2,508	2,446	673	620
Current Affairs	159	160	259	267
Entertainment	433	559	810	781
Sport	670	787	1,028	946
Children's	672	675	1,168	1,353
Drama	1,036	880	166	173
Film	654	839	735	964
Music/Arts	82	53	350	297
Religion	92	86	47	33
Total hours*	8,445	8,467	8,575	8,664

Source: BBC Annual Report and Accounts, 2005–2006, p. 144
Note: * excluding opt-outs.

been Panorama), drama (such as the medical dramas Casualty and Holby City, con drama Hustle and spy drama Spooks), comedy (such as Little Britain and Only Fools and Horses) and sporting events (like the football icon series Match of the Day). BBC Two combines serious factual subjects, including arts output, with original comedy and drama to bring challenging, intelligent television to a broad audience. The channel intends to reflect and contribute to Britain's cultural life and to showcase new talent. For this purpose it covers big cultural events and in 2005–2006 delivered 350 hours of arts and music programming (up from 297 hours in 2004–2005) (see Table 4.4).

As noted by the BBC (2004a, p. 89), in each of the key programme genres the corporation strives to provide a truly high quality offering (well funded and well produced), original (new British content, rather than repeats or acquisitions), innovative and distinctive (breaking new ideas, rather than copying old ones), and challenging (making viewers think). The distinctiveness of BBC news, for example, rests on its range and scope (the provision of news by the BBC has increased substantially during the 1996–2006 Charter period as the BBC launched two continuous news services – BBC News 24 and BBC News Online), the specialists that it employs, its network of news operations across the country, the commitment to coverage of international affairs, and the challenging interviewing. BBC One's spending on news and current affairs has been consistently high over the years and this trend is reflected in the total number of hours devoted to that programming genre (2,508 hours in 2005–2006, up from 2,446 in 2004–2005). Table 4.4 shows that factual output and drama also occupy a significant amount of BBC One's programming, while BBC Two pays more emphasis on formal education, factual and children's programming.

But does the BBC's programming meet viewers' expectations as the corporation claims? Evidence suggests that the BBC offerings entail more innovative and distinctive programmes than those supplied by rivals. The assessment carried out by Oliver and Ohlbaum (2004) demonstrates the BBC's strong commitment to investing on original high quality, national and regional British programming on its channels, which reflects and strengthens cultural identity. The study shows that each BBC television service is offering something distinctive to British audiences when compared with other channels – and often to a distinct demographic. For example, the absence of advertising and imported animation on the BBC children's services is likely to have been attractive to families with children. The May 2004 BBC and Human Capital study (with GfK Martin Hamblin) involved interviews with 2257 people across Britain and revealed that there is overwhelming support for the BBC. Viewers benefit from the values of trust and quality as well as home-produced programmes, especially British comedy, drama and film, the research suggested (BBC and Human Capital, 2004).

However, the current delivery of public channels such as the BBC does not always meet the defined public service criteria. A February 2005 Ofcom review of public service TV broadcasting found that taken as a whole the British terrestrial free-to-air broadcasters, including the BBC, have 'partially but not completely' met the collective remits as set out in the 2003 Communications Act. Although overall the traditional free-to-view broadcasters deliver many of the public policy objectives and consistently produce a broad range of varied programmes that audiences value and enjoy, the analysis identified the following weaknesses:

- A risk-averse approach is reducing distinctiveness and minority content.
- Range within some genres has narrowed, for example in drama where soaps now account for 55 per cent of the output while the proportion of new drama titles has declined steadily over the past

five years; and in factual, where factual entertainment such as reality shows and docu-soaps have displaced some serious factual programming (Ofcom, 2005).

It should also be noted that in prime-time the BBC tends to be more entertainment-led as competition with the main commercial terrestrial network ITV1 becomes fierce. The Leon (2004) study revealed that the BBC is among the European public broadcasters with the highest percentages of entertainment at peak times (54.1 per cent), just behind the Spanish TVE at 56.3 per cent and Italian RAI at 54.5 per cent.

Governance reform

Until 2005 the BBC Board of Governors had a dual role as both strategic directors of the BBC (running the BBC) and regulators (holding it to account). This contradictory role was frequently criticised by those who saw the Board as too close to BBC management to regulate the activities of the corporation in an independent manner. The 2003 invasion in Iraq sharpened this critique as government people felt that the BBC's reporting was biased towards the anti-war position. The row between the BBC and the government highlighted over a report by Andrew Gilligan on the Today programme in which the reporter claimed that the government had 'sexed up' evidence to support that Iraq possessed weapons of mass distraction. The BBC has never demonstrated that the report was not misleading and never answered Downing Street's communications director Alastair Campbell's specific question as to whether it accepts that the 'sexing up' allegation was untrue. According to Cox (2003), the BBC governors are at least partly to blame and their failure can be directly attributed to the impossibly contradictory roles they were required to carry out simultaneously – that of being the champions of the BBC and of being the BBC's main regulators. In the Gilligan affair, Cox argues, they proved themselves 'doughty champions but inadequate regulators'.

Following the Gilligan affair, in March 2005 the government proposed through a White Paper that the governance of the BBC should change to create a clear and structural separation between the management of the BBC and the body charged with setting its strategy and holding it to account (DCMS, 2005). The BBC governors accepted the government's proposal and stated that this structural separation both should increase public confidence and maintain the BBC's independence (BBC, 2005a, pp. 4–5). The March 2006 White Paper (DCMS, 2006) confirms that the BBC will be overseen by a new Trust that is separate from its management and will actively work to ensure the interests of the public are paramount at all times. Two new bodies with distinct and complementary roles are now created: (a) the BBC Trust, independent of BBC management, and responsible for setting overall strategic direction and priorities, and for overseeing the Executive Board, including appointing its Chairman and approving the appointment of non-executive members and the DG; (b) the Executive Board, responsible for delivering the BBC's services within the framework set by the Trust, and for the BBC's operational management. Non-executive members will make up a significant minority of the Board.

Investment in new media

The BBC has launched or experimented in a number of new services, including the website bbc.co.uk, BBCi and the iMP trial. The public service website bbc.co.uk was established in 1994 and offers over 2 million pages of information, including news, sport, programming information, lifestyle, music and education. BBCi is the gateway for digital viewers to access more information, pictures and footage by simply pressing the red button on their remote control. BBCi has now created well over 100 TV programmes around landmark content and major events including Euro 2004 and Fifa World Cup 2006, Wimbledon, Glastonbury and the Proms. iMP (Interactive Media Player) is an application in development offering British viewers the chance to catch up on TV and radio programmes they may have missed for up to seven days after they have been broadcast, using the internet to legally download programmes to their home computers. iMP uses peer to peer distribution technology (P2P) to legally distribute these programmes.

The BBC has invested heavily in the area of digital television technology. Encouraged by the current Labour government[2] which has a vision for an all-digital Britain, the corporation has launched an impressive portfolio of digital services to ensure a smooth transition to digital broadcasting.[3] More specifically, in 1998 it launched the digital news channel BBC News 24 as well as the BBC Parliament. In September 2001 it re-launched its digital services, BBC Knowledge and BBC Choice, as Cbeebies (a service for children under 6), CBBC (another service for

Table 4.5 Allocation of cost of the BBC's TV services (1999, 2002, £m)

Services	1999	2002
BBC One	751.8	961.7
BBC Two	405.9	410.5
Regional services	185.3	252.3
Total, core services	*1.343*	*1624.5*
BBC Four (formerly BBC Knowledge)	29.5	32.4
BBC Choice	33.8	52.6
BBC News 24	50.3	50.3
BBC Parliament	2.2	3.9
CBBC και CBeebies	–	19.7
BBCi on Internet	–	100.4
Digital text and Interactive TV	–	11.2
Total, new services	*115.8*	*270.5*
Total	1.458.8	1.895.0
Cost of new service (% of the total cost)	7.9%	2.0%

Source: Annual Report and Accounts 1998–99, 2001–2002.

children aged 6–13), and BBC Four (aiming at 'anyone interested in culture, arts and ideas'). In 2002 the government approved a further proposed new digital television service for young adults, dubbed BBC Three. These services are funded by the licence fee and are available via digital terrestrial platforms, notably Freeview, digital satellite and digital cable. Table 4.5 shows that the cost of launching and operating these new digital services reached £115.8 million in 1999, the year that the corporation intensified its digital expansion strategy (7.9 per cent of the total allocation for television) and escalated to £270.5 million in 2002, the year that saw the completion of the above strategy with the launch of BBC Three (about 10 per cent of the total allocation for TV).

Criticism on BBC's new services

The public sector's move towards digitalisation has spurred intense criticism at the national level and Britain is no exception. The BBC's plans for digital expansion have drawn disapproval from those who would like to see the corporation more committed to fulfilling its public service mandate. A criticism often put forward regarding the new BBC services is that only a minority of viewers enjoys the full benefits of all BBC digital channels, whereas everybody pays the licence fee. Indeed, in 2005 the new BBC services had a total share of just 3 per cent of all day multi-channel viewing. Critics' concerns date back in the late 1990s when the corporation announced the portfolio of BBC services backed by an unprecedented 30 per cent increase in spending on programmes and services over the three-year period 2001–2004. As Padovani and Tracey (2003, p. 136) remind us, in June 2000, right after the government had increased the licence fee, the BBC lost to ITV the football series Match of the Day, one of the BBC's most popular sport presentations. On that occasion, critics argued that instead of pumping taxpayers' money into the 'scarcely popular' BBC News 24 channel, efforts should have been made to retain the football programme.[4] Along similar lines, Labor politician and member of a parliamentary committee conducting the debate leading up to the 1996 BBC Charter renewal, argued a decade earlier that the BBC has become 'too commercial' and that it spends too much money on new services (Heilemann, 1994).

Another line of criticism focuses on the expansion of online activities and the BBC plans to offer a broad range of its past programmes to viewers for free. Ashley Highfield, the BBC's head of new media, outlined a vision for the future of the BBC on the Internet as follows: 'unlocking the archive is one of the biggest challenges we face and, potentially, one of the richest gifts we can give to the nation' (*The Economist*, 2006, p. 28). Indeed, the benefits to the public are huge if the BBC starts making the numerous programmes it has produced since 1937 available to all, mostly for free. This development will add great value to viewers and should be considered alongside with the BBC plans to introduce the new service, BBC iMP, to allow people to catch up on programmes they missed on its main channels. However, opening up the BBC's archive could amplify the corporation's market-distorting effect. Lots of popular past programmes will be available alongside its current shows and, given that commercial business models are just taking shape for on-demand television and new media, such large intervention by the BBC could stifle innovation (ibid.). If the plan goes ahead the likely outcome will be that Ofcom will investigate the potential market impact.

BBC's new services and the licence fee

Criticism on the BBC's new services often correlates with the unique method of funding these services – the licence fee. Universality has been one of the core principles of public service broadcasting in the past and should remain so in the digital age in order to prevent the emergence of a digital underclass, but so far the new BBC services have not been widely available. This has led influential people, such as Barry Cox, Visiting Professor of Broadcast Media at Oxford University, to argue that the debate over renewing the BBC Charter in 2006 should see the ending of the BBC's privileged position as the sole recipient of the licence fee (Cox, 2003). Cox's critic has two fronts: first, that there is little justification for a compulsory licence fee in an era of an abundance of channels; and second, that few BBC programmes have a truly distinctive cultural and social value. Back in 1985 the Peacock Committee, set up by the Thatcher government to look at alternatives to the licence fee recommended that the BBC should rely to a great extent on voluntary subscription (Peacock Report, 1986).

It can be seen that the unique method of funding the BBC has always been subject to suggestions for radical reformation, but recently these have taken a new dimension to include BBC's digital expansion. In October 2005 the BBC put forward proposals for a generous licence fee settlement in order to fund the additional costs of digital switchover. Income generated both from commercial activities and self-help initiatives have contributed to the funding of the BBC digital strategy. Still, the corporation said that the licence fee should rise from £126.50 in 2005 to about 150.50 by 2013, the year that digital switchover will have been completed. This represents a 2.3 per cent premium over inflation, compared with the last settlement made in 2000, which gave the BBC an increase of the retail price index plus 1.5 per cent (Timms, 2005). The BBC said that this increase is essential to meet the vision laid out in the government's Green Paper on the future of the BBC. The corporation estimates that it would need to spend £5.5 billion between the years 2005 and 2013. According to BBC calculations, most of it (about 70 per cent) will come through cost-cutting measures as well as commercial cash flows, but that still leaves a funding gap of £1.6 billion, which the BBC believes will have to come from the licence fee (ibid.).

Although the licence fee may be viewed as a regressive tax, it is a guarantee that the corporation will not be compelled by commercial pressures to cater to the lowest common denominator. This is particularly true in the digital era, which is producing a sea of change in what the average household can watch on television. In this environment, it is normal for the BBC to lose a growing number of its once loyal viewers.

At the same time though, it should build on the strategy of launching new services to meet increasing audience fragmentation and fulfill its public service remit. However, the BBC cannot afford to have digital ambitions with stagnant resources. It is true that the 1999 licence fee settlement gave the BBC a RPI + 1.5 per cent increase in the licence fee per year. This delivered an additional £1 billion in revenue by the end of 2006. But the 1999 licence fee settlement was set at a level which could facilitate the development of new digital services only if complemented by significant financial self-help within the organisation. Indeed, when the previous licence fee settlement was agreed in February 2000, the BBC set a self-help target of £3.29 billion. As Wells (2003) reminds us, critics forget that in 1999 the government refused to accept a recommendation from a commission led by the economist Gavin Davis – later the BBC chairman – that multi-channel viewers should pay a £5 licence fee supplement to fund the digital expansion. By rejecting the digital surcharge, then culture secretary Chris Smith asked the BBC to generate the extra money through efficiency savings, cutting bureaucracy, being more commercially competitive, and being more accountable over spending. As will be shown below the 2006 settlement provides for similar arrangements.

Commercial activities

The BBC has developed a strong portfolio of businesses operating in the commercial marketplace. The BBC's commercial activities must be within certain standards set out in its guidelines on fair trading and are governed by three main principles: (a) the activity must reflect the same values and editorial quality as those of the public activities; (b) there should be transparency in all commercial activities; and (c) the commercial activities should not present a risk to the licence fee revenues collected by the BBC. As stated in a 2004 BBC document, the principal reason that the organisation engages in commercial activities is to 'help meet its fundamental responsibility to maximise the effectiveness of the public's investment in the licence fee' (BBC, 2004b, p. 106). The activities of these businesses have been rather successful over recent years and increased their contribution to BBC revenues. Since 1996–97, they have almost tripled the financial contribution they make to the BBC's public services, from £53 million to £147 million in 2002–2003 (ibid., p. 108).

The commercial activities, all funded completely separately from the licence fee, are BBC Worldwide (the BBC's content exploitation business), BBC Ventures (that offers technology to the BBC and third parties), and BBC World (the BBC's advertising-funded international news channel). BBC Worldwide develops the BBC's role as the global promoter of British culture and talent. It accounts for virtually all the growth in Britain's television programme exports in recent years and in 2003 was responsible for 54 per cent of all such exports. Sales of BBC programming to overseas broadcasters rose by 13 per cent in 2002–2003, to some 40,000 hours. The most recent example of successful TV programmes sold is The Office, while examples of licensing formats that earned growing reputation as a result of BBC Worldwide's promotion include the Weakest Link and Top of the Pops. Also the company's cross-format strategy translates television ideas into a range of magazines, books, videos, audio products, music and merchandise (ibid., pp. 108–11).

As noted by the BBC (2004a, p. 81), BBC Worldwide intends to continue to roll-out this cross-format strategy into more territories and this will be supported by new international partnerships, such as the magazine publishing joint venture with The Times of India, announced in 2002, and the joint company with Penguin in global children's books. At the same time, the BBC plans to expand existing commercial partnerships with companies such as Discovery Communications in the US, Alliance Atlantis in Canada and Foxtel in Australia. BBC World, which delivers the BBC's global news strategy through strong, authoritative international news reporting, has seen significant audience growth in recent years – from 72.5 million households in 1999 to 127 million in the year 2004. According to the BBC, it is one of the very few worldwide TV news channels that aims to present an impartial view of international events. Following the September 11 attack, demand in the United States from Americans wanting to receive BBC World has risen substantially (ibid., p. 80). Finally, BBC Ventures Group brings together the BBC's commercial business-to-business companies – BBC Broadcast, BBC Resources and BBC Technology – and offers a full range of media management and distribution services.

The government encourages the BBC to take commercial activities. In a government Green Paper (DCMS, 2004, p. 14) it is stated that 'the BBC should be encouraged, as now, to generate income from commercial activity . . . related in some way to the BBC's public purposes'. As the Green Paper acknowledges, the BBC's commercial activities bring significant financial benefits to the BBC. Indeed, over the years 1996–97 and 2003–2004 the cash-flow benefit from commercial activities has risen from £53 million to £135 million (BBC, 2005a, p. 88). The increased income from commercial activity helps to keep the financial burden on licence fee payers low. This is very important as the BBC entered the digital era and has been able to fund a large part of its digital strategy by improved commercial cash flows from BBC Worldwide.

Of course the other means for funding the digital initiatives is by achieving efficiency savings across all operations. The fundamental changes in the media landscape described in Chapter 2 mean that the BBC, similarly to other public television broadcasters, must transform itself to stay ahead. This requires implementing radical plans and going through thorough restructuring to improve value for money. This is the area that the next section turns to.

Restructuring

In the past years the BBC has embarked upon restructuring plans in order to become more efficient and effective. Such a radical plan (involving the biggest organisational change in the BBC's history) was the 'Producer Choice' launched by former DG Lord Birt and referring to a trading system designed around an internal market which was introduced at the BBC over the years 1991–94. As noted in Chapter 3, the adoption of Producer Choice reflected a philosophy based on choice and competition which would drive costs down. The former command economy was replaced by an internal market which separated providers (producers and technicians) from purchasers (commissioning executives). The financial benefit was great. As Cowie (1999) suggested, during the period 1992–96 the BBC saved about £300 million, of which £233 million was reinvested in programmes.

However, further steps needed to ensure the BBC's survival as a public service broadcaster, funded by a compulsory license fee paid by all households with terrestrial television receivers. In order to reduce costs even more the BBC management proceeded to drastic cuts in workforce. The number of employees in the BBC home services in 1987–88 was 24,230 but this fell 18 per cent to 19,882 in 1995–96. This resulted in annual efficiency savings of £130 million and according to Cowie (1999) the surplus was intended to finance the production of new programmes.

In June 2004 the current Director General of the BBC, Mark Thompson, announced an even more ambitious (and painful, for the BBC employees) restructuring program. Identifying key areas of opposition to the BBC, the DG launched reviews of self-inflicting changes before the government took advantage of the review of the BBC's Royal Charter to impose similar initiatives through compulsory means. These changes would be:

- A target for job cuts to 3,780.
- 15 per cent cuts in all budgets to deal with claims that the BBC was 'fat and inefficient'.
- An effective voluntary quota of 40 per cent for independent TV productions.
- Transfers of production departments including Sport and Children's to Manchester, to address claims that the BBC was 'London-centric'.
- Sale of many of the BBC's commercial subsidiaries in the face of complaints from competitors that the corporation was using the licence fee to intrude on their territory. In this context BBC Resources and BBC Broadcast are facing privatisation and the 2,350 staff in these subsidiaries are facing uncertainty about their future.

It is expected that these changes will result in annual savings in the region of £320 million within three years – all of which the BBC promises would be directed (once again) into programmes. Other restructuring plans include the introduction of a 'window of creative competition' (WOCC) which allows independent companies to bid against in-house departments for commissions. This measure intends to answer concerns raised by the independent production sector, which currently has a legal right to provide 25 per cent of BBC TV programmes but wants a higher quota (Levy, 2006). The WOCC will run alongside an 'indie' guarantee – the proportion of commissions that the BBC must offer exclusively to independent production companies. In parallel with the WOCC, BBC production departments are cutting in-house capacity from 75 to 60 per cent, almost guaranteeing that the independent sector will provide at least 40 per cent of BBC programmes.

Prospects for the BBC

The BBC is facing sharply increased competition as the number of digital channels grows rapidly. Audiences to BBC One and BBC Two have fallen and the rising numbers watching the digital channels BBC Three and BBC Four are unlikely to make up the losses. There is some evidence that the corporation's output has become more commercial, particularly when it comes to BBC One's prime-time schedule. Yet the BBC still invests more on home-grown original production than its rivals and consistently produces a broad range of varied programmes that audiences value and enjoy.

The BBC has recovered from some recent crises. Ofcom, the new media regulator was questioning not so long ago whether the licence fee was still justifiable in the era with hundreds of new channels and falling shares for traditional networks, including the BBC. In 2002–2003 the government and Ofcom seemed determined to define the BBC's purpose according to economic principles alone and reduce the BBC's role to correcting market failures. Furthermore, in the depths of the BBC's crisis over an inaccurate report about the Iraq war in 2003, the future of the corporation looked dark (*The Economist*, 2006, pp. 28–31). In the end, the government decided to go on with the tested Lord Reith's BBC formula to 'educate, entertain and inform', albeit it expanded it by including 'sustaining citizenship' and 'bringing the world to the UK and the UK to the world' as new purposes.

The government's 2006 White Paper (DCMS, 2006) proposes a ten-year Charter and secure funding for the BBC via the licence fee. This is a strong endorsement of the BBC as a cornerstone of public service broadcasting in Britain. After two years of public debate, many foresaw that the White Paper would rein the BBC and limit its scope. In fact, it endorses a very different vision for the BBC – strengthening and enriching its existing services, developing on-demand and other digital services, playing a central role in building the infrastructure and the promotion and public awareness needed to create a digital Britain. Above all, the government proposes that the BBC will be funded by the licence fee for the next ten years, therefore retaining the contract between the BBC and, ultimately, the public for the delivery of content that furthers public purposes. Most of the credit for achieving a successful Charter settlement for the BBC should go to DG Mark Thompson and Chairman Michael Grade. However, in November 2006, in a shocked move weeks before the government was due to fix the level of the licence fee, Michael Grade decided to depart to take the role of the new head of commercial rival ITV with a brief to save the 50-year old broadcasting organisation from meltdown following a downturn in advertising revenues and lower ratings.[5]

The maintenance of public funding will allow the BBC to remain firmly committed to taking risks on both new ambitious programmes and new technologies. Jana Bennett, the director of television at the BBC, noted that because the corporation does not have to think about advertising or a commercial return, it can experiment with new forms of television or invest in major projects, like Pompeii, that can take years to create. She also argued that the BBC launch of DTT platform has shifted the TV landscape by making digital channels more widely available and given the BBC new opportunities to better use its vast programming output (Winslow, 2005a, p. 2). But although the government has granted the BBC its wishes on many areas, there will be some changes. First, the licence fee settlement announced in January 2007 means the BBC still receives substantial, guaranteed income of more than £20 billion over the next six years, but it leaves a gap of around £2 billion over the next six years between what the corporation believed it needed to deliver its mission and what will actually be available. More specifically, the BBC asked for PRI +1.8 per cent and £600 million to fund the targeted help scheme and the government is giving the BBC the equivalent of PRI −1.5 per cent and £600 million, as the Treasury has been resisting the BBC's bid for an above inflation-rate increase. Second, Ofcom will for the first time play a part in deciding whether to allow further expansion of BBC services. For each new service there will be a public value test carried out by the BBC Trust, followed by a market impact report conducted by Ofcom. Third, the setting up of the BBC Trust, will mark a step change in the way the BBC is run and held into account and will eventually address widespread criticism of the BBC's in-house governance. It is also expected to stave off calls for independent regulation of the BBC, although some critics say the changes are simply cosmetic. Without doubt, the Trust's task will be difficult and the expectations high – as Barnett (2006) put it, there will be intense pressure on the Trust to restrict the BBC.

Finally, public support of the BBC (and its method of funding) is overwhelmingly positive. The loyalty of most British citizens towards the BBC is typically fierce. The BBC, they will tell you, is a national treasure: impartial and intelligent, serious but not solemn, popular but not populist (Heilemann, 1994, p. 1). An April 2006 independent report by Professor Patrick Barwise concluded that there is a high level of support for the BBC, its role in driving digital Britain, and most of its new services, and a willingness to pay a licence fee of £150 (in 2005 prices) by 2013–2014 in order to fund it (Barwise, 2006). The report has drawn on four earlier research studies, which also demonstrate strong support for the PTV broadcaster (BBC and Human Capital, 2004; MORI, 2005; Opinion Leader Research, 2006; BMRB Omnibus Survey, 2006). The BBC and Human Capital, for example, carried out a survey (together with GfK Martin Hamblin) to measure the value that the public broadcaster creates and revealed that 81 per cent of the British population believe that the licence fee represents good value for money with over 40 per cent being prepared to pay twice the current licence fee or more. Young men with multi-channel television value the BBC the most highly, the research found.

5
France

Population: 60.7 million (UN, 2005)
Monetary Unit: Euro
GNI per capita: $24,730 (World Bank, 2005)
Households with television: 22.16 million
Average daily TV viewing: (ages 4 years and over): 229 minutes
Penetration of cable TV: 15%
Penetration of satellite TV: 19%
Number of pay-TV subscribers: 5.4 million
Number of digital viewers: 9 million
Supervisory body: Conseil Superieur de l' Audiovisuel (CSA)
Households with Computers: 56% (Mediametrie)
Households with Internet Access: 30.1% (Mediametrie)

General characteristics of the TV market

The structure of the French television market differs significantly from that of Britain in that it is characterised by a large number of 'players': the seven over-the-air broadcasters France 2, France 3, France 5, Arte, Canal Plus, TF-1 and M6 plus numerous thematic channels supplied by the two satellite pay consortia Canal Satellite and TPS (now merged). The TV industry is also subject to a continuously changing regulatory framework launched by the government in power. French television and politics have been intertwined for decades and political intervention in the sector has become the norm (Kuhn and Stanyer,

2001, pp. 2–15). The 1960s, in particular, was known as 'the decade of state intervention' (EUMAP, 2005, p. 229), where each new government usually changed or amended existing regulations and appointed directors of their liking to the public sector. In the 1980s French broadcasting entered an era of commercialised state TV, while broadcasting today is a dual public private system, as in most European countries. What is unique is that the commercial sector in France is dominated by one single operator, the formerly public channel TF-1.

The television market in France has experienced spectacular changes since the mid 1980s while it is currently in transition. In 1982 the French government passed a law that ended the state television monopoly and made provision for the establishment of the High Council of Broadcasting (Conseil Superieur de l'Audiovisuel – CSA), as an independent supervisory body. The first private channel to be licensed in 1984 was the pay-TV service Canal Plus, controlled by Vivendi Universal (later acquired by General Electric and renamed NBC-Universal).[1] In 2004 Canal Plus operated in France and in eight more countries and had about 14 million subscribers, but since then has sold nearly all of its international operations except those in Poland, cutting a major source of losses caused by overspending of former President of Vivendi Universal Jean-Marie Messier (Iosifidis, 2005a). In France it controls the terrestrial channel Canal Plus, the digital satellite platform Canal Satellite, as well as the cable network Numericable. Terrestrial Canal Plus has an audience share of around 4 per cent (see Table 5.1), while subscribers to premium content (signing mainly due to soccer and films) total nearly 11 million.

The two commercial, advertising-funded terrestrial channels, TF-1 and M6, have a strong presence in the French TV market. The previously public free-to-air, general-interest and family-oriented TF-1 is the market leader with 32.1 per cent audience share in 2005. TF-1 has enjoyed this dominant position by airing popular shows (such as La Ferme Celebrites, which was a ratings hit in 2004) and soccer (it acquired, among others, the rights for the Euro 2004). The year 2003 marked the end of a depressing ten-year steady fall in advertising share for TF-1 and boosted hopes that real growth can be achieved. During the period 1993–2002 the channel lost 8.4 per cent in terms of advertising share, but in 2004 it managed to achieve a very high 55 per cent share of the advertising market. Parent company TF-1 Group controls the news channel La Chaine Info (LCI), Eurosport, which broadcasts across Europe, the documentary channel Odyssee, TF6, Serie Club and the regional channel TV Breizh. It is also the majority shareholder in the pay digital satellite platform TPS with a 66 per cent stake (M6 owns the balance). M6 is the second most popular commercial channel with an audience share of 15 per cent in 2005. M6 targets young audiences as well as housewives under the age of 50. In 1998 the channel set up the thematic services M6 Musique and Club Teleachat.

Packages of channels are mainly supplied by the newly merged Canal Satelite/TPS consortium, whereas cable consortia provide a broad range of programmes in different combinations. Digital terrestrial television (DTT), initially planned to start in 2003, was eventually launched in March 2005. The package originally included 14 free-to-air channels and in 2006 two bouquets of pay-TV were added. However, several factors adversely affect take-up and deployment of DTT, including low initial technical coverage of 60 per cent (although this should eventually reach 85 per cent of French TV homes by 2007), and a lower programming investment and offer variety than that offered by the satellite consortia. By the end of 2006 an estimated 5.8 million households had DTT.

The regulatory framework

With the Law 86-1067 on Freedom of Communication passed on 30 September 1986, the French government brought to an end the state monopoly in broadcasting. This law, as amended several times, most recently by the Law on Electronic Communications of 9 July 2004, still constitutes today the main broadcasting regulatory framework in France. Three main actors are involved in the regulation of French broadcasting: the Government, the Parliament and the regulatory body CSA, established by the 1986 Law. The government is in charge of designing policies, drafting broadcasting laws and issuing decrees to implement them. Parliament's task is to pass broadcasting laws and determine the funding of public channels. The CSA is an independent supervisory body and consists of nine members who are responsible for granting licences to private broadcasters, appointing the heads of public broadcasters, and supervising the programming of all broadcasters. However, the regulatory body is not adequately equipped in terms of staff and technical expertise and it is often captured by the industry. Also, and in contrast to Britain, citizens are rarely involved in the CSA's decision-making process (EUMAP, 2005, p. 229).

In terms of ownership regulation, France has in place a complex and detailed set of ownership restrictions in order to secure diversity of views and the free communication of thought and opinions. The 1986 Law stipulates that the maximum holding in national terrestrial television channels (reaching more than six million inhabitants) is limited to 49 per cent of the capital. The maximum holding in local or regional television channels (reaching fewer than six million inhabitants) is limited to 50 per cent of the capital. Other provisions relating to multiple television ownership provide that if a person owns more than a 15 per cent of a television channel, then the holding of a second channel is limited to 15 per cent, and the holding of the third to just 5 per cent. For digital services, the 49 per cent limit only applies if the channel has a share of the total television audience exceeding 2.5 per cent. Satellite television ownership is limited to a maximum holding in a single channel of 50 per cent, maximum holdings in two channels of 50 per cent in the first and 33.3 per cent in the second, and maximum holdings in three channels of 50 per cent in the first, 33.3 per cent in the second, and 5 per cent in the third (Giudicelli and Derieux, 2001, pp. 55–7; Iosifidis *et al.*, 2005, p. 74).

Content regulation is also evident with a dual objective: to set editorial standards and to promote programme quality. There is a concern that French citizens should be protected from harmful content and for this reason the CSA aims to 'safeguard fundamental principles such as respect, human dignity and public order'. The need to encourage and support content quality and domestic production through regulatory intervention is felt most acutely in France, which retains an intense commitment to some form of 'cultural exception' (Lovegrove and Enriquez, 2002, p. 108). France has also introduced positive domestic content regulation that takes the form of broadcast quotas (by setting a 60 per cent quota), as well as support of the production of films and other audiovisual works. These provisions are intended to protect the French culture and language.

Article 43-11 of the 1986 Law lays down the objectives of the public channels, which are the following:

- The provision of entertainment, cultural and educational programmes.

- The offering of a wide range, diverse programmes which would reflect the social and cultural trends in French society.
- The provision of independent and pluralist news and current affairs programmes.
- Innovation and pioneering in programme production.
- The advancement of French language and culture through French productions and their diffusion abroad.
- Contribution to the democratic debate within French society, as well as to the social inclusion of citizens.

Public television

As a result of the privatisation of the formerly public channel TF-1 in 1987, France Télévisions, the public broadcaster, established by the Law on Freedom of Communication 2000, now consists of the following channels:

- The national general interest TV channel France 2 (previously Antenne2).
- The national TV channel France 3 (previously FR3), which covers both national and regional issues. France 2 and France 3 have between them an average audience share of just below 38 per cent.
- The national educational and cultural channel France 5 (previously La Cinquieme) with a 3.1 per cent audience rating, which shares the frequency with the bi-national French-German channel Association Relative a la Television Europeenne (Arte). Arte has an average daily rating of 1.9 per cent (see Table 5.1).

Table 5.1 Audience shares of the national terrestrial TV channels in France (1995–2005)

Channels	1995	1999	2001	2003	2005
TF-1	37.3	34.2	32.7	32.7	32.1
France 2	23.8	21.2	21.1	21.1	20.8
France 3	17.6	15.9	17.1	17.1	17.0
Canal Plus	4.4	4.7	3.6	4.0	4.0
La Cinquieme/France 5	1.4	1.9	1.9	2.9	3.1
Arte	1.2	1.6	1.6	1.8	1.9
M6	11.5	14.3	14.0	13.5	15.0

Source: Médiamétrie (2006).

It can be seen that the main public channels France 2 and France 3 enjoy good ratings, and that despite intense competition since 1995 mainly from the three commercial channels, TF-1, M6 and Canal Plus, their share has only dropped slightly. France 2 and France 3 are the second and third most watched TV channels with a 20.8 per cent and 17 per cent shares respectively. France Télévisions has proven far more resilient to the relatively new subscription services than TF-1, which lost 8.4 per cent during 1993 and 2002 (IsICult, 2004). However this has been achieved by airing more entertainment-oriented programming (see below).

Funding

France Télévisions is funded by a mixed system of commercial revenues (mainly advertising) and the licence fee. Occasionally the public broadcaster receives special state subsidies to pursue specific objectives, such as the dissemination of French programmes abroad. The public channels have little control over their funding method and the level of funding; these are determined by the Parliament with the prior approval of the Prime Minister. In order to avoid the financial uncertainties resulting from this process, the Law of 1 August 2000 introduced the principle of annual contracts between the government and the public broadcasters – known as *Contrat d'Objectifs et de Moyens* (Objectives and Means Contracts)[2] (EUMAP, 2005, p. 670). Following this Law, in December 2001, the Ministers of Finance, National Economy and Culture, jointly decided that the licence fee would increase by 3.1 per cent for 5 years, on the condition that the public broadcaster would improve its performance regarding the quality, innovation and variety of the programmes.

France Télévisions totaled revenues of 2.4 billion Euros in 2004, of which licence fees represented 1.6 billion, while advertising and sponsorship trailed at 820 million – that is 21.8 per cent of the total TV ad spend in France (James, 2005). It is clear that the licence fee represents the major source of income for the public broadcaster and advertising complements it. While the level of the fee has increased by about 38 per cent since 1990 (from 84.5 Euros in 1990 to 116.50 Euros in 2005), revenues from advertising were subject to a steep decline and in 2005 represented only 29.3 per cent of the total revenues, down from 39.7 per cent in 1999 (sponsorship represented 2.2 per cent of total revenues).[3] The fall in France Télévisions' advertising revenue could be attributed to the letter of Law of 1 August 2000 which gradually limited the advertising the public channels could air during peak hours from 12 minutes to 8 minutes per hour, with effect from 2002. The intention was to free the public channels from dependence on advertising which was thought to be detrimental to programme quality, but this decision was undeniably a major setback at a time of growing competition. It should also be noted that commercial breaks are not allowed during feature films shown on public TV.

The French television system has significant exceptions in the categories of people who pay the licence fee: the elderly with low income (those above 65 years old, representing almost 3.5 million households), and also the disabled (nearly 720,000 households) are exempted from the fee. A significant percentage of households evade the annual fee. France Télévisions estimates that around 1.5 million television households (seven per cent of the total) did not pay the licence fee in 2000. This problem was addressed by the introduction of a new scheme in January 2005 which attached the licence fee to local taxes, where previously licence fees had been collected by a special service, SRA, operated under the auspices of the Ministry of Finance.

Programming policy

One reason commonly cited for France Télévisions' robust showing, as evidenced by the high shares enjoyed by public channels (see Table 5.1), is a distinctive programming policy. According to a report by the Instituto Italiano per l'Industria Culturale, published by Screen Digest, France Télévisions has steered clear of many of the reality TV formats taken up by commercial channels and has instead focused on regional and local issues (especially through France 3), news and current affairs magazines, high-quality fiction and documentaries (IsICult, 2004). However, it is mainly France 5 – which shares frequencies with the high-brow Franco-German joint venture channel Arte, which acts as a guardian of programme quality and diversity, whereas the programming of France 2 and France 3 increasingly emulates that of private rivals.

Table 5.2 compares the annual output of the public channels with that of the national terrestrial commercial channels. It can be seen that France 5, which is tasked with promoting knowledge, culture and employment, devotes as much as 80 per cent of its schedule to

Table 5.2 Annual output of the national terrestrial TV channels in France – breakdown by genre (%, 2002)

Programme types	France 2	France 3	France 5	TF-1	M6
News	21.1	16.7	0.3	11.3	5.0
Current affairs/Documentaries	17.9	27.8	80.1	17.4	5.3
Feature films	3.3	4.6	0.6	3.7	3.0
TV series/docudrama	25.1	25.6	9.7	31.4	35.2
Entertainment/Music shows	17.5	9.0	2.2	16	35.1
Sports	6.1	5.8	–	4.5	0.3
Other including advertising	9.0	10.5	7.1	15.7	16.1
TOTAL HOURS	8,870	8,155	5,845	8,760	8,760

Source: Annual reports of channels EUMAP (2005).
Note: Being mostly a movie channel, Canal Plus is not included.

current affairs magazines and documentaries. In direct contrast, France 2's programming consists mainly of TV series and docudrama (25.1 per cent), entertainment and music shows (17.5 per cent), while a large proportion is devoted to news (21.1 per cent) and current affairs/documentaries (17.9 per cent). France 3's schedule gives more emphasis to current affairs/documentaries (27.8 per cent), TV series/ docudrama (25.6 per cent), as well as to national and regional news (16.7 per cent). The central news bulletin is at seven o'clock in the evening and has a large audience, being watched by working people and the elderly. The age groups that watch France Télévisions are generally older than those that watch commercial programmes. Taken together, the programming of the main public channels France 2 and France 3 differs only slightly from that of the private TF-1 and M6, which give some more emphasis to entertainment and TV series/ docudrama (see Table 5.2).

This is because public broadcasters are increasingly dominated by commercial concerns and managed as private corporations. Their programming over the years tends to resemble those of their commercial counterparts, with the notable exception of France 5 and Arte (EUMAP, 2005). A pan-European study by Leon (2004) found that there are still some differences between French public and commercial broadcasters in the area of cultural programming. Using a wide concept of culture, the study showed that France 2 and France 3 had more cultural output than their competitors TF-1 and M6, but in prime-time the public channels' programming showed a strong orientation towards entertainment, and information to a lesser extent.

This is evidenced by France 2's programming policy. In September 2000, hampered by a continual but not precipitous, fall in audience share, the flagship public channel made dramatic changes in its programming, especially at peak viewing times. A young director was put in charge of news, and drastically changed the format of the central evening news bulletin at eight o'clock in the evening. Preceding this bulletin there is now a talk show called On a tout essayé, presented by well-known comedians and DJs. Prior to these changes, France 2's output consisted mainly of documentaries and educational programmes, but it now has more of an entertainment and less of an educational character. Overall, the cultural and educational programming of France 2 and France 3 represent about 10–12 per cent of their total schedule. Yet, only a tiny part of this offering is available at peak time (18.00–23.00).

While France Télévisions has refrained from going into reality TV, several of its talk shows have repeatedly generated controversy and complaints. C'est mon choix (It's my Choice), a talk-show in which people defend their lifestyle choices sparked criticism from some viewers for being futile and vulgar and finally went off the air in July 2004. Another talk show, Tout le monde en parle (Everybody is talking about it), was very much criticised for asking politicians questions about their sexual preferences. With respect to news, there have been some occasions the public channels failed to report facts accurately as journalists took risks and covered stories without cross-checking their sources, mainly because of pressure to achieve high ratings. However, public channels air top quality regular political shows, such as 100 minutes pour convaincre (100 Minutes to Convince) on France 2 and France Europe Express on France 3. The evening news on France 3, a mix of national and regional issues, offer extensive and in-depth coverage and attract many viewers. Finally, some of the programmes of France 3, including Des Racines et des Ailes (Roots and Wings), a magazine exploring the artistic heritage of landmark cities throughout the world, and Thalassa (The Sea), a discovery magazine covering life in oceans and seas, are widely acclaimed for their quality (EUMAP, 2005).

Thematic portfolio

Over the past decade public channels in France, as elsewhere in Europe, have faced difficulties in adjusting to a continually changing television landscape and employing a clear and stable strategy. This difficulty stems not only from the financial problems that they face, but also because of frequent changes in top administration. For example, in February 1996 the then President of France Télévisions, Jean-Pierre Elkabbach, signed an agreement with private broadcaster TF-1 for a joint setting up of Societe de Television Europeenne de Programmes et de Services (Steps), which would be responsible for launching both thematic channels and online services. Barely nine months later, his successor Xavier Gouyou Beauchamps judged that the plan was not commercially viable and put an end to the ambitious scheme (Fontaine, 1999).

In a study on behalf of public television, Philippe Chazal (1996) identified the following guiding principles that should be adhered to by the public sector in setting up thematic channels:

- The content of the thematic channels should consist of France Télévisions' extensive archive.
- Thematic channels should focus on specialised topics that would meet the preferences of the twenty-first century viewer.
- Emphasis should be placed on showing programmes which, by definition, are not covered by the private sector (education, training, culture).

According to the study, the funding of the thematic channels should be based on subscriptions and not on public money or advertising (the specialised character of their programmes would not generate significant advertising income, the study noted). Most of Chazal's recommendations were inspired by Britain's BBC, but were not adopted by the then president of France Televisions, Beauchamps, who believed that public channels should not contribute to further fragmentation of society by launching niche services.

Since then the public broadcaster has made significant steps in this area and set up several thematic subscription channels, including:

- Festival – it was set up in 1996 and shows French and European fiction. France Télévisions owns 56 per cent of the capital, the

Spanish La 7 owns 11 per cent and another 11 per cent share is held by Britain's Carlton Communications.
- Mezzo – a music service founded in 1998.
- Ma Planete.
- Planete Thalassa.

Historie, broadcasting documentaries, was set up in 1997 but sold to TF-1 Group in 2002. Apart from these subscription channels, France Télévisions is an owner (together with 19 more public channels) of Euronews, the Europe-wide satellite channel which broadcasts international news. It is also involved in the international French-language channel TV5, co-financed by Belgium, Canada and Switzerland, specialising in news and entertainment. Up to 2001 the public broadcaster had an 8.5 per cent share in the digital satellite platform TPS but this was sold in January 2002 to the commercial rival TF-1, as part of a restructuring and deficit reduction programme (see below).

Digital initiatives

Development of DTT

Until recently, the most important digital initiative by France Télévisions was its participation in TPS, the digital satellite platform established in 1996, in which it initially took a 25 per cent stake, then reducing it to 8.5 per cent before finally in January 2002 selling the holding to the TF-1 Group due to financial constraints (TF-1 now holds 66 per cent of the platform and M6 owns the balance). As pointed out in Chapter 3, the fact that public channels were available exclusively and solely on the digital subscription platform TPS generated some discomfort and many scholars argued that the availability of public television on one only platform and therefore accessible to a limited number of subscribers, conflicted with the principle of universal access embedded in the public service mission. For example, Gilles Fontaine (1999) from IDATE pointed out that the public television's decision to opt for additional revenue, rather than a more socially responsible universal access route, resulted in public policy being virtually the same as that of private channels.

Responding to this criticism, the French government approved funding for the development of a digital terrestrial platform, in which both public and private channels would participate. In February 2002 the DGCCRF (the French Office of Fair Trading) announced that the development of the platform would start in 2003 and would be accessible to all households with a one-off payment of about 100–150 Euros for a digital decoder. As in the case of Freeview, set up by the BBC, the service would be subscription-free. The Ministry estimated that within the five-year period 2003–2008, around 2 million households would have bought the service and reported that the cost for developing the platform would rise to 2–4 million Euros. However, since the French broadcasting system is heavily exposed to the winds of political shifts, the DTT ambitious plan suffered a major blow following a change of government in 2003.

In fact, DTT was launched in March 2005, two years later than originally scheduled. In addition to political upheavals, it had to overcome interminable conflicts on standards – candidates were MPEG-2 and MPEG-4 – and eternal differences between France Télévisions, TF-1 and Canal Plus. The new service was entitled TNT and the initial offering consisted of 14 free-to-air channels while later in 2005 two bouquets of pay-TV were added. Take-up of services exceeded expectations and by the end of 2006 5.8 million households were equipped to receive DTT. This early success was partly because the set-top boxes were made available from as little as 70 Euros, and partly because the offering was sufficiently convincing to make people forget the earlier hesitancy. Following the success of Freeview in Britain, this number is expected to reach 7 million households by the end of 2007. But this will be achieved on condition that geographical coverage will increase (in January 2006 the coverage of the French territory approached only 60 per cent of the population), and the offering will improve with the launch of additional channels to match the variety offered by the satellite consortia.

Prospects for France Télévisions

Public television channels in France have had difficulty in recent years adjusting to a constantly changing landscape and mapping out a firm strategy. This difficulty stems from the financial constraints the public channels have been facing, and has been exacerbated by the heavily interventionist regulations and frequent changes of governmental media policies. Despite the modest rise of the licence fee public channels' resources are limited compared to private broadcasters like Canal Plus, M6 and in particular TF-1, which enjoys more than half of the advertising revenues. The financial uncertainties are exacerbated by the fact that each year the budgets for the public channels are drafted jointly by the Ministry of Communication and the Ministry of Finance and then require the approval of the Prime Minister before they are finally presented to Parliament. This is a long process (normally starts in July and finishes in November), in which public broadcasters have little control over their financing and spending as the final decision is taken by politicians (EUMAP, 2005).

In terms of programming France Télévisions is experiencing a profound identity crisis. As in many countries across Europe the dilemma faced by the public broadcaster is how to fulfil its cultural and educational objectives, while also successfully competing with commercial broadcasters. The programming obligations applying to public channels (see article 43-11 of the 1986 law) are not always met and the diversity of French population is not adequately represented on public broadcasters' programmes. While France Télévisions has refrained from many of the reality-TV formats taken up by commercial channels and has instead paid greater emphasis on news, documentaries and regional affairs, it is recognised that the increasingly competitive environment has forced it to become more entertainment-oriented medium, concerned with audience ratings. Thierry Vedel, responsible for compiling the EUMAP report for France, writes: 'Public television stations are caught in a double, and contradictory, blind – while being given public service missions and very exalted cultural aims, they are at the same time required to compete with private channels. The public broadcasters are required to be profitable and are continuously compared to the private channels in terms of ratings, economic performance or professional management' (EUMAP, 2005, pp. 231–2).

The PTV broadcaster has been benefited by a major restructuring programme which led to the formation of France Télévisions to combine the resources of the public channels. This change has improved the organisational and operational profile of the now joint stock company and led to a better exploitation of programmes and personnel, resulting in trimming running costs at a saving of about 50–52 million Euros a year since the beginning of the new century (James, 2005). Overheads were cut and management streamlined, with the result that net debt has fallen from 245 million Euros at the end of 1999 to

109.6 million Euros in 2003 (IsICult, 2004). Heavy losses have turned into a net profit of 14.2 million Euros in 2004. France Télévisions grew its advertising by 4.9 per cent in 2002 to 710 million Euros, while in 2003 advertising grew again by 6.8 per cent to reach 820 million Euros.[4] Much of this success is credited to the then managing director Marc Tessier, a former Canal Plus top executive, who took over the directorship of the public broadcaster in 2000.[5]

France Télévisions holds high audience shares and enjoys good financial results, thanks to organisational changes implemented in the late 1990s. In 2005 the combined audience share for the main public channels France 2 and France 3 was approaching a very respectable 37.8 per cent, but this is expected to drop as the multi-channel environment continues to expand. At the same time, the advertising income, already significantly lower due to regulatory changes (in 2002 advertising on public channels during peak hours was limited to eight minutes per hour, versus 12 minutes before that) is likely to decline even further due to channel multiplication. Since the annual fee represents the major source of the public broadcaster's income (about 68 per cent of the channel's total revenues in 2004, versus 29.3 per cent of advertising), it follows that its financial stability is very much dependent on a generous increase of the fee to meet the escalating costs of producing or acquiring high-quality content. A licence fee increase may be justified given that the French public broadcaster is the recipient of the second lowest annual amount among the six countries examined (116.5 Euros). However, any fee increase would be an unpopular political decision, not favoured by the general public. And any further dependence on commercial income may jeopardise the public character of France Télévisions and alienate it from its audiences.

But is there any evidence of political and public support for the French public broadcaster, as it is the case with the BBC? The government's partial funding for the development of DTT platform in which France Télévisions participates, is an indication of political support, although political upheavals was proved to be one the reasons for its late deployment. The 2000 governmental decision to increase the licence fee at 3.1 per cent annually over the next 5 years also provides evidence of financial backing, although this is conditional on good performance. However, French politics and broadcasting have been closely connected, thus making the public channels dependent on the government of the day for their income and creating uncertainty as to future investment decisions. Public support for France Télévisions is ambivalent. There is some evidence of viewer satisfaction with the public channels' output, given that in 2002, for the third successive year, France 3 was voted the most favourite channel among French households – although the most popular remains TF-1. However, it is paramount for the public broadcaster to know in much more detail what people expect from it and how they evaluate the programmes.

France Télévisions runs a 'barometer' to measure viewers' satisfaction with programmes, but according to EUMAP (2005, p. 674) neither its methodology, nor its content have been made public. The barometer has been criticised by Members of Parliament for being too general and too quantitative. Furthermore, the relative satisfaction with the content of public TV does not mean that French households are also happy with the licence fee payment. As elsewhere in Europe, there is a 'legitimacy crisis' over paying the fee and people openly question as to why they have to pay for watching public television while private channels are free at the point of reception. Another drawback is that public participation in television regulation is extremely low, in contrast to Britain where consultation rounds with the public over media regulatory issues is common. As EUMAP (2005, p. 674) pointed out, 'debate on French media policy is mainly confined to experts and professionals while the general public is absent'.

6
Spain

> Population: 44.1 million (official figure 2005)
> Monetary Unit: Euro
> GNI per capita: $21,210 (World Bank, 2005)
> Households with television: 12 million
> Average daily TV viewing: 218 minutes (CMT, 2004)
> Penetration of cable TV: 6%
> Penetration of satellite TV: 11%
> Number of pay-TV subscribers: 2.8 million (CMT, 2004)
> Number of digital viewers: 6.1 million (incl. DTT)
> Supervisory body: CMT – Comision del Mercado de las Telecomunicaciones
> Households with Computers: 54%
> Households with Internet Access: 30.8 million (CMT, 2004)

General characteristics of the TV market

Television in Spain has been experiencing many changes since General Franco's death in 1975, when the authoritarian regime transformed into democratic government. While in the period of 'Frankism' (1939–75) the medium was fully controlled and used as a propaganda tool by the regime, Spanish TV has witnessed a spectacular expansion in the years that followed with the emergence of new commercial operators and the launch of digital services. Today, the free-to-view TV market can be characterised as 'mature' as it enjoys high household penetration rates and is the principal market by revenue. In 2004 revenue from unencrypted TV channels totalled six billion Euros, up from 5.7 billion in 2003 (nearly 55 per cent of total TV revenues) (CMT, 2004). The public sector is powerful, both in raising financial resources through advertising and subsidies/debt authorisations, and in obtaining of relatively high viewing shares. Television Espanola (TVE) includes two national channels, TVE1 and La2 (formerly TVE2), as well as seven regional channels run by the autonomous governments.

The market liberalised in the early 1990s and the first private network Antena 3 (jointly owned by the Spanish multimedia group Planeta, RTL and the big Spanish bank Banco Santander Central Hispano) began operations in January 1990. Commercial channel Tele 5 (Telecinco), the most watched Spanish TV channel in 2005, launched in March 1990 and is owned by Grupo Telecino (which belongs to the Italian holding company Mediaset). The subscription channel Canal Plus, which also began broadcasting in 1990, belongs to the Sogecable group whose main shareholders are Telefonica (23.83 per cent) and PRISA (25.5 per cent). The introduction of private channels and the rise of pay-TV affected the public broadcaster's audience and advertising share which are continuously decreasing.

As it is the case in most southern European countries the penetration of cable and satellite channels remains low in Spain. However, in recent years the cable and satellite TV markets are expanding steadily, sustained by the recently-launched digital channels and market consolidation. The previously separate digital satellite consortiums Canal Satellite Digital (owned by Sogecable) and Via Digital (owned by the Spanish telecoms giant Telefonica) merged in 2003 in an attempt to reduce operation costs. The deal had been bitterly opposed by cable TV operators who feared that a satellite TV monopoly would make it much harder for them to acquire valuable sports and movie rights and to compete for subscribers. In 2004 there were 1.7 million satellite and 1.1 million cable subscribers, most of them belonging to the market leader Sogecable group. On the contrary, digital terrestrial television (DTT) has been less successful as pay-TV operator Quiero TV closed in 2002, just two years after it went on air in May 2000. The re-launch of DTT in 2005 seems to be more prominent – in early 2007 the TVE-led platform with eighteen offerings had signed around 3.3 million homes, representing a penetration rate of just below 30 per cent.

The regulatory framework

The Spanish media are governed by various laws which cover terrestrial, cable and digital transmission. The decentralised character of the country (that is, the autonomous geographical regions) has facilitated the creation of many regional regulatory bodies. Many laws have been introduced recently and special emphasis has been given to liberalising the cable and satellite market, but also to the rapid installation of digital terrestrial television.

Terrestrial television is governed by the Private Television Act 10/1988 of 3 May 1988 which made provision for:

- The establishment of an independent council for the granting of licences. However, up until 2006 licences were granted by the government itself.
- Content regulations. These derive from Law 4/1980 for public television, and Law 25/1994 of 12 July 1994, for the incorporation of the TWF Directive into national legislation.
- Regulations to limit ownership and protect competition. Article 9 of the 1988 Act prohibits one person or company from holding more than one national terrestrial television channel, whether analogue or digital. It also prohibits a person or company from owning more than a 49 per cent share of a television station.

The cable industry is regulated by Law 42/1995 of 12 December 1995, but there are no specific regulations for digital cable broadcasting. Law 17/1997 of 3 May 1997 covers digital satellite television, and makes provision for the granting of licences (article 3), ownership limits (highest limit of shareholding is set at 25 per cent), as well as conditional access systems. The Telecommunications Committee (Comision del Marcado de las Telecomunicaciones – CMT) defines the technical specifications of the digital decoders.

One of the peculiarities of the regulatory regime is that there is no independent administrative authority with the specific responsibility for overseeing the audiovisual market. The only example of such an authority is the Radio Television Council of Catalonia. The Telecommunications Committee CMT was set up in June 1996 by Royal Decree-Act 6/1996, but is primarily concerned with telecommunications liberalisation. Although it covers the audiovisual sector, its decisions are non-binding and need to be enforced by judicial means. In 2004 CMT declared that the audiovisual market needed systematic reorganisation and suggested the setting up of a legal body that would put an end to the regulatory diversity that not only makes difficult the application of the laws, but also has a negative impact on market growth. In April 2004 the Council for the Reform of the Communication Media, established by the Royal Decree 744/2004, provided for the creation, as soon as possible, of a fully autonomous audiovisual council, with regulatory and sanction capacity that will ensure a harmonious audiovisual system. Yet by 2006 this council had not been established.

Regarding public television, the Administrative Council of the public broadcaster oversees conformity with audiovisual legislation. Law 24/2001 of 27 December 2001 attempted to define the public broadcaster's mission in the era of digital convergence. More specifically, the law determined that TVE should:

- Produce and deliver quality programmes, both of general and specific content, in order to contribute to education and training, entertainment and national culture.
- Increase its efforts to provide more local programmes.
- Contribute to the creation of the Information Society by providing digital interactive services.
- Offer programmes with appeal to Spanish citizens abroad.

In February 2005 the Council for the Reform of the Communication Media published a report for the reform of the public broadcaster and stipulated that its conclusions should provide the basis for a new law on the audiovisual sector. The report proposed that the public broadcaster should:

- Have managerial and editorial independence.
- Be subject to a financial model that guarantees economic stability, avoids indebtedness while impeding excessive advertising pressure on its activities and stimulating greater diversification of commercial revenue.
- Act as the driving force of digital take-up (CMT, 2004).

Public television

TVE operates two national networks, TVE1 (which until 2004 was the most popular general interest channel in Spain) and La2 (with a cultural and educational output). Spanish public TV has unusual characteristics compared to other European public broadcasters:

- Its income derives from a combination of advertising and government funding (TVE is not a recipient of the licence fee).
- It runs a considerable 8 billion Euro debt which increases year-after-year (the debt was just 636 million Euros in 2000).
- It has an ineffective administration. Similarly to other Mediterranean countries, such as France and Greece, where every change in government is accompanied with shifts in top administration of public organisations, the Spanish public broadcaster changed Director Generals (DGs) three times during the period 1996–98. According to Sanchez-Tabernero (1999), the frequent changes of government-appointed DGs have hindered long-term strategic planning and raised concerns about political influence in public broadcasting.
- The system is decentralised – alongside the national service there are seven regional public TV stations supported by the autonomous regional governments with an overall daily viewing share of 17.6 per cent in 2005. The Federation of Autonomous Radio and Television (FORTA) was formed in 1990 to centralise the acquisition of film and sports rights for regional TV stations, to coordinate their planning and programming processes, and to share news coverage.

Audience shares

TVE competes for viewers and advertisers mainly with the two free-to-air, advertising-funded private channels Tele 5 and Antena 3. Between them these two channels enjoy a total audience share of around 43 per cent (22.5 per cent for Tele 5 and 20.8 per cent for Antena 3). The subscription service Canal Plus Espana has a rating of about 2.2 per cent (see Table 6.1). Not surprisingly, competition had a negative effect on the public TV broadcaster's share. Although it enjoys a very respectable 25.4 per cent combined share (19.6 per cent for mainstream TVE1 and 5.8 per cent for culture-skewed La2) and the regional pubcasters attract 17.6 per cent daily viewing, over the 10-year period to 2002, TVE1 alone lost 5.9 per cent of all day audience share. According

Table 6.1 Audience shares of the Spanish TV channels (1999–2005)

Channels	1999	2001	2003	2004	2005
TVE-1	24.9	24.9	22.1	20.8	19.6
La2	8.1	7.8	7.6	6.2	5.8
Regional TV	16.4	17.5	18.5	17.7	17.6
Tele 5	21.0	21.0	21.4	22.1	22.5
Antena 3	22.7	20.3	19.5	20.8	20.8
Canal Plus Espana	2.4	2.3	2.4	2.1	2.2
Others (local, digital)	4.0	6.0	7.6	9.1	9.8

Source: CMT (2004); Variety (2006).

to IsICult (2004) this was the second-worst performance among public channels across Europe after BBC1, which lost 6.5 per cent during the same time period. The poor performance continued in more recent years and in 2005 TVE1 fell to a historic audience share low of below 20 per cent, partly owing to the popularity of Tele 5 and Antena 3, and partly to the rise of local and digital channels.

Things may be worse for the PTV broadcaster in the future. The merger of the digital satellite consortia Canalsatelite Digital and Via Digital and the possible reduction of operational expenses as a result, will generate profits for investment in programmes, something which in turn will attract new subscribers and take away viewers from free-to-air channels including the public broadcaster. Sogecable and Canal Plus have signed agreements with the Spanish football league Primera Liga, giving them exclusive rights to broadcast football matches until 2006 for the price of 300 million Euros per year. Heavily-indebted TVE is unable to match such offers. Indicative of the dire financial position in which TVE had sunk is the fact that in 2002 could not compete against commercial network Antena 3 in raising the sum demanded for the acquisition of rights to cover world football cup matches. The Spanish government declined to pay TVE the 43 million Euros required for the 2002 World Cup rights and said that the priority would be to eliminate the accumulated debts.

Funding

TVE is funded by advertising and state subsidies, which may include subsidies, debt authorisations and capital increases. Revenues deriving from advertising and state grants are balanced. Table 6.2 shows

Table 6.2 Revenues for free-to-air TV in Spain (2004, Euros m)

Channels	Subsidies	Advertising	Other	Advertising share (%)	Total
TVE	740.30	728.98	38.80	24.98	1,508.08
Antena 3	0.00	659.52	30.18	22.6	689.70
Tele 5	0.00	643.03	0.00	22.03	643.03

Source: CMT (2004).

that in 2004 state subsidies represented 56 per cent of the total TVE revenues, whereas advertising accounted for about 42 per cent, but in 2005 the subsidy from the state dropped slightly and accounted for 48 per cent of the total budget.[1] In any case, the public broadcaster depends to a large extend on public funding to survive and prosper in an intensely competitive environment. Meanwhile TVE's share of advertising as a percentage of the total TV advertising was almost 25 per cent in 2004, followed by Antena 3 and Tele 5 at 22.6 per cent and 22.03 per cent respectively. Although advertising-based revenue for TVE has declined over the years (TVE accounted for over 30 per cent of total TV advertising in 2000), it nevertheless retained its market leadership, as Table 6.2 demonstrates.

Programming strategy

The two national public channels differ between them with regard to programming. TVE-1 is a general interest channel and offers light entertainment such as game, chat and music shows, comedy, soap operas, series and serials, but also news and films. According to some analysts (Nicholls, 2004) TVE-1 is going through an identity crisis and this is reflected in its schedule, which includes occasional moments of inspired brilliance, but in general the channel does not seem to know what is wants to be. La-2, in contrast, has a clearer mandate and acts more in accordance with public service criteria. It targets a more demanding public and mainly covers genres such as quality films, less popular sports, arts, culture, science and education (see Table 6.3).

Traditionally, Spanish public television is not renowned either for its balanced news coverage or for its quality. In terms of balanced news

Table 6.3 Public channels in Spain: share of transmissions by genre (%, 2004)

Programme genres	TVE-1	La-2
Fiction	39.0	23.8
Game-shows	6.5	2.5
Music	2.1	3.8
Sports	4.2	16.6
Information/news	27.0	10.2
Cultural/educational	7.3	26.5
Other	13.9	16.6
Total	100.0	100.0

Source: IsICult (2004); RTVE (2004).

coverage, Nicholls (2004) argues that TVE often gives the impression that Spain has barely moved on since the days of Franco. This is illustrated by a 2003 ruling from Spanish National High Court which condemned TVE's coverage of the general strike of June 2002. According to Nicholls, further evidence of the way the channel has become little more than a government mouthpiece was provided by Alfredo Urdaci, the former news director of TVE who was relieved of his duties shortly after the change of government. Furthermore, a European parliament report investigating freedom of information refers to unprofessional practices used to foster unbalanced, biased or manipulated provision of information between 28 February and 5 March 2003 on the military intervention in Iraq. The report goes on to state that the government pressure on TVE resulted in blatant distortion and ignoring of the facts regarding responsibility for the appalling Madrid terrorist attacks of 11 March 2004 (ibid.).

In terms of quality in programming, the introduction of competition and the challenges involved in attracting advertisers have had an enormous effect on TVE's output. Public and private broadcasters alike are in constant search for content that will generate large audiences; meanwhile, ambitious and risky programming formats become a rarity. TVE's dependence on commercials has led to programme uniformity between mainstream public and private channels, thus confirming a Europe-wide trend suggested by several commentators. Leon (2004) found that the diversity of genres in prime-time is quite similar between the Spanish flagship public channel TVE1 and the commercial channels. In fact, TVE1 had one of the highest percentages of entertainment

(56.3 per cent) among its European counterparts, followed by the Italian RAI1 (54.4 per cent) and the BBC1 (54.1 per cent), while at the other end of the scale the public channel with the least entertainment programmes in prime-time was the Greek ET1 (10.5 per cent).

As Ramon de Espana, journalist of the *El Pais* daily, put it: 'Television is, in fact, the most democratic system for propagating culture that ever existed. If we prefer to fill it with soccer games, foolish quiz shows and holiday series it is because we live on the planet Earth and not in the Garden of Eden. . . . If we have this sort of television it is because our country is what it is' (de Espana, 2001, pp. 7–10). Indeed, the Spanish public is attracted by football games and well-known TV series and reality shows. Record- breaking audiences watch football matches of the Spanish or European leagues and the channels have been involved in bidding wars to acquire live coverage of this exclusive product. With regards to TV series and reality shows, TVE1's Operacion Triunfo (Operation Victory) format, in which viewers choose the Spanish representative for the Eurovision song contest, has been a big hit on the public channel since 2001 and allowed it to compete against Tele 5, which transmits the popular series Gran Hermano (the Spanish edition of Big Brother).

The need to fuel its ratings has led TVE to sign volume deals with Warner Bros and Buena Vista. The Warner Bros accord gives the public broadcaster weekend children's programming block La Hora Warner plus dramas and feature films. TVE is linked with Buena Vista on dramas, feature films and Zon@Disney, another weekend type omnibus. With the deals come Desperate Housewives, (averaging a 17.8 per cent share and 1.9 million viewers), Lost (16.9 per cent share), Six Feet Under and the OC (each recording strong shares of 6.5 per cent and 6.2 per cent respectively), all shown by mainstream TVE-1. Other popular series broadcast by the main public channel include The West Wing and One Tree Hill (de Pablos, 2006).

However, under RTVE DG Caffarel and TVE director Estremera, appointed after the PSOE socialist election victory in 2004, TVE is already taking a more public service programming path and has largely refrained from acquiring populist TV formats or making heavy-duty deals with Hollywood. It has improved its performance in documentaries (for example, TVE1 shows event-documentary Homo Sapiens in prime-time), current affairs (new slots include TVE1 debate showcase 59 Seconds and current affairs programme Enfoque), and films

(TVE was planning to buy 60 Spanish films for the season 2005–2006, including Almodovar's Volver, Aragon's Virgin Rose and Oristrell's No es lo mismo). This improvement was made possible through an increased 1.54 billion Euros budget which ranks the national PTV broadcaster with pay-TV giant Sogecable as Spain's biggest TV company. According to TVE1 programme director Pablo Carasco, this spending on films will deliver value in a country where access to pay-TV remains relatively low at just 26 per cent of households. Spaniards are film fanatics and the country's cinema-going is among the highest in Europe, with 2.9 admissions per capita in 2005 (De Pablos and Hopewell, 2006).

Digital initiatives

In July 1999, the public TV broadcaster established the Department of Development and Thematic Channels. This department, enjoying relative autonomy, introduced the digital service TVE Tematica, which includes numerous thematic channels initially funded by subscription and broadcast through the digital satellite platform Via Digital in which TVE had a 17 per cent stake. In 2004–2005 the package included:

- TVE Internacional aiming at Spaniards living abroad,
- the 24-hour news service Canal 24 Horas,
- the 24-hour sports channel Teledeporte,
- the classical music channel Canal Clasico,
- the documentary service Docu TVE,
- The children's channel Clan TVE (launched in November 2005 and broadcasts from 7.00 am to 9.00 pm),
- TVE 50 Anos (it shares the same frequency as Clan TVE and broadcasts programmes from the TVE archives (Leon, 2006).[2]

The above channels are now available through the recently launched TVE-led free-to-air digital terrestrial platform. In late 2005 the Spanish cabinet approved the digital terrestrial television technical plan which allocates a minimum of nine channels to TVE, four to Tele 5, Antena 3 and Sogecable, and two each to the current digital providers, Veo TV and Net TV. However, private broadcasters are sceptical that the heavily-indebted provider will be able to manage the expansion. It should be noted that together with Britain and Sweden, Spain led the initial deployment of DTT, but its pay-TV model operated by Quiero TV failed as a result of poorly perceived service offering, much like ITV Digital in Britain (Iosifidis *et al.*, 2005, pp. 115–16). Spain re-launched its DTT services on 30 November 2005 with twenty unencrypted services, available to 80 per cent of the population. As already mentioned, in early 2007 3.3 million households were already enjoying DTT. As it is the case in Britain and France, the free-to-air model in Spain is likely to be proved compelling to many households who are sceptical about pay-TV. The Spanish broadcaster has also introduced interactive educational services, as was specifically required by Law 24/2001.

Restructuring attempts

TVE has been in deep financial difficulty since 1990, when the government legalised commercial television. Over the years there have been some attempts to address the public broadcaster's financial problems. In December 1999, in an attempt to improve its finances, TVE offered for sale its 17 per cent share in the satellite platform Via Digital, valued at 85 million Euros. This helped the company in the short term, but did not prove adequate to amortize the accumulated debt, which by the end of 2001 had risen to 636 million Euros. The year 2001 witnessed a first serious attempt to face TVE's financial burden with the setting up of the Comite de Implementacion y Seguimiento del Plan (CIS). CIS consisted of four members of the public broadcaster and four members of Sociedad Estatal de Participaciones Industriales (SEPI), which was charged with administering the public broadcaster. CIS's purpose was to implement the Marco plan, tasked to eliminate the broadcaster's deficit by 2004. This business plan envisaged structural changes (creation of business units and modernisation in the organisational structure; privatisation of organisational teams; provision for sharing production resources to increase productivity), as well as a review of the public broadcaster's mission, so that it could respond to the demands of the digital era (Law 24/2001 makes provision for this review).

Likewise, the plan envisaged the introduction of new forms of funding, such as sponsorship, as well as an increase in revenues from the sale of new products. A newly-established department of the Ministry of Finance was made responsible for the public broadcaster's budget and the management of its operational expenses. However SEPI administrators' claims that the broadcaster would be put on a firm financial footing in three years were not realised. Even though the Spanish government increased its contribution to the organisation by 13.5 per cent in 2002 to about 75 million Euros, its debt grew to 6.2 billion Euros by the end of 2002. The debt could be higher if the public broadcaster did not sign an agreement with the Morgan Stanley consultancy for the issuing of bonds for a three-year period (2002–2005), enabling it to raise 768 million Euros.

Given the broadcaster's ever growing financial troubles a group of experts (Committee of Wise Men) was set up in 2005 and published a report on its future prospects. The report suggested that the state could take on the public broadcaster's accumulated debt of 8 billion Euros and continue to subsidise the channel's spending on 'public service' activities. The report also proposed that the amount of advertising contracted by TVE should be cut, thus reducing dependency on advertisers and allowing it to pursue a more public service oriented programming strategy. However, the report has been subject to heavy criticism. Fernando Gonzalez Urbaneja, president of the Reporters Association, argued that the Wise Men's proposals simply continue the status quo without cutting TVE's joy of spending, its poor use of human resources, its bureaucratic disorder or lack of commercial spirit. Pedro Schwartz, professor at the University of San Pablo-CEU argued that these proposals do not provide much incentive to reform and he went even further to say that the only viable solution would be to privatise the public channel (Schwartz, 2005). A similar controversial proposal for partially privatising the network had come in June 2004 from the secretary of state for the Treasury, inevitably sparkling union protests.

On 29 July 2005 the Spanish cabinet approved a draft public broadcasting law which laid down the future make-up and financing of the public broadcaster. The draft legislation stipulated that Radio Television Espanola will become a public limited company with state capital, controlled by the parliament and a newly-formed broadcast media council. It provided for the setting up of an independent board of directors to oversee the PTV broadcaster. The directors will be appointed by the parliament for a term of six years, and the DG should be a 'professional' appointee, rather than a political one, and if the broadcaster overspends its budget for two years in a row, the board will be asked to resign. It should be noted that the demand for greater autonomy and enhanced accountability gained momentum after the 11 March 2004 terrorist attacks in Madrid. Following a controversy over the public broadcaster's misleading pro-government coverage of the attacks, the socialist government has promised to strengthen TVE's editorial independence and return it to its public-service roots (Winslow, 2005b). Soon after the attack and the ensuing general election that swept the socialists back into power, the new government brought Carmen Caffarel, a university professor with little management experience, as DG of RTVE, and in December 2004 Manuel Perez Estremera replaced Juan Menor as director of TVE's television division. This is regarded as a positive step as Estrevera was a key executive under DG Pilar Miro in the late 1980s, the last time RTVE made an effort towards more public service broadcasting.

The new management has pledged to put an end to the era of television serving political parties and has committed to bring independence and pluralism to news services. However, many doubt as to whether this will be achieved, for every other new DG before them had flirted with public broadcasting independence shortly after being elected. Some analysts point to the new management's lack of experience in television and doubts have been cast on the appropriateness of Caffarel in charge of deciding how a public body should run. Also many have voiced concerns that the government-appointed experts committee, made up of five academics, is nothing more than a talking shop for highbrow theorists who have little or no contact with the real world and minimal experience in the media field (Nicholls, 2004). People are wondering whether calling in the academics is such a wise move, but in light of all previous unsuccessful efforts for reform and failures to provide any critical appraisal of TVE's policies, it should be considered a positive factor to rely on these professionals in forming proposals which cover a system for appointing directors, the way in which programmes are oriented, and the funding model.

In terms of funding, the experts group proposed that the state should assume the broadcaster's accumulated debt and increase up to 50 per cent its annual state subsidies, while at the same time reducing advertising time from 12 minutes per hour to nine minutes (similarly to changes in France). Other options suggested by the experts group to reduce the deficit included a return to the licence fee system, which was abolished in 1965, but DG Carmen Caffarel argued that a TV licence would not be welcomed by the Spanish society as the country is not used to the idea. Another controversial proposal was drastic cuts in the workforce, following hundreds of redundancies at the BBC. In March 2006 the TVE management presented a restructuring plan that involves lay-offs for 3133 employees (most of them over 50 years old who will get pre-retirement benefits) and eliminates a further 1300 temporary contracts (Leon, 2006). The cuts, which will hit 39 per cent of the workforce, are opposed by the unions and the European group of the International Federation of Journalists who argue that this draconian planning does not defend independence, professionalism and quality in the public sector. The Spanish Parliament was scheduled to debate the report in late 2006.[3] Despite these efforts to find ways of creating a healthier and more independent operation, only a few have hopes of any great change so long as public TV depends on government grants and its DG is chosen by a parliamentary committee.

Prospects for TVE

TVE is plagued by low-quality programming, news manipulation and chronic debt, which has resulted in a most serious financial problem. It does not receive a licence fee; instead it depends on commercial income and state grants. Funding through these means rather than a licence fee is insufficient to cover TVE's operational costs. To plug the deficit that ballooned soon after the arrival of commercial rivals, the public broadcaster has been relying on state-guaranteed loans, allowing it to accumulate debt of around 8 billion Euros. In the past years there have been some steps for the restructuring and modernisation of the organisation, such as the implementation of the 'Marco' business plan, but these steps were largely unsuccessful. With Spanish Socialist Workers' Party in power in 2004, new initiatives have been taken in search of a viable solution, such as the appointment of a new DG from the academia who pledged to carry out a wide-ranging reform of TVE, as well as an experts group charged with developing a new public TV model. Following suggestions from the experts group the government was planning to absorb the broadcaster's debt, restrict its advertising income, but continue to subsidise it.

TVE has adopted a programming strategy based on entertainment, to the detriment of culture and education and has therefore been openly accused of not differentiating itself enough from its private competitors. The 1989 introduction of private TV in Spain did not result in audience segmentation and/or enhanced viewer choice, but rather led to programming convergence. This is because TVE opted for profitability and neglected the citizens' cultural and social needs, therefore competing in a manner that was contradictory to its public service remit. By taking the safe road to profits the public broadcaster has produced low-quality programmes and has become more vulnerable to public opinion. As Nicholls (2004) puts it, 'high quality public television does not cost too much; what costs is television which broadcasts practically the same as private stations'. However, under the new management TVE has committed to take a more public service-oriented programming approach, raise the standards of quality content and diminish its reliance on imports (such as Hollywood blockbusters) in favour of home-grown cinema. The new programming offering will require some time until it finds audience acceptance.

Every effort to reform the company is at risk because of the cost of digitalising its network. TVE has been tasked with leading the development of digital terrestrial television in the country and has invested heavily in upgrading the infrastructure to support digital services. A new company – RTVE Digital y Multimedia – is now responsible for the digitalisation of the signal and new thematic channels, such as Canal 24 Horas, are devoted to continued information or offer educational, cultural, sports or children's programmes. The installation of DTT is forecasted to be as successful as it has been in Britain and France and trigger demand for new programmes and interactive services. Moreover, the public broadcaster plans to reshape its website (enrich the content and make it user-friendly), and it is in the completion phase of supplying new services adapted to mobile telephony, cable, satellite and the Internet. The financial implications of these actions for the already heavily indebted public broadcaster will be devastating, unless the above-mentioned far-reaching changes in TVE's financial structure can pay off.

Yet at the moment TVE remains an important 'player' in the Spanish television market. Audience ratings remain at good levels in a highly competitive market. TVE's role will remain important in the years to come as the public broadcaster has taken various initiatives as part of its new re-defined mission to respond to the demands of the Information Society (see Law 24/2001). The modernisation of the organisation, the launch of the new services and the recent programming changes are expected to bring the PTV broadcaster closer to the viewers. Its editorial autonomy may also be enhanced if the DG is appointed by the board of directors (as suggested by the experts group) and not as it is today by the government. This will certainly ease some of the concerns about governmental influence over the PTV broadcaster. At the time of writing this has yet to be implemented and it is doubtful if it ever will, for political control of the media is a vice that is hard to kick.

7
The Republic of Ireland

> Population: 3.8 million
> Monetary Unit: Euro
> GNI per capita: 14,000 euros
> Households with television: 1.35 million (ComReg, 2005)
> Average daily TV viewing: 184 minutes
> Penetration of cable TV: 62%
> Penetration of satellite TV: 22%
> Number of pay-TV subscribers: 839,000 (ComReg, 2005)
> Number of digital viewers: 389,000 (ComReg, 2005)
> Supervisory body: Broadcasting Commission of Ireland (BCI); Commission for Communications Regulation (ComReg)
> Households with Internet Access: 50.7% (Internet World Stats, 2006)

General characteristics of the TV market

The Irish television landscape has been dominated by the public broadcaster, Radio Telefís Éireann (RTÉ), which provides a comprehensive service in both English and Irish. RTÉ's main national channel is RTÉ One (broadcast from both Cork and Dublin), while RTÉ Two (formerly known as Network 2) is the secondary national channel. Both channels broadcast in English, but a third (TG4 – Teilifis na Gaeilge) broadcasts in Gaelic. RTÉ competes with the British TV channels which are widely available to most parts of the Republic via various means (terrestrial, cable, satellite or MMDS – Multipoint Microwave Distribution System). The presence of the British channels constitutes an important obstacle to the development of domestic private television channels.[1] The first Irish national commercial broadcaster, TV3, was licensed as late as in September 1998. Entertainment-led TV3, the only indigenous terrestrial competitor to RTÉ, is backed financially by the Canadian TV company CanWest Global (also present in Australia and New Zealand) and the British media group Granada Media, which dominates the ITV network.

Most Irish homes have access either to Sky Digital or multi-channel cable TV, or MMDS.[2] UPC Ireland (the local affiliate of Liberty Global), which comprises the networks of NTL Ireland and Chorus Communications is the country's largest cable service provider. In 2005 NTL offered cable broadband and digital TV services to over 350,000 customers in Dublin, Waterford and Galway and Chorus had a reach of 320,000 homes. However, cable companies are finding it hard to compete against Sky's satellite TV platform, for the satellite operator has increased the number of subscribers it had in Ireland by 102,000 from 2004 to 2006, bringing the total number of subscribers to 465,000 in December 2006. The powerful presence of Sky and the wide availability of cable TV were facilitated by the suspension of the 1998–99 development plan to create a domestic digital terrestrial platform, in which it was intended that the public RTÉ would participate in cooperation with private broadcasters. Digital Terrestrial Television was not available in the country in late early-2007, although RTÉ and the Department of Communications, Marine & Natural Resources were trialling a DVB-T based system. The BBC-led Freeview can be received in many parts of the Republic.

It can be seen that the British TV channels whose signals spill into Ireland, including those on digital terrestrial and satellite platforms, have a strong determining role on the Irish TV landscape. As digital becomes more mainstream in the coming years, Irish viewers will have access to hundreds of channels and the RTÉ-only diet will be an issue of the past. Already RTÉ faces competition from the decade-old national channel TV3 and Channel 6 (an entertainment-oriented channel launched in early 2006, available nationally via cable), the regional player City Channel (available on NTL digital platform), and of course a plethora of satellite and cable digital services. The new reality, notably audience fragmentation and competition, has brought immense new challenges for both the public broadcaster and the main commercial broadcaster TV3. As will be shown below, RTÉ's audience and advertising shares have plummeted. Meanwhile, CanWest, one of the backers of TV3 put its 45 per cent stake up for sale in early 2006. The Irish TV business is in a current of flux at the moment with unforeseen consequences for the companies and the viewers alike.

The regulatory framework

The Radio and Television Act 1988 for the first time made provision for the granting of licences to private broadcasting stations. It also provided for the establishment of the Independent Radio and Television Commission (IRTC) to supervise them, following the model of the British Independent Television Commission (predecessor to Ofcom). The Broadcasting Act 2001 updated broadcasting law and paved the way for the introduction of digital terrestrial television in Ireland, with the participation of the public broadcaster, but the government did not implement RTÉ's business plan in relation to digital television. The Act of 2001 also changed the name of the independent supervisory authority to the Broadcasting Commission of Ireland (BCI), whose role was upgraded, now being responsible for the provision of licences for digital terrestrial, cable and satellite television broadcasting.

The Communications Act 2002 established the Commission for Communications Regulation (ComReg), whose main role in the broadcasting sector is to: (a) develop and issue licences for broadcast distribution; (b) devise new licensing regimes and draft appropriate secondary legislation; and (c) monitor and enforce compliance with licence terms and conditions. According to McGonagle (2005), ComReg's independence is questionable as it can be subject to policy intervention from the Minister of Communications. A more recent piece of legislation, the Broadcasting (Funding) Act 2003, establishes a broadcasting funding scheme for: (a) new programmes on Irish culture, heritage and experience; (b) programmes to improve adults' literacy; and (c) the development of archiving of broadcast programme material. The scheme is developed and administered by the BCI.

In relation to public services, the public service broadcaster RTÉ was established under the Broadcasting Authority Act 1960. The Authority referred to in the title of the Act is the RTÉ Authority, the administrative council comprising a chairman and nine members appointed by the Cabinet upon the recommendation of the Minister for Communications, Marine and Natural Resources. The RTÉ Authority is both the owner of RTÉ and also its regulator; it is therefore charged with control and management of RTÉ (McGonagle, 2005).[3] The members of the council convene once a month and their decisions determine the public broadcaster's aims, organisational structure and operation. The administrative council appoints the general director of RTÉ, who is responsible for its day to day running.

As part of a package of measures, agreed by Government in December 2002, in response to RTÉ's application for a licence fee increase (see below), it was agreed that RTÉ would operate under a Public Service Broadcasting Charter, much like the BBC. The Department of Communications, Marine and Natural Resources published the Charter in June 2004 and it will be formally reviewed after five years. According to the Charter, the public service remit of the broadcaster is to: (a) reflect the democratic, social and cultural values of Irish society and to preserve media pluralism; (b) reflect fairly and equally the regional, cultural and political diversity of Ireland and its peoples; and (c) aim to avoid editorial or programming bias in terms of gender, age, race, disability, sexual orientation, religion or membership of a minority community (DCMNR, 2004).

Public television

As mentioned before, Radio Telefís Éireann has been dominating broadcasting in the Irish Republic since regular TV broadcasts began in December 1961. The first channel RTÉ One went on air on New Year's Eve, 1961 and the second channel RTÉ Two launched in November 1978. The Irish language TV service, TG4, began broadcasting in 1996 and operates as a subsidiary of RTÉ, but the Government has proposed an independent status and ultimate separation from RTÉ. These channels are also available in Northern Ireland via terrestrial overspill or on cable, or Sky Digital (encrypted). In 2004 the public broadcaster employed 2,169 people, up from 2,025 in 2003 and 1,867 in 2002 (Hunt, 2005; O'Connor, 2005), an increase reflecting growth in in-house programme production alongside with increased statutory employment obligations bringing about a requirement to award employment contracts to certain individuals rather than self-employed contractor engagements, as was the past practice (RTÉ, 2005).

Audience shares

RTÉ may still be considered dominant in the Irish TV market, but like its European counterparts its audience share has declined owing to intense competition and the rise of multi-media market. Table 7.1 shows that the most affected channel was RTÉ Two, which lost about nine per cent of all day share in the years from 1998 (the year that saw the launch of commercial rival TV3, essentially the first commercial television channel with national coverage) to 2005. Meanwhile RTÉ One's ratings also went down by about six per cent of all day viewing. In stark contrast, the share of commercial channel TV3 saw a sharp rise from five per cent in the first year of its operation to 13.5 per cent in 2005 (see Table 7.1). However, RTÉ performs much better during peak-time (6.00pm–11.30pm) with a high 32.3 share for the flagship channel RTÉ One and an 11.6 share for RTÉ Two. Commercial broadcaster TV3 is the closest rival to RTÉ with a 13.5 per cent all day share and 13.8 per cent peak-time share, followed by BBC One and UTV, a multi-media company offering broadcasting, Internet and telephony services.

Table 7.1 National individual all day and peak-time channel shares in Ireland (%, 2005)

Channels	All day channel shares	Peak-time channel shares
RTÉ One	25.8 (32.1% in 1998)	32.3
RTÉ Two	12.4 (20.9% in 1998)	11.6
TG4	3.1	2.7
TV3	13.5 (5% in 1998)	13.8
BBC One	6.6	6.1
UTV	6.5	7.6
Channel 4	4.2	3.9
BBC Two	3.8	3.2
Sky One	3.1	3.1
Sky News	1.6	0.9
Sky Sports 1 & 2	1.8	1.5
E4	1.4	1.1

Source: AGB Nielsen Media Research (Jan.–Dec. 2005).

Funding

While in 2001 RTÉ had a deficit of 71 million Euros, in a reversal of fortune in 2004 the public broadcaster earned a net surplus of 6.8 million Euros, building on the organisation's recovery in 2003 which reported a 2.3 million Euros surplus (RTÉ, 2005). In turn this followed the successful restructuring programme which had been undertaken in 2002, with a view to addressing the substantial deficits incurred over the course of the preceding three years (see below). Improved earnings were also the result of an increase both in public funding and commercial revenues, the two main sources of income for the public broadcaster. More specifically, public funding in 2004, in the form of licence fee revenue, increased by 8.7 million Euros and commercial revenues were buoyant in most areas resulting in an increase of 21.5 million Euros, with TV advertising accounting for 15.3 million of this overall growth.

The level of the TV licence, paid by all households with a television receiver,[4] has increased significantly in recent years and makes just below 50 per cent of RTÉ's revenue (the rest comes from commercial income). As will be shown below, RTÉ was required to undertake specific commitments as a condition for the granting of a higher TV licence. Table 7.2 shows that while in 1998 revenues from the licence fee totaled about 80 million Euros and accounted for 33.6 per cent of RTÉ's income, in 2005 TV licence revenues more than doubled, thus comprising a little less than 50 per cent of the total income. This is mainly due to a change in government policy towards the public broadcaster. In more particular, in November 2002 RTÉ tabled a full proposal to the government, in which it asked for a generous increase in the TV licence. RTÉ argued that the level of the licence fee was very low in comparison with other European countries and this low income did not allow the broadcaster to produce quality programmes that could contribute to the public interest (RTÉ, 2002). Following intense lobbying, the government

Table 7.2 RTÉ's income sources (1998–2005, Euros m)

Income sources	1998	2001	2003	2005
TV licence fees	80,717	94,940	157,425	170,131
Commercial income	159,616	158,680	155,247	199,757
Total revenue	240,332	253,620	312,672	369,888

Source: RTE, 2005.

finally accepted RTÉ's claims and decided to grant the broadcaster a 40 per cent increase in the licence fee (an increase of 43 Euros to a figure of 150 Euros per annum) effective from January 2003. Furthermore it was suggested that the annual adjustments to the TV licence fee would be based on a CPI minus X formula (Consumer Price Index less a specified figure X).

This formula is used to take account of rising costs but it also reflects performance on execution of a change management agenda and performance against programme commitments. In November 2004 PricewaterhouseCoopers reviewed RTÉ's performance and sought to inform the Government's decision with regard to the 2005 increase in the licence fee (PWC, 2004). The consultants were required to assess the extent to which RTÉ has delivered upon its commitments with regard to performance, output and organisational change and found that the set of performance objectives have been fulfilled to the full. Following this report the government fixed the licence fee at 155 Euros a year for 2005–2006. RTÉ One is the largest beneficiary of the licence fee, accounting for 45 per cent of the licence revenue received by RTÉ in 2004, or 61.44 million Euros. In the meantime RTÉ Two received 32.28 million Euros, or 24 per cent of the total (RTÉ, 2005).

The second major source of RTÉ's income is commercial revenues, notably advertising. Table 7.2 shows that the share of commercial revenues dropped slightly in the years from 1998 to 2003, but it recovered in the following years and in 2005 it comprised more than 50 per cent of the total RTÉ revenue. Revenue from advertising accounted for the lion share (40 per cent), while the sale of products via the public broadcaster's commercial department represented 12.1 per cent of RTÉ's total income.

Programming policy

Similarly to most other European PTV broadcasters RTÉ One and RTÉ Two provide round-the-clock broadcasts seven days a week, comprising coverage of news and current affairs, drama, music, sport and light entertainment. RTÉ has produced popular programmes that attract large audiences. It is noticeable that in 2005 nine out of the 10 most watched TV programmes broadcast by the public channels (see Table 7.3).

The Director of TV programmes at RTÉ Claire Duignan (2005) informed us that since 2003 RTÉ has branded its TV programmes

Table 7.3　Top 10 TV programmes in Ireland in 2005

Rank	Programme	Channel
1	The Late Late Toy Show	RTÉ One
2	You're a Star Live – The Result	RTÉ One
3	Rose of Tralee 2005 – Final	RTÉ One
4	All Ireland Football Final (Kerry v Tyrone)	RTÉ Two
5	Rip-off Republic	RTÉ One
6	A Killinaskully Christmas carol	RTÉ One
7	RTE News: Nine O'Clock	RTÉ One
8	World Cup Qualifier (Rep. of Ireland v Switzerland)	RTÉ Two
9	Coronation Street	TV3
10	Fair City	RTÉ One

Source: AGB Nielsen Media Research.

under a number of different genres. Each genre operates under a Commissioning Editor, except for RTÉ News and Current Affairs which are separately structured and controlled: RTÉ Arts produces documentaries on well-known Irish figures (for example, Sean O'Casey and Patrick Kavanagh) and a weekly magazine show, The View; RTÉ Diversity produces religious, disability, Irish language and minority programming; RTÉ Drama produces soap operas such as the Fair City; RTÉ Education's programmes aim at students and adult literacy; RTÉ Entertainment produces chat-shows the flagship of which is The Late Late Show as well as game shows such as You're a Star; RTÉ History, RTÉ Music, RTÉ Sport and RTÉ Young Peoples (mainly on RTÉ Two) are additional television genres.

RTÉ has undertaken specific content commitments as set out in its 2004 commitments to its audience (RTÉ, 2004). The Statement of Commitments is based on the Public Service Broadcasting Charter contained in RTÉ's 2002 submission for a licence fee increase (RTÉ, 2002). It is in effect an understanding between the public broadcaster and its audience. The specific content commitments are measured and independently verified at the end of each year. Strategy advisory services PricewaterhouseCoopers assessed RTÉ's 2004 content commitments and found that the public broadcaster either met or exceeded all of its commitments. In more particular, RTÉ One made commitments to broadcast over 1140 hours of indigenous content (Drama, News/ Current Affairs, Entertainment/Music, Factual) during peak viewing

Table 7.4 Indigenous hours of content on RTÉ in peak-times by genre (2004)

Genre	RTÉ One	RTÉ Two
Drama	117	56
News and current affairs	582	94
Entertainment	208	66
Music	25	24
Young people	0	15
Sport	6	313
Education	16	5
Religious	26	2
Arts	24	0
Other factual	251	47

Source: RTÉ Annual Report 2005.

time in 2004 and in fact it broadcast just over 1200 hours of indigenous programming, across the four specified genres (see Table 7.4). Indigenous content target (for the four genres) for peak-time viewing in 2005 was some five per cent up on 2004 output. The wide availability of RTÉ One's indigenous content partly explains its significantly higher audience share as against its closest rival TV3.

RTÉ Two also exceeded its indigenous output commitments at peak-viewing time for 2004, but such commitments were by far more modest at 193 hours of indigenous content for Drama, News/Current Affairs, Entertainment/Music and Factual (see Table 7.4). As part of the re-branding and re-positioning of RTÉ Two in 2004, it is the management's intention to: (a) increase home production; (b) offer real alternative choice in the schedule; (c) identify and develop new on-air talent; and (d) give a new and more contemporary 'look and feel' to the channel. A strengthening of RTÉ Two's overall proposition and market share position during 2005 was a key priority, given that commercial broadcaster TV3 by-passed RTÉ Two both at peak-time and on an 'all-day' basis (see Table 7.1) due to transmitting some of parent company Granada's popular content (Coronation Street, Emmerdale). However, to deliver this strategy RTÉ Two would require a significant up-lift in funding and resourcing (PWC, 2004).

RTÉ has also made output commitments for the schedule overall, across a number of genres (News and Current Affairs, Young Peoples,

Sport) and once again it exceeded all commitments in this regard. It has also demonstrated strong performance against more qualitative aspects of content – originality, experimentation, risk in creativity, development of talent, high standards and quality. The consultancy PricewaterhouseCoopers were required to capture some of the key highlights of RTÉ's performance under each heading above and across the different genres and concluded that the PTV broadcaster has delivered its specific commitments for 2004 (ibid.).

Independent production

RTÉ has a special relationship with Independent Producers of programmes. As it is stated in the RTÉ Corporate Responsibility in 2006, the development of a secure, profitable and stable independent production sector in Ireland enhances the interests of broadcasting, including those of RTÉ. Under legislation RTÉ must expend annually a specific sum to fund independent TV programmes. In 1999 the amount was set at about 20 million Euros, but in 2005 this was increased to 29.4 million Euros. However, during that year RTÉ spent in excess of 74.6 million Euros with this sector, significantly exceeding the required amount. One of the reasons of RTÉ's growing independent commissioning trend is to meet the indigenous content commitments outlined above. RTÉ commissions independent programming across all genres with Commissioning Editors managing programming for their own area. The business, financial, legal and administrative aspects of RTÉ's commissions is handled through the Independent Production unit (RTÉ, 2006).

Organisational development

RTÉ has been through major changes in recent years. In 1998 the Transformation Plan[5] was introduced in an attempt to reduce costs by cutting staff numbers and establishing new work practices, but these changes did not stem revenue losses. However, a completely fresh organisational structure was created at the dawn of the new millennium, resulting in six Integrated Business Divisions (IBDs): RTÉ Television; RTÉ Radio; RTÉ News and Current Affairs; RTÉ Network; RTÉ Publishing; and RTÉ Performing Groups (O'Connor, 2005; Hunt, 2005). Head of Public Affairs at RTÉ Patricia Galvin (2005), whose position was created to alleviate the 'tensions' between the PTV broadcaster and the government/regulatory agency following the re-organisation of RTÉ, argued that the setting up of business divisions has established better efficiency and smoother running within the broadcaster. Feeney (2005) and Hunt (2005) believed that operational improvement has resulted in better planning, more efficient use of technology, superior marketing, more efficient programme production, as well as staff flexibility. Manager of publishing O'Doherty (2005) and managing editor of RTÉ e-publishing Murphy (2005), also highlighted the benefits from the new divisions created at RTÉ and insisted that even though their own division is not profitable (it is not funded by the licence fee), its existence is nevertheless of utmost strategic importance.

The consultancy PricewaterhouseCoopers first proposed the movement to the IBD structure in 2003 and argued that this would improve both financial transparency and the management of RTÉ's activities. In its 2004 review the consultancy found that the IBD structure was successfully bedded-in and brought greater accountability at IBD level in terms of revenues, costs and decision-making. More specifically, the review revealed that each IBD set out 10 initiatives undertaken in 2004 that express significant change to the manner in which they conduct their business. While the initiatives vary from IBD to IBD, success could be measured quantitatively (in terms of cost savings or headcount reduction) and qualitatively (for example, a different way of working). The set of objectives is underpinned by business needs, which in turn determines the training and development needs. One of the key objectives for the PTV broadcaster, for example, is value for money, so it is important that all training is relevant, cost effective and aligned to the business objectives. Regarding the management of manpower process, the consultancy review noted that over the past six years there has been significant staff churn via various redundancy programmes and departures, and while RTÉ management believe that more recent employee contractual agreements afford greater manpower flexibility, this has come with a significant cost, with the costs of various redundancy programmes totaling 83 million Euros (PWC, 2004).

In sum, the consultants argued that RTÉ has now moved from the financial difficulties of the early 2000s and the then imperative of cost reduction, including personnel costs. RTÉ management expects to increase its workforce in the next years; in the meantime it anticipates greater flexibility from the newer employees. To achieve this, PricewaterhouseCoopers noted that RTÉ needs to: (a) document the full range of existing skills within each IBD; (b) set out the high level requirements for additional skills going forward; (c) plan for the management of older/less used skills; and (d) implement a performance management system throughout all levels of the organisation (ibid.). According to Murray (2006) the IBD system cultivated a business ethos among management, encouraging management and staff to think about costs, revenues and output together. It may be that the IBDs are structured in such a way that each division must ultimately be concerned with revenue, but public service remains a stated objective of the organisation.

Involvement in new technologies

Digital terrestrial television

In 1998 RTÉ proposed a plan for the introduction of DTT in the Irish Republic. Taking into consideration factors such as topography, population density, existing infrastructure, size of the market, social and cultural factors, RTÉ estimated that DTT constituted the most cost-effective and viable solution for Ireland. The country has just 3.8 million inhabitants, who live as much in urban centres as in provincial towns. Ireland's geography, more specifically the existence of high mountains, causes problems in the broadcast of the television signal and as a result the choice to develop digital cable television was rejected as non-viable financially. A digital satellite platform may constitute a better option in terms of topography, although there is a danger of control by multinational companies, broadcasting mainly foreign output. The need to purchase additional equipment by the consumer (satellite dishes) renders satellite broadcasting uneconomic for a small country like Ireland.

RTÉ's estimate for the total cost of modernising its existing infrastructure was 70 million Euros. According to government statements during the two-year period 1999–2000, the funding was not to be covered by an increase in the licence fee, but RTÉ had to raise funds from other sources, for example the selling of its minority share in the cable channel NTL, the privatisation of a part of its transmission network, and a gradual reduction in head count by 300–400 people up to 2002. Although the resources that would be generated by these initiatives were significant, they were not enough however to cover the total cost of setting up the digital platform. Precisely for this reason,

RTÉ proposed collaboration with private broadcasters and in particular the setting up of a consortium in which RTÉ would hold a majority share (40 per cent). In terms of output, the DTT would offer a linked sequence of choices, beginning with free-to-air programming, and ending in a wide spectrum of pay services. According to the then General Director of RTÉ, Farell Corcoran digital technology would help the organisation develop a strategy to expand its services, and thus allow it to face the challenges of the digital revolution. Digital technology allows innovations in the production and use of programmes, thus significantly benefiting the independent producer sector. Also the digital terrestrial platform offers the capacity for new advanced and interactive services and the supply of additional educational programmes (Corcoran, 2000).

RTÉ moved forward from 1998 with careful planning of these business activities. In May 1999, a draft Broadcasting Bill approved these initiatives, but in February 2000 the Government decided to re-examine the business plan, taking into consideration the negative opinion expressed by interested broadcasters who argued that RTÉ's 40 per cent share in the platform violates competition rules. In contrast to the British government and the green light it gave the BBC to develop a widely available DTT platform, the Irish government was hesitant to approve a similar plan. John Hunt, Patricia Galvin and Anne O'Connor, all interviewed in April 2005, noted that the DTT scheme failed due to wrong timing and listed the following reasons for this failure: the twin tower attacks that resulted in a global slowdown; the dotcom burst (Ireland was directly affected due to its affinity with new technologies); and the failure of the digital terrestrial pay-TV platform ITV Digital in Britain. For these reasons not many bidders emerged and those who did bid were then cancelled. According to Corcoran (2000, 2003), this state and business inertia conflicted with the majority of Irish households that wanted the development of a domestic platform and future independence from British services.

Eight years later DTT has yet to be developed in Ireland. This inertia has given competitive advantage to private cable networks, which already offer triple-play services, including digital TV. In the field of satellite Sky Digital has continued to increase its subscriber base, while RTÉ simply lags behind these developments and has lost its competitive advantage in the digital era. According to O'Connor (2005), Hunt (2005) and Murphy (2005), RTÉ needs to take a leading role in DTT, otherwise it will be left to the peril of the private sector (by using their platforms) to deliver its own content. More recently, the government announced its intention to facilitate the development of DTT as a free-to-air platform, promote digital take-up and meet the 2012 digital switchover deadline set by the European Commission. Following the June 2005 announcement to develop DTT, in 2006–2007 the Minister for Communications, Marine and Natural resources, Noel Dempsey, was seeking applications from content producers interested in participating in the DTT trial. It seems that the Irish government is now more committed to roll out a DTT service nationally, although details of the scheme are not yet available.

Multimedia services

According to McLaughlin (2005) from the regulatory agency ComReg, RTÉ will have a critical role to play as a multi-media content provider in the digital landscape, as evidenced by the broadcaster's collaboration with mobile telephony company Nokia to bring to 3G customers the latest entertainment news, reviews and reports on films and music. In 2006 RTÉ was conducting technical trials of a mobile TV service. Based on BT Movio, BT's wholesale mobile TV service that piggybacks on the Digital Audio Broadcasting network to broadcast pictures to handsets, the service was due to become available in Dublin. Those behind the trial would be running a full portfolio of services, including the two public TV channels RTÉ One and RTÉ Two (The Register, 2006).

Thematic channels

The Irish PTV broadcaster has not launched any thematic channels and according to O'Connor (2005), Hunt (2005) and Murphy (2005) it is doubtful that this will change in the near future. The above interviewees believe that the market is saturated already as there are plenty of satellite and cable TV services, as well as several free-to-air channels either due to spill-over from Britain or from local stations.

Prospects for RTÉ

RTÉ has played an important role in the development and promotion of Irish culture. It has managed to maintain high audience ratings and a leadership position, despite the competition it has always faced from

British channels widely available to Irish citizens. Domestic competition comes mainly from national commercial operator TV3, whose audience ratings have been increasing over the past years owing to the management's strategy to attract a specific target group, notably age groups between 15 and 45 years old. Repercussions for RTÉ will be significant if it loses a part of these age groups who are important to advertisers. In 2005 advertisers funded about half of RTÉ's needs, but as audiences scatter across the spectrum RTÉ may no longer be able to attract viewers on a scale that makes it uniquely attractive to advertisers. RTÉ also competes with newlyformed entertainment-oriented Channel 6 with national coverage, regional player City Channel, as well as multi-channel cable and satellite consortia.

Despite the intense competition, RTÉ is particularly strong at peak-time slots due to its commitment to home-grown programme production. Viewers are happy with this emphasis on Irish-made programming and continue to support their PTV broadcaster for the pursuance of an indigenous cultural agenda. The robust performance can also be attributed to certain key decisions made at the beginning of the current decade. The decision to set up business divisions for television, radio and publishing meant that each division had sole responsibility for revenue and output so there is now a much more of a virtual circle. Geralnine O'Leary, Head of TV sales at RTE, argued that the virtual circle works like this: 'if and when we make money it goes back into programming, it generates an audience, which in turn makes more money, which goes back into programming and so on' (Skelly, 2006).

The public broadcaster is also financially healthy. While in 2001 it had a deficit of 71 million Euros, it is now projecting surpluses of between nine and 10.3 million Euros for the next four years. RTÉ has subsequently been able to reverse its fortunes thanks to a major increase in the licence fee from just 107 Euros per household per annum in 2002 (one of the lowest in Europe) to 155 Euros in 2005. RTÉ's relationship with the state has not always been rosy, but as of late this relationship is improving, as evidenced by the licence fee increase. The Strategy Advisory Service PricewaterhouseCoopers 2004 report says that about 112 million Euros has been embarked for capital projects between 2005 and 2009, including the development of DTT.

In terms of RTÉ's future prospects, the PricewaterhouseCoopers 2004 review is very positive. It noted that RTÉ has moved from a period of *crisis management* to one of *operational management* whereby the new Executive Board has:

- Focused on restructuring the organisation into more manageable IBDs with clearer financial transparency and accountability.
- Greatly improved the quality and level of indigenous programming and the composition of its schedules.
- Improved the connectivity between the development of the schedules and advertising/commercial revenue optimisation.
- Rolled-out a number of redundancy programmes and regularised its contractual relationship with its employee base, resulting in more flexible workforce.
- Started to get a better understanding of the investment needs in broadcasting infrastructure (PWC, 2004).

In sum, RTÉ proved that mainstream channels can survive in the new environment providing the management take prompt action with regards to programming choices and internal re-organisation. The accountability of the public broadcaster has also enhanced. In 2004 RTÉ and the Minister for Communications, Marine and Natural Resources agreed that in future RTÉ would operate under a Public Service Charter. The public broadcaster is now legally obliged to agree a Charter every five years and publish a statement of commitments every year. These commitments include the production of high quality home produced programmes and fostering of new talent, as well as providing comprehensive transparent financial information on the performance on public funding spending. This practice will help RTÉ to live up to its purpose as a creative, innovative and trusted broadcaster who accounts for itself, its values, standards and performance to the public.

8
Sweden

> Population: 8.9 million (UN, 2005)
> Monetary Unit: Swedish Krona (9.9 Euros)
> GNI per capita: 31,460 Euros
> Households with television: 3.9 million
> Average daily TV viewing: 162 minutes
> Penetration of cable TV: 56%
> Penetration of satellite TV: 19.5%
> Number of pay-TV subscribers: 3.2 million
> Number of digital viewers: pay-TV: 2.4 million; DTT: 654,000 (January 2007)
> Supervisory body: Radio and Television Authority (licensing); Broadcasting Commission (content)
> Households with Internet Access: 67%

General characteristics of the TV market

The Swedish terrestrial TV market is centralised and dominated by national broadcasters – two public service channels and one commercial. As in most European countries, television in Sweden was introduced as public service medium. Public television is run by Sveriges Television (SVT), whose first television programme was transmitted in 1956. The first competition for SVT came in the late 1980s with the launch of free-to-air satellite channels TV3 and Kanal 5, each of them reaching over 60 per cent of the population via cable or satellite. Swedish language TV3 (owned by the Modern Times Group – MTG) and Kanal 5 (owned the Scandinavian Broadcasting System) are broadcasting from Britain in order to avoid the Swedish broadcasting law which restricts advertising heavily.[1] However, SVT's main competitor is TV4, the only major terrestrial commercial channel which leads the ratings. Entertainment-oriented TV4 was launched in 1992, at a time when Sweden was caught up in a major turn to the right; the Social Democrats lost the 1991 election and a bourgeois coalition came to power to pursue deregulatory policies (Dahlgren, 1998). TV4 does have a more popular profile than public channels, but from its inception it had to operate within a highly regulated framework, much the same as ITV in Britain, so it could be seen as a quasi public service (ibid.). TV4 runs two additional services – TV4 Plus (a lifestyle channel) and TV4 Med i TV (aimed at young people).

Today Swedish audiences enjoy a wide variety of commercial broadcast services, though until relatively recently public TV had a near monopoly of the airwaves. Satellite TV services are provided via Viasat (a subsidiary of the MTG) and Canal Digital (controlled by the Norwegian telephone company Telenor). The cable industry is also well developed, with four cable companies accounting for 85 per cent of total subscriptions (ComHem, Kabelvision, UPC Sweden and Sweden On-Line). Digital terrestrial television commenced in 1999 (Sweden, along with Britain, Finland and Spain was among the first EU countries to launch DTT), but the service had a slow start in a heavily cabled market (Iosifidis *et al.*, 2005, p. 108). Other reasons explaining the initial low take-up (100,000 households, or two per cent of total Swedish households in 2001) were that the offer did not include TV4, the country's most popular commercial terrestrial channel, and it was not sufficiently differentiated from the analogue offer. Also, decoders were expensive, ranging from 300 to 450 Euros (ibid.). However, the re-packaging of the content in 2004 to include the two public channels SVT1 and SVT2 and commercial operator TV4 (all offered free-to-air) and SVT24, Kunskapskanalen (the Knowledge Channel) and Barnkanalen (a children's channel) at not extra cost, as well as the ramp up to digital switchover (Sweden is expected to switch-off the analogue airwaves by early 2008), have resulted in an increase in subscriber numbers which in January 2007 totaled 654,000.

The regulatory framework

The Swedish broadcasting sector is primarily regulated by the 1996 Radio and TV Act. The Ministry of Culture issues licenses for national terrestrial TV channels for a period of five years and Radio-och TV-verket (Radio and Television Authority) bears responsibility for cable and satellite TV operations. The cable and satellite sectors are only slightly regulated and in direct contrast with most regulatory regimes across Europe, licenses are not required for cable and satellite broadcasters, although they must register and report their activities (Loebbecke and Picard, 2005). Television programmes are formally overseen by the Broadcasting Commission, which is a government agency. Also relevant is the Fundamental Law on Freedom of Expression (a law with constitutional power), which protects the rights of free opinion and expression in all electronic media.

Since the opening of the broadcasting market to competition, ownership concentration has been one of the main issues. The main players are Bonnier Group (originally a publishing company which has diversified to broadcasting and TV production) and MTG, which owns several satellite TV channels. A special government committee, the Council for Pluralism in the Media was formed in the early 1990s to address the phenomenon, but its work has progressed slowly due to political split. As elsewhere in Europe, the issue of media concentration in Sweden has raised intense political controversies, especially between the Social Democrats and the Centre Party, which favour more regulation and the Liberal and Conservative parties, which pursue a more deregulatory approach.

SVT programming is also regulated by the 1996 Radio and TV Act and the exact terms are set out in the Charter between the public broadcaster and the state, as well as internal programming guidelines. In terms of programming, the Charter states that SVT must produce (a) quality and varied programmes that contribute to a democratic society; (b) programmes that are not exclusively aimed at increasing audience ratings; and (c) output that would satisfy all interests, including those of minorities. Furthermore, the Charter guarantees SVT's independence from all pressure groups – political, commercial or special-interest. A key provision is that SVT should have the freedom to 'scrutinise public agencies, organisations and privately-owned businesses which exert influence over public policy, and to report on the activities of these and other bodies'.

Public television

The Swedish public broadcasting system is in many respects modeled after the British one and publicly-funded SVT has many similarities with its British counterpart, the BBC – both are powerful, non-profit media enterprises serving the national audiences; both are acclaimed for their independence and funded almost exclusively by the licence fee; both face the same competition including one main terrestrial competitor and a few smaller commercial channels. The three public service broadcasting companies, SVT (public television), SR (public radio) and UR (educational broadcasting company) are owned by an independent public foundation (and not the state), the board of which is appointed by the government after consultations with the parliamentary parties. The foundation has no influence on the programming; its main purpose is to serve as a buffer between the state power and the content companies (Bjorkman, 2005). In other words, the foundation has been specially formed to defend editorial autonomy of the public service companies from political influence. Decisions on the general aims of the company are made by the SVT Board, while programme content is entirely the responsibility of the SVT Management (the managing director and the head of programmes).

In 2000 Sam Nielsen left SVT after been Director General for seventeen years and Christina Jutterstrom (previously Head of Drama) became DG, but was later (in 2006) replaced by Eva Hamilton (SVT's Head of Fiction). These infrequent changes at top-level management enabled the organisation to plan for the longer term and contrast sharply with frequent changes of DGs in PTV broadcasters from southern European countries. Another scheme that distinguishes SVT from most other PTV broadcasters is that all managers gather together outside the SVT premises once or twice annually and brainstorm to create strategies up to the year 2012. As trend-setters SVT managers wish to lead the way to the digital future and be pro-active in areas such as programming, technology and internal restructuring (Bjorkman, 2005).

Funding

Similarly to other Nordic public service broadcasters, Sveriges Television's mission is to fulfill the democratic, social and cultural needs of the Swedish society. SVT operates two national channels, SVT1 and SVT2, launched in 1956 and 1969 respectively. Their revenues derive

Table 8.1 Breakdown of income for Swedish SVT (1998, 2000)

Source	1998		2000	
	euros (000)	%	euros (000)	%
Licence fee	344.392	94.0	395.456	91.0
Commercial income	22.010	6.0	24.830	5.7
Sponsorship	2.339	0.6	3.873	0.9
Sales of programmes	14.460	3.9	15.490	3.6
Merchandising	106	0.0	–	0.0
Other commercial income	5.104	1.4	5.467	1.3
Other income	–	0.0	14.351	3.4
Total	366.402	100.0	434.637	100.0

Source: SVT Annual Report, 2002.

almost in total from the annual fee which is obligatory and placed in a special account at the Bank of Sweden. The public service companies – SVT, SR and UR – receive a sum of that account (decided by the government) on an annual basis. In 2000, income from the licence fee neared 400 million Euros, with television as always absorbing the largest share (58.9 per cent was allocated to SVT, 34 per cent to SR and 4.7 per cent to UR). In 2005 the level of the fee was 1968 Swedish Krona – SEK (approximately 214 Euros) per year. Table 8.1 shows that the licence fee is the major source of funding for the Swedish public broadcaster, accounting for more than 90 per cent, with commercial revenues far behind at 5.7 per cent.

Audience shares

For a long time SVT2 was the most popular channel in Sweden, but in 2001 many popular programmes, such as the news programme Rapport and the Saturday night entertainment, were moved to SVT1, thereby making it the broader mainstream channel. SVT2 became a narrower channel, often overturned by TV3 and Kanal 5 in the overall ratings (see Table 8.2). SVT2 (and SVT1) are behind in ratings compared to the terrestrial commercial channel TV4, which since 1994 has become the nation's most viewed channel.

Reorganisation

Up to the end of 1995, the two public channels were competing openly with each other, with SVT1 (then named Kanal 1) showing

Table 8.2 Audience shares of television channels in Sweden (%, 2001, 2005)

Channels	Share (2001)	Share (2005)
SVT1	19.9	24.3
SVT2	23.9	13.7
Total (SVT)	*43.8*	*38.0*
TV3	11.4	10.7
TV4	26.4	26.0
Kanal 5	6.3	8.0
ZTV	1.6	1.8
TV8	0.5	0.9
Others	10.1	14.6

Source: Personal interviews.

Stockholm-based programmes and SVT2 (named TV2 at the time) broadcasting programmes from other parts of Sweden. In January 1997 the two channels were reorganised under a common administration and have since cooperated closely in the areas of production and broadcasting. In 2000 new programme schedules were introduced for each service which aimed to make it easier for viewers to find and watch services that they wish (as mentioned above, this led to the popularity of SVT1). Public television acquired a more local character, so as to satisfy local interests. Today, branches of public television consist of STV South, SVT West, SVT North and SVT Central. The broadcaster has also set up a special department for news, current affairs and documentaries (SVT News and Documentaries), another for production and technology (SVT Production and Information Technology), and a third for strategic planning (SVT Planning). There are six production departments: News and Documentaries, Sports and Entertainment, Culture, Children, Drama and Factual (Stromqvist, 2005).

Another reorganisation strategy concerns redundancies or early retirement plans. In 2004 SVT had roughly 2700 employees in twenty eight regions. A year later 150 staff left the company as part of SVT's strategy to streamline the company by cutting staff by 400 in the period 2004–2006. Most staff reductions have involved people from the production and administration units and according to head of research at SVT this strategy will continue in the coming years (Bjorkman, 2005). A related issue is that about 40 per cent of SVT's staff is aged 55–65. This is a predicament because in Sweden early retirement plans are expensive to carry our and retraining may also be ineffective or not viable because the people are at a more advanced age (ibid.).

New services

In the context of this restructuring, the regional channels were shut down in the beginning of 2002 and were replaced by SVT Extra (special events channel), which was later renamed SVT24. December 2002 witnessed the introduction of Barnkanalen, a children's channel. Overall, the six channels operated by SVT in 2006 were the five national SVT1, SVT2, SVT24 (a 24-hour news and sports channel), Barnkanalen (a children's service until 18.00), and, in cooperation with UR, the knowledge channel Kunskapskanalen (shown on the same frequency as the children's service but from 19.30), and one European, STV Europa. Only SVT1 and SVT2 are transmitted in the analogue terrestrial network, whereas the other major transmission platforms, analogue or digital, carry all the national SVT channels.

In autumn 2005 Sweden commenced a region-by-region phasing out of the analogue terrestrial network and the effort is slated for completion on 1 February 2008. The first three regions that went digital in 2005 were Gotland, Motala and Gavle. Head of research Bjorkman (2005) argues that SVT should be available on all platforms to maintain the universal coverage requirements in the digital age. SVT is putting pressure on the government for the switch-off to happen as scheduled to avoid the high cost of prolonged simulcasting (ibid.). However, both interviewees Bjorkman (2005) and Stromqvist (2005) see web-based technology as the future for television. In fact, the PTV broadcaster has invested in new digital equipment, metadata and a tape-less environment and in 2005 there were talks (much as in Britain) about creating an open-archive system available to all Swedes either for free or for a small fee. The newly established department SVT-i deals with new media, WAP and live streaming, but other experiments such as the creation of a media lab and a green house production (for new programming) have not survived.

Programming strategy

SVT programming covers the whole genre spectrum and is non-commercial, but popular – as stated in the SVT 2005 annual report,

95 out of the 100 most popular Swedish TV programmes during 2005 came from the public broadcaster. But why the Swedish public trusts SVT? In terms of news, public channels contain more dense information when compared to the news programmes of commercial channels, with Rapport (Report) and Aktuellt (Current) being the two main SVT news programmes. Rapport, in particular, originally shown on SVT2 (moved to SVT1 in 2001) has been the most popular news programme in Sweden for almost 30 years. Regarding drama, Rederiet (1992–2002) has been a popular Swedish soap opera, but new drama imports include Veronica Mars and what acquisitions executive Per Ogren calls British garden detective stories, such as The Inspector Lynley Mysteries and Walking the Dead, as well as Yank series Without a Trace (Lundberg, 2006).

Although the British influence is evident, local entertainment has also done really well for SVT. For example, Melodifestivalen (pre-selection for the European song contest) is very popular and the final generally gets more than four million viewers. The reality show Survivor (named Expedition Robinson) was first broadcast by STV in 1997 and before it ceased in 2003–2004 it was breaking audience records. Other popular shows include Pa sparet (run from 1987 till present and based where celebrities answer questions related to different locations), Sa ska det lata (the Swedish version of The Lyrics Board), Allsang pa Skansen (a show based on a crowd singing folk music) and Antikrundan (the Swedish version of Antiques Roadshow). Conversely, the American dominance of the schedules is evident in commercial stations TV3 and TV4, which both launched their most expensive marketing campaigns ever in early 2006 for Prison Break and Commander in Chief, respectively. Commercial channels also feature reality shows, like Big Brother, The Farm and Fame Academy on a daily basis and TV4 continues to broadcast current hits Lost and Medium.

But what is SVT's programming mission and how the PTV broadcaster attempts to fulfill it? As it is stated in the SVT's Charter, the public broadcaster exists to enrich the lives of all Swedes through a wide range of quality programming that spans news, entertainment, education and the arts, accessible to all, regardless of their background, orientation or aptitude. Head of programme policy and scheduling Stromqvist (2005) informs us that SVT's output consists mainly of domestic productions (85 per cent), whereas foreign acquisitions account for only 15 per cent. From that, 70 per cent is in-house production; the work of

Table 8.3 SVT programming genres (%, 1991–2004)

Programme genres	1991	1998	2001	2004
News	21	21	20	18
Factual	25	26	26	29
Fiction/feature Films	24	22	25	24
Entertainment	9	8	9	10
Sport	14	15	14	12
Arts/music	7	7	6	5
Other	0	1	0	2
Total	100	100	100	100

Source: SVT Annual Reports; Nordic PSB (2004).

independent producers accounts for about 30 per cent. According to Stromqvist (2005) a problem when using independent producers is to explain the difference between public service and commercial content, which is not always clear to them. SVT intends to increase the independent production output, even though it looses 25 per cent VAT for outsourcing (ibid.).

In 2004 SVT broadcast 8987 hours of programmes, 6500 of which were original productions. Table 8.3 shows that SVT broadcasts a variety of programmes that give emphasis equally to entertainment, news and current affairs, but also sciences, the arts, culture and sport.[2] As explained in Chapter 3, this programming diet has only slightly changed during the past decade, indicating that growing competition had minimum impact on the PTV broadcaster's output. Research has shown that this is the case even at peak-time slots. For example, Leon's 2004 study on prime-time programming found that the Swedish flagship public channel SVT1 devotes 20.5 per cent of its prime-time programming on fiction, 20.4 per cent on news/current affairs, 5.2 per cent on sports and 5.1 per cent on quiz shows, and completely refrains from showing reality shows or infotainment. As a result, it has higher indices of diversity (53.9 per cent) as against commercial channels at 39.5 per cent.

Prospects for SVT

Similarly to other European countries, the advent of commercial television in Sweden completely altered the position of public channels. The launch of satellite services TV3 and Kanal 5 in the late 1980s paved the way for the introduction of the commercial terrestrial channel TV4, which until today is the major competitor to SVT. Also the wide availability of cable and satellite channels alongside the development of the DTT platform have meant that the former mixed, public-private system has been replaced by intense competition. How the non-commercial channels have adjusted to the new reality? As Dahlgren (1998) notes, the response has not at all been what the alarmists had feared. In terms of ratings, public TV has managed to maintain very respectable audience shares at around 40 per cent. Research (McKinsey, 1999; Leon, 2004) has shown that SVT1 and SVT2 continue to maintain an impressive level of programming diversity, with many programmes clearly intended for niche audiences. The PTV broadcaster is the most trusted Swedish medium (although commercial rival TV4 is the most watched channel) and enjoys very good support from the Swedish TV audience.

Public support can be attributed to the broadcasting of quality, varied and balanced programmes that satisfy all preferences including those of minorities. As mentioned in Chapter 3, SVT's funding model by the licence fee did not push it to concede to commercial pressures and allowed the PTV broadcaster to provide a balanced programming diet. Alongside ensuring its survival, this robust source of financing has enabled SVT to meet its public service obligations, take certain risks and devise more distinctive forms of programming. While continuing to maintain a strong public service profile, SVT improved its scheduling strategy in order to respond to the growing fragmentation of the Swedish society, which is in dynamic flux as economic, political, ethnic and cultural factors continue to accentuate fragmentation and differentiation. Support from the public is growing after the operational restructuring that took place in 2000 (especially the creation of local branches that give emphasis to local events). As head of programme policy and scheduling Stromqvist (2005) put it, 'SVT has the credibility and audiences will listen to the PTV broadcaster first for important issues'. He added: 'SVT wants its audience to perceive it not merely as an information provider, but as an experience provider'.

Undoubtedly, SVT faces many challenges, the most important of which is the cost of digitalising its operation. However, the burden of this financial challenge is smaller than most other PTV broadcasters across Europe. The Swedish government supports SVT's digital expansion, as evidenced by the April 1999 generous allowance of 500 million SEK that allowed it to create the second digital terrestrial platform in

Europe (Britain was first). But government funding does not stop there. From the year 2000 a sum of the annual licence fee covers the investment for the parallel transmission in analogue and digital frequencies. In 2002, for example, 10.74 million Euros (out of a total of 391.33 million Euros licence fees) were extra fees SVT obtained for distributing programmes both in analogue and digital means. This scheme will come to an end in February 2008, when the analogue frequency is expected to cease.

9
Greece

> Population: 11.1 million
> Monetary Unit: Euro
> GNI per capita: 12,000 Euros
> Households with television: 3.5 million
> Average daily TV viewing: 260 minutes
> Penetration of cable TV: 1.5%
> Penetration of satellite TV: 5%
> Number of pay-TV subscribers (analogue or digital): 500,000
> Number of pay digital viewers: 350,000 (*Nova* satellite package)
> Number of free-to-air digital viewers: 800,000
> Supervisory body: National Council of Radio and TV
> Households with Internet Access: 18%

General characteristics of the TV market

Television broadcasting in Greece was introduced in 1966, with the first network, ERT (Elliniki Radiofonia Tileorasi) broadcasting out of the capital Athens, as a state-owned monopoly. However, through-out the 1980s, as the country began to reform and modernise at an unprecedented pace, audiences demanded a wider choice of viewing options, following the example of other European countries which had already allowed private television. Also, as a member of the European Union, Greece had to adapt to TV market liberalisation policies pursued by the European Commission. But similarities with other European TV markets stop there, for the development of the Greek TV sector is distinctly different from that of most EU member states. In more particular:

- Public television took its first steps during a military junta (which ruled Greece between 1967–74), in an environment hostile to the development of objective TV broadcasts.
- The direct dependence of public television on political authority continued even after the restoration of democracy and undermined the validity and reliability of ERT. The problem was intensified by frequent changes in ERT's management (much like in Spain) during the period 1984–94 when the Socialist party PASOK ruled. This was not conducive to long-term planning and action-taking.
- The process of liberalisation at the end of the 1980s was conducted without any prior economic analysis of the consequences on existing companies. Taking advantage of regulatory loopholes and the ineffective licensing regime, the Mayors of the three largest Greek cities of Athens, Piraeus and Thessalonika (all affiliated to the opposition conservative party New Democracy) set up unlicensed local TV stations, which offered more choice and lured the public. ERT was the main victim of this de-facto liberalisation as it lost a significant part of its advertising income almost overnight and today has in fact the lowest audience share of all PTV broadcasters reviewed in this study (below 15 per cent).
- The first attempt to regulate the TV sector occurred in the mid-1990s, but even at the time of writing private TV channels are operating under a quasi legal state as they only have provisional licenses.
- The penetration of cable and satellite services is negligible, mainly because of the wide availability of free-to-air national channels.

The restoration of democracy in 1974 brought new impetus to the Greek media landscape and television became the dominant medium of information and entertainment, penetrating citizens' everyday life. The TV sector is characterised by cataclysmic changes which have continued with undiminished intensity since the end of the 1980s, when the first private television stations MEGA (owned by Tylepypos, a consortium of the major newspaper publishers Lambrakis, Tegopoulos and Pegasus) and ANT1 (owned by ANT1 TV S.A. with interests also in radio, publishing and recording) went on air. Alongside these pioneer private services and the three public channels ET-1, NET and ET-3, there is a multitude of national terrestrial private channels, funded mainly by advertising, the most important of which are Alpha TV (formerly Sky TV), Star Channel and Alter TV.

Private TV grew and expanded rapidly, but it strives to adjust to a pluralistic profile in a highly politicised and commercialised environment, driven by an increasing populism. In 1994 Multichoice Hellas (owned by multinational NetMed BV) started offering analogue subscription TV services and in 1999 introduced the digital service Nova, now occupying a monopoly status in the digital satellite pay-TV market after the collapse of rival digital satellite platform Alpha Digital Synthesis (Iosifidis et al., 2005, p. 117). Nova has acquired the rights to broadcast latest blockbusters as well as live football matches from the Greek League and Champions League and consequently managed to sign about 350,000 customers.

The regulatory framework

Law 1730/1987 allowed private radio stations and paved the way for the end of state monopoly in TV broadcasting. It also united public TV into one corporate body titled ERT S.A. (Hellenic Broadcasting Corporation). Law 1866/1989 permitted local private TV channels and made provision for the establishment of an independent regulatory agency, the National Council of Radio and Television (NCRTV), to oversee the operation of broadcast media, grant licences to private stations and supervise programmes. The Council's members are appointed by political parties represented in Parliament, but its independence has been questionable as until the 2004 general elections it was the Ministry of the Press and the Mass Media that granted the licenses and the NCRTV only had a consultancy role.[1] In 1993 Law 2173 was finally passed allowing for the establishment of national private TV channels, therefore legitimising the stations that had entered the market without a licence. Today, the basic operational framework of private television media is defined by the Law 2328/1995, in essence the first serious attempt to regulate the market effectively. Law 2644/1998 makes provision for the supply of broadcasting subscription services and regulates all new pay-TV services regardless of their process (digital or analogue) and means of broadcast (terrestrial, cable or satellite).

The Greek media are subject to strict ownership rules. Law 2328 from 1995 stipulates that a physical or legal person can hold only one broadcast licence and only up to 25 per cent of the capital of the company, while ownership of more than one electronic mediums of the same type is prohibited. The same rules apply to relatives of physical persons of up to the fourth degree. Concerning cross-media ownership, a 'two out of three' rule exists, meaning that a single company or individual cannot participate in more than two traditional media categories (TV, radio or newspapers). The participation of non-Europeans in the shareholding of media companies is also limited to 25 per cent of the capital (Terzis and Kontochristou, 2004). However, this strict regulatory framework has not prevented high levels of concentration of media ownership, as evidenced by the control of electronic media (particularly MEGA) by powerful publishing interests.

Public television

ERT A.E., with 2,500 full-time and another 2,500 part-time employees, is the Greek unified body of broadcasting and its activities include the four television channels ET-1 (mainstream), NET (mainly news), ET-3 (covering events from northern Greece) and ERT world (aiming at the Greek community abroad). As mentioned above, the public broadcaster was forced to pass, completely unprepared, through an anarchic process of liberalisation of the television market. The de-facto TV market deregulation did not allow sufficient time for ERT to prepare in terms of organisation, funding or programming and scheduling. Its traditional bureaucratic operation, overlap of responsibilities at managerial level among departments, as well as frequent changes in administration, made virtually impossible any efficient exploitation of its resources. In addition, the absence of a developmental planning to enable the company to respond to the social, economic and technological shifts that occurred during the critical phase of the abolition of the state monopoly pushed ERT to the sidelines and alienated it from the public.

Audience shares

Consequences of this were an unprecedented reduction in ERT's appeal and a sharp fall in audience ratings – from 50 per cent in 1989, the time before liberalisation, to 18.9 per cent in 1992 and just 9 per cent in 1995 for the three services ET-1, NET and ET-3 combined – ERT's lowest ever accumulated share on record. Meanwhile, audience shares for the two largest commercial stations, MEGA and ANT1 reached in total the very high level of 64.3 per cent in 1992, although this has been falling from 1994 onwards, mainly because of the arrival of more commercial stations, such as Alpha TV, Star Channel and Alter TV. In this highly competitive market the PTV broadcaster has improved its position in relation to audience ratings. Table 9.1 gives us a snapshot of the trends in audience shares in the period 1992–2005, indicating that ERT went up by about seven percentage points in 2005 compared to its performance in 1995, thanks to an ambitious restructuring plan which changed the programming profile of the two main services (ET-1 became a general interest and NET a purely news channel) so there is no longer any overlap between them.

ERT's income

ERT is primarily funded by the licence fee, paid by all Greek households via their electricity bill. Revenues from the licence fee have only slightly increased since 1997 – amounting 176.4 million Euros in 1997, 188.7 million Euros in 2001 and 215 million Euros in 2005 (see Table 9.2).

Table 9.1 Annual % audience shares of the Greek TV channels (1992–2005)

Year	ET-1	NET	ET-3	ANT1	MEGA	Alpha	Star	Alter
1992	10.5	5.9	2.5	30.7	33.6	–	–	–
1995	4.7	3.3	1.0	25.5	25.6	10.8	11.7	–
1998	6.1	4.0	1.2	24.1	21.2	15.8	14.3	–
2001	5.9	4.1	1.5	22.9	21.3	14.6	12.7	3.2
2005	4.2	8.7	2.0	20.6	18.4	13.1	11.6	10.8

Source: AGB Nielsen Media Research.
Notes: NET was previously named ET-2 and Alpha was previously named Sky.

Table 9.2 ERT's income (in million Euros, 1997–2005)

Type of income	1997	2001	2005
Licence fee	176.4	188.7	215.0
Commercial revenues	8.5	18.5	23.0
Government grants	1.9	2.6	2.6

Source: KPMG (2003) personal interviews.

Table 9.3 Advertising expenditure of TV channels in Greece (million Euros, 2000, 2003)

Channels	2000	2003
ET-1	25.2 (3.8%)	16.9 (2.3%)
NET	5.8 (0.9%)	15.4 (2.1%)
ET-3	4.3 (0.7%)	1.3 (0.2%)
ANT1	180 (27.0%)	222 (30.7%)
MEGA	203 (30.6%)	193 (26.8%)
Alpha	101 (15.2%)	106 (14.6%)
Star	131 (19.7%)	101 (14.0%)
Alter	9.0 (1.4%)	61.4 (8.5%)

Source: Media Services S.A. (2004).

However, ERT's licence fee income in 2006 is expected to reach 281 million Euros, following a government decision to increase the TV licence at 31 per cent (the first significant increase for a number of years – the last TV licence increase at 33 per cent was allocated in April 1997). Commercial income, mainly from advertising and sales, totalled 8.5 million Euros in 1997, 18.5 million Euros in 2001 and 23 million Euros in 2005. Government grants, the third source of income, totalled 1.9 million Euros in 1997, 2.6 million Euros in 2001 and remained unchanged in 2005.

It can be seen that advertising accounts for only 10 per cent of the company's total income as ERT never recovered from the loss of about 80 per cent of its advertising revenue in the decade 1989–99. It is striking that in 2003 advertising expenditure for ET-1, NET and ET-3 combined amounted to 33.6 million Euros, while the expenditure for the dominant players ANT1 and MEGA was 222 and 193 million Euros respectively (see Table 9.3). Meanwhile, in 2005 ERT had an accumulate deficit of about 130 million Euros (mainly as a result of the early retirement programme described below), which is expected to decline due to the generous licence fee increase.

Restructuring efforts

In the past three decades certain studies have been carried out and proposals have been put forward referring mainly to the organisational and administrative modernisation of ERT. Sir Hugh Green's proposals in

1975, the study by the BBC experts Alan Hart, Michael Johnson and Peter Marshount in 1990, the findings of Ernst and Young consultants in 1992, as well as the proposals of the Panhellenic Confederation of Trades Unions of ERT (POSP/ERT) in 1997, all highlighted ERT's operational, organisational and financial difficulties. The conclusions of these studies boiled down to the following:

- ERT was characterised by centralised decision-making and lack of clarity in objectives and allocation of responsibilities.
- The main services ERT-1 and ERT-2 (now ET-1 and NET) operated autonomously and were never integrated into a unified, coordinated ERT A.E. There was also overlap in programming between ERT's services.
- Political interference and frequent changes of personnel in strategic managerial positions hindered the smooth operation of the company.
- The general directorate of administration and management was disproportionately large compared to the other directorates.
- There was no administrative mechanism to evaluate the performance of organisational units and to create incentives to improve it (for example, through cost reduction).
- ERT did not have the necessary marketing and sales infrastructure.
- The work of the Director General was significantly overloaded, as 16 organisational units were reporting directly to him.

The studies' recommendations for the organisational improvement of ERT (particularly that of Ernst and Young, 1992) can be summarised as follows:

- ERT should set up a unified general directorate of news and current affairs and a unified general directorate of programme production.
- The general directorate of administration and management should be split into three general directorates: technical, financial and administrative services.
- ERT should establish an internal body to assess performance in programme production.
- The public broadcaster should re-position and change the profile of the three public television networks: shaping ET-1 into a general interest channel, NET into mainly news network and transforming ET-3 into a regional channel.

- ERT should pay more emphasis in producing programming for the youth market and women, as well as output aiming at households in semi-urban regions and the countryside.
- Steps should be taken towards the reinforcement of ERT's programme quality and objectivity, the cornerstones of its distinct, non-competitive nature *vis-à-vis* private television.

Without doubt, public television, as seen from the conclusions of the studies above, has significantly improved in recent years and in general terms has become more accountable, with a change of character, change of mentality in the way it is run, and some independence from asphyxiating state control. Contributing decisively to this was the formation of a strategic management plan for the five-year period 1998–2003 (the first in the company's history) carried out by consultants KPMG, aiming at the organisational, managerial and financial renovation of ERT. In KPMG's 2003 assessment of the plan, it is stated that the company met most of the economic objectives (reduce debt through a share capital increase from the state) without extra funding (the level of the annual licence fee between 1997–2002 remained unchanged at 36 Euros per household). In more particular, the following were completed and achieved:

- Paying off the company's accumulated debt and the drawing up of its first profitable balance sheet.
- Development of a new service organisation for the company, with a significant reduction in the number of departments.
- Completion of a study for the development of ERT's property portfolio, as well as the organisation of its archives.
- Passing a law for the early retirement of 1,100 permanent employees of ERT.

In addition to sorting out its balance sheets, ERT improved its programming offerings especially in the areas of news and current affairs, as evidenced by the creation of the news and current affairs service NET (which replaced ERT-2). This enabled the company to gain back a significant number of viewers, as demonstrated in Table 9.1.

The implementation of the early retirement programme

One of the major, chronic problems of ERT has been the large number of its permanent staff. In 1996 the permanent workforce numbered

3,500 people, a rather large figure in relation to a small country like Greece of 10.6 million inhabitants. This large number of employees left scant margin for improvement in ERT's finances and therefore produced a serious competitive disadvantage. It is striking that in the period 1996–97, around 75 per cent of ERT's revenues had to be used to cover operational expenses and workforce costs, while the remaining 25 per cent was available for investments in new technologies and programme production. At the end of the 1990s the state took measures to face up to this bureaucratic situation. More specifically, Law 2747 of 1999 made provision for the implementation of a programme of early retirement of the ERT's personnel (voluntary and compulsory). The early retirement programme started in December 1999 and with the consent of trade unions in the four-year period 1999–2002 a total of 826 employees left the company. Up until June 2000 the monthly benefit accruing from this staff reduction, in relative prices, came to 1.7 million Euros, while the annual benefits totaled 24 million Euros. However, in 2003 ERT had an obligation to pay 96 million Euros in the form of pensions to the retired employees (KPMG, 2003).

The implementation of the early retirement programme has both brought financial benefits to the company and contributed to a reversal in the ratio of operational cost versus investment in programming, which in all previous years was dominated by operational cost. An increase in investment spend is essential in the new era, as ERT has already started to modernise and digitalise its network. This increase in spend on entertainment, news, education and training programmes has increased ratings and added prestige to the company. But the early retirement programme has also offered an opportunity to restructure the workforce and to place employees in positions depending on their qualifications and experience. According to a former ERT Director General, its personnel was badly distributed across organisational posts, with the result that in some places there was over-supply and in others a serious lack (Panagiotou, 2000).

Next phase of ERT's modernisation

It is clear that important steps have been taken in this thorough-going renovation of ERT, without of course meaning that its organisational and operational problems have been overcome completely, for the public broadcaster has to go through the next phase of modernisation. In fact, KPMG was contracted by ERT to carry out a new five-year strategic management plan to cover the period 2003–2008 which includes the following objectives:

- Upgrading ERT's infrastructure to meet the requirements of the digital era.
- Improving financial performance through further structural change and rationalisation. This will enable the company both to invest in digital technologies and repay the 96 million Euro debt to retired staff.
- Reinvestment of revenues into programme production in order to increase public acceptance and achieve a total share of 20 per cent by 2008.
- Introducing a mechanism to measure performance in terms of programmes provided to make it more accountable to the public (KPMG, 2003).

According to the consultants, the above actions will generate in the five-year period 2003–2008 a sum of 235 million Euros, which both can be used to cover pensions to the staff due to early retirement and allow ERT to prepare for the digital age. Precondition for this was the increase in the annual licence fee (which the government accepted) and RPI + 1 per cent increase in the licence fee per annum (which was not agreed). A second precondition was the reformation of the regulatory regime, particularly with regards to defining with more clarity ERT's public service obligations. At the time of writing no action has been taken in this area.

Programming strategy

The introduction of competition between the public and private TV channels led ERT to compromise on quality by increasing programme homogeneity and limiting viewer choice. This is the outcome of an empirical study conducted by Tsourvakas (2004), which analysed ERT's programming strategy before and after TV market liberalisation. The findings suggest that the PTV broadcaster changed its strategy to offer types of programmes similar to that of private counterparts, shifting the focus of its programming strategy from an informational direction to a more commercial orientation. While during 1987–89 (just before competition) ERT pursued an informational profile, immediately after the entry of private channels (1989–92) it paid more attention to entertainment programmes, such as foreign and Greek police series, foreign and Greek sitcoms, Greek movies and game shows – basically similar programme types of those offered by private rivals.

Yet as noted above in more recent years ERT embarked upon an ambitious restructuring plan to change the profiles of the three services. Under that plan initiated in the late 1990s, ET-1 became the mainstream channel appealing to a broad audience, NET operated solely as a news channel and ET-3 became a regional service covering events from Northern Greece. These changes are reflected in Table 9.4 which shows that since the period 1998–99 news and current affairs have dominated NET's output. In contrast, ET-1's programming contains diverse genres to appeal to a broad audience.

Table 9.5 reveals that the era of programming convergence between public and private channels has come to an end, for public channels

Table 9.4 ERT's programming mix by genre (1998–99 and 2004–2005)

Genres	ET1 (1998–99) (%)	ET1 (2004–2005) (%)	NET (1998–99) (%)	NET (2004–2005) (%)
Series	10.8	3.0	1.7	9.6
Films	20.0	7.3	8.0	11.4
Light entertainment	1.3	0.3	0.3	0.4
Arts/Culture	5.7	12.1	11.3	3.8
News/Information	35.5	50.9	76.7	66.7
Children's	11.8	13.2	0.3	1.3
Sports	10.9	7.7	2.7	5.6
Other	3.9	5.5	0.7	1.2

Source: AGB Nielsen Media Research (2005).

Table 9.5 Programming mix by genre – ERT, MEGA, ANT1 (2004–2005)

Genres	ET1 (%)	NET (%)	ET3 (%)	MEGA (%)	ANT1 (%)
Series	3.0	9.6	1.0	28.1	26.2
Films	7.3	11.4	6.3	19.5	14.1
Light Entertainment	0.3	0.4	0.4	6.5	6.7
Arts/culture	12.1	3.8	9.8	1.1	0.7
News/information	50.9	66.7	65.3	39.3	45.6
Children's	13.2	1.3	3.6	1.1	2.1
Sports	7.7	5.6	9.7	1.8	2.2
Other	5.5	1.2	3.9	2.7	2.4

Source: AGB Nielsen Media Research (2005).

Table 9.6 Top 10 TV programmes in Greece (2005)

Programme title	Channel	% share
Eurovision	NET	82.3
Soccer (Greece v Albania)	MEGA	64.8
Soccer (Greece v Ukraine)	MEGA	62.3
To Kafe tis Haras	ANT1	57.5
Soccer (Greece v Brasil)	NET	57.1
Fame Story	ANT1	55.6
Mi Mou Les Antio	ANT1	53.6
Vera sto Dexi	MEGA	49.4
Lampsi	ANT1	43.2
Koinonia Ora 8	MEGA	32.5

differ tangibly from their private counterparts in terms of types of programmes broadcast. In particular in 2004–2005 the three public channels covered a far greater amount of news/information, children's programming and arts/culture than commercial channels. The latter paid more emphasis on news/information, but also on series, films and light entertainment.

In terms of popular programmes, the sitcom To kafe tis Haras (Cafeteria), the drama series Mi Mou Les Antio (Don't Say Goodby), long-standing soap opera Lampsi (Light) and the reality game Fame Story 3, all showed on leading commercial channel ANT1, achieved high viewing figures. MEGA, which in 2005 remained in the second place but with a significant increase in share, improved its ratings with the new morning magazine Koinonia Ora 8 (Society at 8am) and soap opera Vera sto Dexi (Wedding Ring). The popularity of these programmes shows that Greek viewers prefer domestic productions to imported programmes, especially at peak-times, something that verifies a Europe-wide trend. The public channels attempted to remain competitive in the post-Olympics season by showing more sports, especially football, which had become ever more popular after the Greek national team won the Euro 2004. However, the programme with the highest ratings was the final of the European Song Contest, which was won by the Greek participation (see Table 9.6).

Criticism

ERT may have improved its ratings, but this has come at a cost. The acquisition of the rights to show live football matches of the home games of the two top Greek football teams Olympiakos and Panathinaikos, together with the rights to broadcast Champions League matches, has sparked a row. In more particular, ERT's two-year deal with the two Greek clubs cost 27.3 million Euros (the previous two-year deal with private channel Alpha TV had cost just 11 million) and the Champions League two-year deal fixed at 30 million Euros. Meanwhile ERT has acquired the rights to show the successful TV series Loufa kai Parallagi (a military-based series based on successful movie), with each episode costing about 120,000 Euros. It has also bought the game-show Tois Metritois (Cash) for 3 million Euros and pays 14,600 Euros per show for the mid-day reality show I Zoi Einai Paixnidi (Life is a Game). On top of that, ERT has signed a three-year 27 million Euro deal with Disney for the rights to broadcast a series of cartoons (Nasopoulos, 2006). Critics argue that the PTV broadcaster should take steps to reduce its 130 million Euro deficit, rather than spending large amounts of money to broadcast live football and populist shows.

Digital initiatives

ERT, together with OTE, the Greek telecommunications incumbent, and the commercial channel Alpha TV had agreed to set up a digital satellite platform. According to the then head of technical services, Tsakiris (2000), in 2000 ERT was feverishly preparing for its participation in the digital platform, but on the way the partners abandoned the plan. In retrospect it seems that the market was not mature enough for the introduction of digital services and the political will for ERT's participation in the scheme was not strong. The public broadcaster finally launched digital terrestrial television services in 2006, encouraged by the European Commission plans which wants all member states to embark upon DTT in order to release spectrum and motivated by the introduction of DTT platforms across Europe. In more particular, in March 2006 ERT began broadcasts of ERT Psifiaki (ERT Digital), a bouquet of three thematic TV services broadcasting digitally, initially in the capital Athens, the second largest city Thessalonika and central Greece. The services include CINE+ (movies), SPOR+ (sport channel) and PRISMA+ (focusing on people with special needs). These channels are free-to-air and their reception only requires the purchase of a set-top box, costing about 130 Euros. ERT's involvement in digital terrestrial television is expected to accelerate consumer take-up of digital services (especially if the public broadcaster takes advantage of its rich audiovisual archives to offer a complete range of programmes), thus making more achievable the government's target of switching off the analogue frequency by 2012.

Prospects for ERT

In March 2005 the current Director General of ERT, Panagopoulos, outlined in a Parliamentary session the five areas in which the PTV broadcaster needs to prioritise: improvement of the programming in the core channels, especially in the news and current affairs and cultural output; improvement of the programming in the satellite service world (formerly ERT SAT) SAT; investment in new technologies and preparation of the company for the digital age; improvement of the web site and online services; and commercial exploitation of the company's productions (Kathimerini, 2005). It can be seen that most of these priorities had already been put forward by KPMG, indicating that ERT is determined to follow the consultant's recommendations for internal restructuring and programming reformation. This does not mean that there are no setbacks. For example, 1,800 people have been recruited since 2001, when the early retirement scheme completed, revealing that bad practices continued to exist and that overstaffing problems may return.

One area in which ERT has improved substantially since the early days of the TV market liberalisation is that of programming supply. While under the highly restricted state monopoly system the PTV broadcaster's output was influenced by the political elites and in the early days of market liberalisation ERT emulated the programming of commercial channels in order to secure advertising revenue, in more recent years ERT's content tends to be more openly diverse than that of its private rivals. The public broadcaster's news bulletins are the most trusted and more and more Greeks turn to ERT for accurate and reliable news. This is a substantial improvement considering that the news output of the monopoly public channel was subject to strong control by the political executive. One of the reasons for this change is that the PTV broadcaster is less dependent on commercial revenues and therefore increasingly free from the so-called 'tyranny of the ratings'. Another is a change in management practices which were influenced by KPMG's report and enabled ERT to gain professional competence. In the highly competitive nature of the contemporary

Greek TV market, where television is the single most important medium of political information, ERT provides a degree of pluralism and equity in the amount of political coverage.

But while ERT is no longer equated with 'government television', it would be misleading to contend that public TV shows no evidence of overt and intended partisan bias, for there has been little change in the form of the relationship between governing elites and public TV. Political output on Greek public television largely reflects a loose ideological consensus on the part of mainstream political elites. This has led left-wing political parties, particularly the Communist party KKE, to the assertion that TV fails to give appropriate weight to alternative and oppositional perspectives. Also and in spite of the establishment of a regulatory authority in 1990, the responsibility for appointing the Director General of the public network still rests with the government, signalling that the practice of political intervention is still apparent. Successive DGs, including the current one who was appointed by the rulling party New Democracy, have been regarded with suspicion by opposition political parties and are not accepted across the political class.

Despite an improvement in the overall programming supply in terms of range and diversity, the public broadcaster does not seem to have clear programming objectives, for it decided to compete for product and programme rights in areas such as feature films and sport, particularly football. There are two problems with this policy. First, the large sums of money spent to acquire the rights of these programme genres is likely to prevent ERT from producing or acquiring content of a clear public service nature (educational and cultural programmes, or programmes aiming at minorities). The precise definition of public service television in Greece is currently a challenge and a there is a need for understanding of the role of ERT in the digital age. Second, the competition for film and sports rights between ERT and commercial channels, free-to-air (MEGA and Alpha TV) or encrypted (Nova), has resulted in an unprecedented increase in the cost of acquiring these rights. ERT's spending in these areas is driven by ratings considerations, but this tactic may lead to more debt and a deeper financial crisis. It is true that consistently low ratings make the public broadcaster vulnerable to criticism from viewers, sections of the media and politicians. However, the PTV broadcaster must not increase its share at any cost, and in any case the current audience share of around 15 per cent provides ERT with the opportunity to play an important role in forming models of quality in entertainment, news and education.

10
Discussion and Conclusion

It has been the intension of this volume to analyse some of the trends in the European television industry as they are highlighted in in-depth, semi-structured interviews with key management personnel from public broadcast organisations and regulatory agencies, broadcasters' annual reports, EC official documents, conferences, press releases and other published documents, and look at the impact they have had on public television broadcasters. To this end, there has been a detailed review of the technological, economic, political, ideological and regulatory changes which have shaped television markets in Europe and an investigation into the pressures these changes have placed on PTV broadcasters across Europe with regard to their financing, organisational structures, technological initiatives and programming choices. This work argued that the public television sector can provide a forum for democratic debate and cultural exchange against a background of a deregulated global media system, inevitably influenced by market forces and dominated by large multinational enterprises. The TV market is now opened, but major media formations of economic and political influence cannot ensure access to all voices. Public channels, independent from both capital and political interests, can function as instruments for articulating objective societal values.

What should the mission of PTV broadcasters be? Should they aim for comprehensiveness or rather complement the market? What type of content should they adapt? What resources should they use to fulfill their mandate? These are important, albeit difficult questions to answer, particularly in a context where public channels are in direct competition with private rivals for commercial revenues and therefore strive to combine public service with popularity. Perhaps the starting point would be to ask what kind of society we want to live in. It is this author's view that the values that should be protected in a society with a human face are pluralism, independence, accessibility, content quality, social cohesion and protection of privacy. PTV broadcasters' mission should not merely be to inform, educate and entertain but also to empower the citizens by aiming for distinctiveness in the range and quality of offerings. Not only that. PTV institutions should invest in many categories of content. As Jakubowicz (2006) argued, there is a big difference between simple variety and genuine choice and public channels should cover many genres that are underrepresented, such as current affairs, the arts and religion. Most importantly, public channels must treat their viewers as citizens, not just as audiences. This is so because the audiences for PTV broadcasting are a public, not a market (Raboy, 1996).

But what funding model should they adopt to achieve this? The studies examined in this volume show that the licence fee remains the most reliable and stable source of funding that is relatively free from political constraints. Although the rationale of maintaining public funding has weakened in the present era, this funding method frees public broadcasters from market pressures and guarantees innovation, distinctiveness and quality in programming as evidenced by the British and Swedish cases, thus helping public institutions to fulfill their mandate. PTV broadcasters who are highly dependent on commercial revenues behave similar to their commercial competitors and focus on majority preference low cost programming choices, as evidenced by the Spanish TV broadcaster. No one likes to pay taxes, but the licence fee is accepted as the least worst option to maintain the independence of the public channel and novelty in content; it is, in other words, an 'imperfect beauty'.

However, it is clear that public television is under attack – its monopoly status is long gone, its legitimacy is eroded and its public mandate is questioned. Public channels formerly enjoyed protected environments but are now faced with unprecedented levels of competition from new channels. The resulting shift of viewing towards the small and niche has put great strain on established broadcasters, including PTV broadcasters. There is a double challenge: first, PTV broadcasters are operating in a new multi-cultural and more individualistic society in which they have to adopt; second, new technologies have brought about major changes in the programming, scheduling and company organisation. With regards to social changes, the television audience is now fragmented and shared with other media outlets. An advanced consumer culture fosters 'nichification', or even 'neo-tribalism', as some observers put it, as the pluralisation of tastes, interests and lifestyles in modern society accelerates. Referring to Sweden, Peter Dahlgren (1998) argued that many Swedes find themselves in various degrees of what he called 'domestic cultural shock', meaning that people have difficulty orienting themselves in this period of rapid social transition, where the older coordinates are less helpful. The result is the erosion of the unified and homogeneous national society in which public service was originally embedded. PTV broadcasters must look ahead to a society that is in dynamic flux and where economic, political, ethnic and cultural factors will continue to accentuate fragmentation and differentiation (ibid.).

With regards to programming, multi-channel growth and declining share has left some public channels, particularly those of southern European countries, with no choice but to replicate services of commercial competitors. Adapting to declining audiences by scheduling similar programmes to their commercial rivals would result not only in less viewer choice but would also constitute a distortion of the market in so far as the public channels use public money to fund programmes that the market provides in abundance. The strategy of the so-called 'programming convergence', adapted by the Greek and Spanish PTV broadcasters in the early days of TV market liberalisation led to marginalisation and alienated them from their viewers. PTV broadcasters should address the full range of audience interests and remain a major engine of offering original, home grown high quality output, rather than recycled or bought-in mainstream programmes. The case studies revealed that public service content in the digital age is not abundant as some technology gurus predicted, but scarce. Public channels should therefore be more relevant, more rooted to people's lives and serve as a model for all broadcasters, by catering for innovation in programming, providing diverse, independent news, and offering thematic channels of plural content in an accessible and affordable manner. As Jakubowicz (2006) argued, public service broadcasting is regaining monopoly on public service content and may remain the only free-to-air pluralist channel to do so.

Meanwhile, PTV broadcasters should separate services with clear public service content – which can be publicly funded – from services of a commercial nature – which should be funded by commercial means (an important example of separation of public from commercial activities is found in the BBC's Charter). Where this separation is not clear public channels are subject to criticism. In fact, in 2004 a powerful pro-market lobby within the European Publishers Council published a report on the financing and regulation of publicly funded broadcasters which called the member states to correct the fundamental distortions caused by dual funding of broadcasters so that a competitive, liberalised market can evolve. The EPC urged the European Commission to ensure that the principle of economic efficiency is fully applied to public broadcasters' expenditure (EPC, 2004). There are clearly two approaches on public broadcasting: for some it is a problem, but for others public broadcasting is a solution to solve a problem. While it is undeniable that financial transparency and EC competition provisions should apply to all broadcasters, one should also recognise the specific programming obligations that are imposed on publicly funded channels. In Britain, in exchange for the recent ten-year extension of the licence fee, the BBC was told it had to preserve the quality and distinctiveness of its output and avoid chasing ratings through copycat programming. At an EU level it is accepted that programming that serves the public interest could be funded by the licence fee. The Protocol on public broadcasting attached to the 1997 Amsterdam Treaty recognises that the mission entrusted to public broadcasters is culturally important and entitles them to appropriate funding.

PTV broadcasters should also ensure that this wide, diverse range of output is provided free at the point of reception to all households. New technology can ensure that public service content is available on all platforms. Citizens expect to access it free of charge, as the France Télévisions case revealed, when in the late 1990s the public broadcaster was available in one only pay-TV platform. Free-to-air digital terrestrial television and the leading role that public channels are taking in its development may be the answer to universally available content as the public institutions seek to adjust to the digital era (Iosifidis, 2006b). Most PTV broadcasters have taken advantage of the launch of DTT to expand their supply of programming, with the BBC in the forefront. For the BBC, in addition to the corporation's historic mission statement to 'inform, educate and entertain', six new purposes were added including building a 'digital Britain'. In Spain, France and Sweden the respective PTV broadcasters have been tasked to accelerate

DTT take-up. Public channels in France and Spain do not enjoy the same status or legitimacy in their respective media landscape that the BBC has in Britain, and this impacts on their expansion to new services. Of course universal content and universal accessibility is no longer attainable in the digital age, for there are different levels of accessibility: universal channels; thematic channels; and personalised channels. As the Digital Strategy Group of the European Broadcasting Union put it, 'universality of access can no longer be understood as a couple of terrestrial channels available to the entire population, but as presence on relevant media and platforms with significant penetration, but also the ability to deliver a "personalised public service" in the "pull", online and on-demand environment' (DSG, 2002). In other words, public channels should aim for 'must offer' but certainly not for 'must use', for not everyone will use their services.

PTV broadcasters must be independent from the state. Typically in southern European territories there has been varying degrees of interdependence between public TV and political actors. Referring to France Télévisions, Kuhn (2006) argued that in part this is because the experience of the government model in the first age of French TV prevented public broadcasting as a whole from developing a tradition of independence which would allow the organisation to foster a positive relationship with civil society and embed itself in popular consciousness as a national icon. The scholar went on to say that in more recent years the state monopoly ownership has given way to a framework of regulated competition in which the state is still a key actor, while government control of television news has been replaced by a pluralism of official sources where the views of the executive and mainstream political parties tend to predominate. Yet Papatheodorou and Machin (2003) inform us that in Spain and Greece state media policy is determined as ever by the persistent culture of political expediency, as political elites still seek to influence the content of political coverage. Despite the seeming plurality of voices brought about by media multiplication, state paternalism continues to play a pivotal role in the structuring of Greek and Spanish markets. Needless to say, such a close connection between broadcasting and party politics has given rise to an ethos of subjectivity and imbalanced journalistic practices within TVE and ERT, the respective PTV broadcasters, who need to take further steps towards political independence.

PTV broadcasters' Charter, internal reorganisation as well as the establishment of an effective and efficient regulatory framework would ensure that public channels remain independent and are held accountable for the services they provide. For example, the primary task of the BBC Trust, the new supreme body to govern the BBC, is to ensure that the corporation fulfils its public purposes and demonstrates it through published plans on how it intends to meet them and regular reporting on their delivery. The BBC Trust offers an opportunity to increase the BBC's accountability to licence fee payers, and improve processes and structures that deliver openness and transparency. More specifically, the BBC will have to pass a 'public value test', carried out by the Trust, for all new services it seeks to launch, or if it wants to make major changes to existing services. The independent media watchdog Ofcom will carry out a 'market impact assessment' of what future BBC plans could mean to rival companies. This structural change follows complains from companies such as ITN (Independent Television News) that the BBC effectively stifled the market in emerging areas like online news services by giving content away on its news site.

Enhanced accountability is only one area in which PTV broadcasters need to improve to ensure the genuine support of the public for their continued existence, which in turn may prompt a more favourable public policy towards public channels. Other areas include internal restructuring to make public institutions more cost efficient and effective but without sacrificing their public service values. RTÉ's case is striking. RTÉ's reorganisation into business divisions (the IBD system) introduced a business-like approach to the organisation's activities, encouraging management and staff to 'align' costs and revenue, but the interviews undertaken with senior management staff reveals a clear sense of a public service ethos. The restructuring may have created a climate in which commercial objectives are occasionally prioritised in order to help the broadcaster to survive in the current environment – according to Murray (2006), for example, RTÉ is scheduling strategically to ensure maximum return on its investment – but the definition of public service in terms of particular functions and programme types is equally strong. This is reflected in RTÉ's commitment to offering a full range of content, prioritising in home-grown programmes.

In short, over the past thirty years public television in Europe has in general terms stabilised its position in a rapidly changing media environment and even engaged in an expansion of its TV supply. It has weathered the storm which followed the introduction of private channels and has learnt to compete with the private sector. The intense competition has inevitably resulted in a reduction of audience and (where applicable) advertising shares and this led some PTV broadcasters to emulate the management practices and resemble the output of commercial rivals. However, publicly-funded channels especially from northern European countries have retained a distinctive programming output and found a balance between seeking internal restructuring and keeping strong public service principles. All public broadcasters covered in this study have embarked upon digital technologies and launched new services to reflect the multi-cultural and multi-ethnic composition of contemporary European societies. One thing is certain: the technological, financial, organisational and programming challenges will intensify in the coming years. Yet the public service broadcasters' relationship with the audience remains strong and ensures their viability and relevance in the digital age.

Notes

1 Introduction, Aims and Methodology

1. The Media Plus programme was originally scheduled to run until 2005 with a budget of 400 million Euros. The proposal to extend it was approved by the Council of Ministers on 26 April 2003, in line with the modifications made by the European Parliament, to take account of the effects of enlargement from 2004.
2. This book largely uses the term 'public' rather then 'state' television because this term fits better its social remit and contribution to the 'public interest'. However, the research takes into account the differences between state broadcasters, closely connected to political regimes (characteristic of most broadcasters in the southern Europe) and more independent public broadcasters of the northern countries.
3. Many scholars argue that 'quality' is the defining feature of public broadcasting (McQuail, 1992; Iskikawa, 1996; Brands and de Bens, 2000). A widely accepted definition of quality programming is content that is distinctive, informative, socially relevant and accessible to all. It is of course difficult to measure in any quantitative and objective way how well the programmes screened by public channels meet the standards of quality. For this purpose the McKinsey & Company (1999) report measured the amount of time devoted to factual and cultural programmes, as well as to shows for children and called this kind of programming 'distinctive'. The British media regulatory agency Ofcom (2004) considered total spend by programme genre, spend per hour by genre and the level of first-run origination by genre as contributions to an evaluation of the quality of output, as they indicate the level of resources being spent on each genre. Whatever the definition of quality, most market reports and media scholars agree that quality does not automatically generate viewers.
4. The package includes the following elements: a directive on the common regulatory framework for electronic communications networks and services (framework directive); an authorisation directive; an access and interconnection directive; a directive on universal service and users' rights relating to electronic communications networks and services; and a decision on a regulatory framework for radio spectrum policy.
5. However, in July 2006 the Court of First instance (Europe's second highest court) overturned the Commission's decision to allow the two record labels to merge. It ruled that the EC's arguments supporting the Sony/BMG merger in 2004 were not of 'the requisite legal standard' and were marred by 'a manifest error of assessment' (see http://www.out-law.com/page-7111 accessed August 2006).

6. Although the notion of the 'public interest' in the media field is multi-dimensional, it is this author's view that television channels serve the public interest only when they: (a) provide programming diversity that can satisfy all viewers, including the minorities; (b) offer high-quality content; (c) ensure viewer access to programmes regardless of geographical locations; and (d) guarantee accuracy and impartiality, especially with regards to news and current affairs.
7. The three large countries of Britain, France and Spain, with about 160 million inhabitants, account for almost one third of the total population of the EU 25.
8. These countries were Poland, Czech Republic, Hungary, Slovak Republic, Lithuania, Latvia, Slovenia, Estonia, Cyprus and Malta. Romania and Bulgaria joined the EU in January 2007.

2 Factors Affecting the Development of Public Television

1. Initially, Freeview was jointly owned by the BBC, BSkyB and transmission company Crown Castle, but in October 2005 ITV and Channel Four each took a 20 per cent stake. The Freeview platform is strategically important to both companies since ITV1 and Channel Four perform relatively well in share terms in DTT homes, where viewers have fewer channels to choose from, compared to satellite and cable. The BBC, BSkyB and National Grid Wireless are the remaining shareholders (Ofcom, 2006).
2. Member States' switchover plans are available at: http://europa.eu.int/ information_society/topics/ecomm/highlights/current_spotlights/switcho ver/national_swo_plans/index_en.htm (accessed February 2006).
3. A company is said to be in a dominant position when it has control of the total process, from raw material to distribution to sales. This situation implies power to seize out potential competitors and distorts the economy with monopolistic control over prices.
4. For example, the public broadcasters of the Nordic countries have collaborated with private operators and reached an agreement on a common, open standard for set-top boxes in the region (the NORDIG cooperation).
5. There have been various terms to describe the emerging shape of the television landscape – de-regulation, re-regulation and light touch regulation. Perhaps 're-regulation' or 'light touch regulation' most appropriately describe today's broadcasting landscape, because what is being witnessed, as Murdock (2000, p. 41) has pointed out, is not a total dismantling of rules but a shift of emphasis towards relaxation.
6. One of the main proponents of the conservative camp was Veljanovski (1990), but even left-wing scholars, such as Garnham (1978) and Kean (1991) have taken a critical stance against the practices of some of the public broadcasters and suggested that public institutions should take steps to reform and get away from direct state control and coercion in order to fulfil their public service mission.

7. The media address their audiences as 'citizens' when they seek to involve them in social issues, while the basic meaning of 'consumer' is that of 'potential buyer of products and services'. The consumer-citizen dichotomy has been challenged by Syvertsen (2002, cited in Meijer, 2005) who proposed replacing it with a division of about ten audience groups. Meijer (2005) also questioned the relevance of this dualism and argued that the media could conceive the members of the audience as 'enjoyers' (what impact particular programmes have on them), rather than as members of pre-given groups.
8. However, the purchase led to a record $98.7 billion loss in 2002 and caused the shares to tumble as the promised profit and sales growth never emerged (see http://www.washingtonpost.com/wp-dyn/content/article/2005/05/20/AR2005052001512.html, accessed September 2006).
9. For example, in the 1980s the two US media content giants Disney and Viacom acquired the American television networks ABC and CBS respectively. At the same time the Japanese electronics company Sony entered the American film production and distribution market.
10. Until 1989 the EC had powers to act against anti-competitive mergers and acquisitions only after they have taken effect and a restrictive practice or dominant position is established or strengthened. For many years the EC had argued that it should have new, pre-emptive powers that would remove the uncertainty of retrospective action for the parties involved. In fact, competition rules that intervene after a problem of imbalance has arisen (for example, an anticompetitive practice has been established or a dominant position has already been created) may not be able to remedy the situation. The Merger Regulation was intended to deal with that problem.
11. Of course there are several limitations with regard to any consumption of moving images, which may lessen the value of such services. These limitations include the quality of images and sound, the high cost of usage linked to technology, and the limited battery/power capacity.
12. Commercial broadcasters in Spain (1992, 1993), France (1993), Portugal (1993, 1996, 1997), Italy (1996), Germany (1997, 2003), Britain (1997, 1999), Ireland (1999), Denmark (2000) and the Netherlands (2002) have filed complaints against a European PTV broadcaster. These complaints largely concern State Aid issues and some of them are still unresolved.
13. The Commission's approach in its Communication on the Application of State Aid rules to public service broadcasting (EC, 2001) is to require member states to define the remit of their public broadcasters, to entrust their remit to one or more broadcasting organisations, and to establish effective means of monitoring its fulfilment.
14. Apart from the Amsterdam Protocol, the Resolution of the Council of 25 January 1999 also stresses that public broadcasting must be able to continue to provide a wide range of programming in order to address society as a whole; in this context it is legitimate for the public sector to seek to reach wide audiences.

3 Competition and Dilemmas

1. These factors are listed as possible explanations of ERT's chronic problems in a number of reports conducted in the past 30 years: former BBC DG Sir Hugh Green's suggestions in 1975; the report of BBC experts Alan Hart, Michael Johnson and Peter Marshount in 1990/91; the conclusions of a 1992 Ernst & Young report; and the proposals of the Committee of ERT's employee's POSP in May 1997.
2. However, the EPC's study found that advertising revenues for the same period only increased by 2.9 per cent, compared with the 4.7 per cent rise of public revenue. When calculating public revenue for broadcasters the EPC includes state grants and subsidies, in addition to the licence fee.
3. This is why the European TV market is characterised by high levels of concentration as different operators join forces to stem huge advertising losses. Recent technological developments, such as *TiVo*, which allow the viewer to skip advertisements, have exaggerated the problem. Some television channels have searched for alternative funding sources by, for example, introducing subscription.
4. The only exception being Greece, in which the public broadcaster ERT has also been subject to political intervention.
5. These trends can be identified in other Mediterranean countries. In response to competition from commercial rival SIC in the early 1990s, Portuguese public channel RTP-1, which is more mainstream than the culturally oriented RTP 2, adapted a more populist tone and began screening more infotainment, game shows, and Brazilian telenovelas, especially in prime-time.
6. A thorough investigation of these activities in all six European countries under study is provided in the second part of the book.

4 Britain

1. In 2006–2007 this was increased to £131.50 (about 194 Euros) for colour TV and £44 (65 Euros) for a black and white TV. There are a number of concessions, namely free licences for people over 75 years of age and a 50 per cent Blind Concessionary Licence and the Accommodation for Residential Care.
2. The government has always recognised the central role which the BBC had to play in convincing people to switch to digital. The February 2000 funding settlement was intended to support the BBC in this role: allowing a balance to be struck between maintaining the quality of core services and investing adequately in new ones.
3. In Britain, the switchover from analogue to digital broadcasting should start in 2008 and end by 2012. The BBC will take the leading role in ensuring that the transition is smooth. This will involve executing a comprehensive communications strategy and providing financial assistance to those who have practical difficulties in making the switchover.

4. Since then the BBC has re-acquired the popular sport presentation.
5. ITV has been locked into a spiral of decline over the past three years and in November 2006 the cable group NTL, in which Sir Richard Branson is the largest shareholder, launched a takeover bid. That was rejected after BSkyB, controlled by Rupert Murdoch, stealthily built up an 18 per cent holding. This was widely interpreted as a blocking move to NTL and provoked Sir Richard into accusing his rival of damaging competition (Gibson and Allen, 2006).

5 France

1. As mentioned in Chapter 2, in October 2003 Vivendi agreed to merge Vivendi Universal Entertainment with the US television network NBC, a unit of General Electric, in a 43 billion Euro transaction to create a new entertainment industry giant with significant market power. The deal brought together assets including Vivendi's Universal Pictures with NBC's broadcast network and cable channels CNBC and Bravo. General Electric now owns 80 per cent of the merged company while Vivendi holds 20 per cent.
2. Article 53 of the Law on Freedom of Communication 1986, as amended by Article 15 of the Law of 1 August 2000. The 'Objectives and Means Contract' is available (in French) at: http://www.francetelevisions.fr/data/doc/synthese_com.pdf (accessed April 2006).
3. In contrast, the share of advertising enjoyed by the commercial channel TF-1 in 2005 neared 55 per cent and that of M6 exceeded 20 per cent.
4. However, the advertising market share of France 2 and France 3 combined in 2003 was 19.8 per cent, much lower than the share of TF-1 at 54.7 per cent and M6 at 22.4 per cent.
5. The current managing director of the public TV organisation is Patrick de Carolis, selected by the Higher Audiovisual Council.

6 Spain

1. Information extracted from communication with Leon (2006) as well as RTVE's web site at www.rtve.es/informe/10.html (accessed September 2006).
2. For further information see http://www2.noticiasdot.com/publicaciones/2005/1105/3011/noticias/noticias_301105-08.htm (accessed October 2006).
3. For further information see http://www.elmundo.es/elmundo/2006/03/10/comunicacion/1141950931.html (accessed October 2006).

7 The Republic of Ireland

1. Cultural nationalists, Irish-language groups and the Catholic Church were additional bodies which expressed concerns about the influence of private TV on such an isolated country.

2. Cable/MMDS household penetration is 40 per cent, satellite penetration is 22 per cent, while free-to-air only households account for 38 per cent (ComReg, 2005).
3. This arrangement may generate much of the concern about the detrimental effects of having the same group of people both running and holding the organisation into account. That was the case with the BBC Board of Governors who had a dual role as both strategic directors of the BBC (running the BBC) and regulators (holding it to account).
4. The TV licence fee is free for those over the age of 70. Responsible for the collection of the fee is the Post Office.
5. The Transformation plan relied on the recommendations of a report 'Review of RTÉ's Structures and Operations' by RTÉ management and trade union representatives. The main recommendations included structural change, implementation of new work practices and job cuts of about 350. However, not all of these recommendations were implemented.

8 Sweden

1. All channels that broadcast from Sweden are prohibited by law from any commercials that promote the use of tobacco and alcohol. Also they cannot broadcast commercials or sponsored programmes directly targeted at children.
2. It should be noted that SVT collaborates for sports and Hollywood content with commercial channel TV4 and a negotiation takes place among themselves as to what is shown by whom (Stromqvist, 2005).

9 Greece

1. In 2005 the Ministry ceased to exist and was replaced by a General Secretary of Information and Communications.

Bibliography

AGB Nielsen Media Research (2005) *Yearbook* (Athens).
A.T. Kearney *Plan Strategy* (2001) Report for France Télévisions, February.
Aufterheide, P. (1992) 'Cable Television and the Public Interest', *Journal of Communication*, 42 (1) 52–65.
Aufterheide, P. (1999) *Communications Policy and the Public Interest* (USA: Guilford Press).
Bagdikian, B. (1992) *The Media Monopoly*, 4th edn (Boston: Beacon Press,).
BARB (Broadcasters' Audience Research Board), 2001 Report.
BARB (Broadcasters' Audience Research Board), 2006 Report.
Barnett, S. (2006) 'Public Service Broadcasting: A Manifesto for Survival in the Multimedia Age' Paper submitted to RIPE@2006 Conference (Amsterdam and Hilversum: 16–18 November).
Barwise, P. (2006) 'The BBC Licence Fee Bid: What Does the Public Think?' An Independent Report for the BBC Board of Governors, (London: April). Available at: http://www.bbcgovernors.co.uk/docs/rev_licence_bid.html (accessed October 2006).
BBC (2004a) 'Building Public Value: Renewing the BBC for a Digital World' (London: June).
BBC (2004b) 'Review of the BBC's Royal Charter: The BBC's Response to the DCMS Consultation' (London: June) (this document and others relating to Charter Review can be found online at www.bbc.co.uk/thefuture).
BBC (2005a) 'Review of the BBC's Royal Charter: BBC Response to A Strong BBC, Independent of Government' (London: May).
BBC (2005b) 'The Tipping Point: How Much is Broadcast Creativity at Risk?' An independent report commissioned by the BBC, The Work Foundation (London: July).
BBC Annual Report 2005–06. Available at: http://www.bbcgovernors.co.uk/annreport/index.html (accessed November 2006).
BBC and Human Capital (2004) 'Measuring the Value of the BBC' (London: October 2004). The fieldwork was done by Gfk Martin Hamblin. Available at: http://www.bbc.co.uk/thefuture/pdfs/value_bbc.pdf (accessed October 2006).
Bjorkman, P. (2005) Head of Research, SVT, Interview (Stockholm: 4 May).
BMRB Omnibus Survey (2006) 'Measuring Reaction to Targeted Help (London: March 2006). Available at: http://www.bbcgovernors.co.uk/docs/reviews/bmrb_omnibus.pdf (accessed November).
Born, G. (2003) 'Uncertain Futures: Public Service Television and the Transition to Digital – a Comparative Analysis of the Digital Television Strategies of the BBC and Channel 4', Electronic Working Paper (London: Media@lse). Available at: http://www.lse.ac.uk/collections/media@lse/mediaWorkingPapers/ewpNumber3.htm (accessed February 2006).

Brands, K. and E. de Bens (2000) 'The Status of TV Broadcasting in Europe', *Television Across Europe: A Comparative Introduction*, eds J. Wieten, G. Murdock and P. Dahlgren (London: Sage), 7–23.
Broadcasting Act 1996. London: Her Majesty's Stationery Office. Available at: http://www.opsi.gov.uk/ACTS/acts1996/1996055.htm (accessed November 2006).
Broadcasting Act 2001, 'Number 4 of 2001'. Available at: http://www.bci.ie/documents/2001act.pdf (accessed November 2006).
Broadcasting (Funding) Act 2003, 'Number 43 of 2003'. Available at: http://www.bci.ie/documents/2003fundingact.pdf (accessed November 2006).
Carnegie Commission 1967, *Public Broadcasting's Original Mission*. Available at: http://www.cipbonline.org/carnegie.htm (accessed November 2006).
Chazal, P. (1996) 'Le Pole Public de Programmes Thematiques', (Thematic Channels of Public Television Stations), Study on behalf of France Televisions (Paris: May).
CMT (Comision del Mercado de las Telecomunicasiones) 'Annual Report – The Industry in 2004' (Madrid: 2004). Available at: www.cmt.es/cmt_eng/index.htm (accessed June 2006).
ComReg (Commission for Communications Regulation) Annual Report 2005. Available at: http://www.comreg.ie/publications/annual.asp?s=5&NavID=100#?s=5&navid=100 (accessed November 2005).
The Communications Act 2003 (c.21), 17 July 2003. Available at: http://www.opsi.gov.uk/acts/acts2003/20030021.htm (accessed July 2006).
Coppens, T. and F. Saeys (2006) 'Enforcing Performance: New Approaches to Govern Public Service Broadcasting', *Media, Culture & Society*, 28 (2) 261–84.
Corcoran, F. (2000) Director General – RTÉ, Telephone Interview (20 March).
Corcoran, F. (2002) 'Digital Television in Ireland: Local Forces in a Global Context', *Javnost/The Public*, 9 (4).
Corcoran, F. (2003) Director General – RTÉ, Telephone Interview (7 January).
Council of Europe (2004) 'Report on Public Service Broadcasting in Europe', Parliamentary Assembly, Recommendation 1641 (Strasburg: 2004). Available at: http://assembly.coe.int/Documents/AdoptedText/TA04/EREC 1641.htm (accessed December).
Council of the European Union (1997) 'Treaty of Amsterdam – Protocol on the System of Public Broadcasting in the Member States' (Brussels: August).
Council Regulation (EEC) No 4064/89 of 21 December 1989 on the control of concentrations between undertakings. Official Journal L 395 of 30 December 1989.
Council Regulation (EC) No 1310/97 of 30 June 1997 amending Regulation (EEC) No 4064/89 on the control of concentrations between undertakings.
Cowie, C. (1999) Policy and Planning – BBC, Interview (London: 13 December).
Cox, B. (2003) 'The Reformation of the BBC', *Guardian Unlimited* (February). Available at: http://media.guardian.co.uk/broadcast/comment/0,7493,888678,00.html (accessed October 2006).
CSA (Conseil Superieure d'Audiovisuel) (1998) 'La television publique en Europe', La Lettre, No. 111 (Paris: December).

Dahlgren, P. (1998) 'Public Service Media, Old and New: Vitalising a Civic Culture?' The 1998 Spry Memorial Lecture. Available at: http://www.com.umontreal.ca/spry/spry-pd-lec.html (accessed November).

Dahlgren, P. (2000) 'Key Trends in European Television', *Television Across Europe: A Comparative Introduction*, eds J. Wieten, G. Murdock and P. Dahlgren (London: Sage) 23–34.

Dataxis (2006) *EU Market for Digital Television*. Available at: http://europa.eu.int/information_society/policy/ecomm/doc/info_centre/studies_ext_consult/digital_tv_final_report_cec.pdf (accessed November 2006).

DCMNR (Department of Communications, Marine and Natural Resources) (2004) 'Public Service Broadcasting Charter', (Dublin: June 2004). Available at: http://www.dcmnr.gov.ie/Broadcasting (accessed November 2004).

DCMS (Department for Culture Media and Sport) (1999) 'The Future Funding of the BBC' – Report of the Independent Review Panel chaired by Gavyn Davis (London: July).

DCMS (Department for Culture Media and Sport) (2004) 'BBC Royal Charter Review: An Analysis of Responses to the DCMS Consultation (June 2004). Available at:http://www.bbccharterreview.org.uk/pdf_documents/ubiques_analysis_bbccr_responses.pdf (accessed November 2006).

DCMS (Department for Culture Media and Sport) (2005) 'Review of the BBC's Royal Charter: A Strong BBC, Independent of Government (London: March).

DCMS (Department for Culture Media and Sport) (2006) 'A Public Service for All: the BBC in the Digital Age', White Paper, Cm 6763, (London: March).

De Bens, E. and H. de Smaele (2001) 'The Inflow of American Television Fiction on European Broadcasting Channels Revisited', *European Journal of Communication* 16 (1) 51–76.

De Espana, R. (2001) *La Caja de las Corpresas. Una Historia Personal de la Television* (Barcelona).

De Pablos, E. (2006) 'US Deals Help RTVE Fill Channels' Programming Blocks' *Variety's Festivals and Markets*, (2 April). Available at: http://www.variety.com/index.asp?layout=features2006&content=jump&jump =story&dept=mip&nav=Fmip&articleid=VR1117940697 (accessed August 2006).

De Pablos, E. and J. Hopewell (2006) 'Local Giant Shapes Spanish Daily Life' *Variety Weekend*, (2 April). (Available at: http://www.variety.com/index.asp?layout = features2006&content=jump&jump=story&head=mip&nav=Fmip&articleid=VR1117940702 (accessed June 2006).

Deloitte & Touche (2005) 'Web TV: The Channel of the Future' (29 June 2005). Available at: http://www.deloitte.com/dtt/press_release/0,1014,cid=87176&pv=Y,00.html (accessed July).

DSG (Digital Strategy Group) (2002) 'Media with a Purpose: Public Service Broadcasting in the Digital Era', Digital Strategy Group of the European Broadcasting Union (Geneva: November). Available at: http://www.ebu.ch/CMSimages/en/DSG_final_report_E_tcm6-5090.pdf (accessed November 2006).

Duignan, C. (2005) Director of TV Programmes – RTÉ, Interview (Dublin: 13 April).

EAO (European Audiovisual Observatory) (2005) *Improvement of the Economic Situation of European Television Companies – But the Brunch as a Whole Remains in Deficit* Press Release (Strasburg: 12 September).

EC (European Commission) (2001) 'Communication on the Application of State Aid Rules to Public Service Broadcasting, JO C320 of 15 November (Brussels: Commission of the European Communities).

EC (European Commission) (2003) 'Communication on Digital Switchover – Transition From Analogue to Digital Broadcasting, From Digital Switchover to Analogue Switch-off', COM(2003) 541 final, 22 September (Brussels: Commission of the European Communities).

EC (European Commission) (2004) 'Harmonisation of transparency requirements in relation to information about issuers whose securities are admitted to trading on a regulated market and amending Directive 2001/34/EC', commonly known as the Transparency Directive 2004/109/EC (Brussels: Commission of the European Communities).

EC (European Commission) (2005) 'Communication on Accelerating the Transition from Analogue to Digital Broadcasting', COM(2005) 204 final, 24 May (Brussels: Commission of the European Communities).

The Economist (2006) 'Reshaping the BBC: Back on Top' (18 March) 28–31.

EEC 'Television without Frontiers' (1997) Directive (89/552/89), as amended by Directive 97/36/EC, OJ L 202, 30 July (Brussels: Commission of the European Communities).

EIAA (European Interactive Advertising Association) 'Media Consumption Study II – 'Pan European Results October 04', Conducted by Millward Brown. Available at http://www.t-online.de/uebertonline/marktforschung/eiaa-10-2004.pdf (accessed January 2006).

Enders Analysis (2005) 'Digital Terrestrial TV in France', Study conducted by Francois Godard (April).

EPC (European Publishers Council) (2004) *Safeguarding the Future of the European Audiovisual Market – A White paper on the Financing and Regulation of Publicly Funded broadcasters* (Brussels: EPC, March).

Ernst & Young, (1992) Ekthesi Anadiorganosis – ERT A.E. (Report on ERT A.E.'s Restructuring) (Athens).

EUMAP (EU Monitoring and Advocacy Program) (2005) *Television Across Europe: Regulation, Policy and Independence* (Brussels: OSI's EUMAP and Media Program, 11 October). Available at: http://www.eumap.org/topics/media/television_europe (accessed January 2006).

Feeney, P. (2005) Head of Public Affairs Policy – RTE, Interview (Dublin: 12 April).

Fontaine, G. (1999) IDATE – Communication via e-mail (8 October).

Galvin, P. (2005) Head of Public Affairs – RTE, Interview (Dublin: 12 April).

Garnham, N. (1978) *New Structures of Television* (London: British Film Institute).

Garnham, N. (1986) 'The Media and the Public Sphere', *Intermedia*, 14 (1) 28–33.

Garnham, N. and G. Locksley (1991) 'The Economics of Broadcasting', eds G. Blumler and Nositer, *Broadcasting Finance in Transition* (Oxford: Oxford University Press).

Gibson, O. and K. Allen (2006) 'Beleaguered Broadcaster Pulls off Secret Coup – Departure Weeks Before Licence Fee Ruling' *Media Guardian*, 24 November, p. 1.

Giudicelli, L. and E. Derieux (2001) 'France', *Television and Media Concentration – Regulatory Models on the National and the European Level*, ed. S. Nikoltchev (Strasbourg: European Audiovisual Observatory) 55–62.
Habermas, J. (1979) 'The Public Sphere', eds A. Mattelart and S. Siegelaub, *Communication and Class Struggle*, New York: International General.
Habermas, J. (1989) *The Structural Transformation of the Public Sphere*, (Cambridge: Polity Press).
Heilemann, J. (1994) 'Can the BBC Be Saved?' (March). Available at: http://www.wired.com/wired/archive/2.03/bbc.html (accessed October 2006).
Hesmondhalgh, D. (2002) *The Cultural Industries* (London: Sage).
Hoynes, W. (1994) *Public Television for Sale. Media, the Market, and the Public Sphere* (Boulder: Westview).
Humphreys, P. (1996) *Mass Media and Media Policy in Western Europe* (Manchester: Manchester University Press).
Hunt, J. (2005) Head of Operations – RTE Television, Interview (Dublin: 13 April).
IDATE (2004) *Overview of the TV Markets in the 10 New EU Member States* (Montpellier: November). Available at:http://www.idate.fr/jii04/bio04/actes/IDATE_Gilles_Fontaine_EU.ppt#1 (accessed July 2006).
Internet World Stats (2006) *Internet Usage in Europe*. Available at: http://www.internetworldstats.com/stats4.htm (accessed July 2006).
Iosifidis, P. (1999) 'Diversity Versus Concentration in the Deregulated Mass Media Domain', *Journalism & Mass Communication Quarterly* 76 (1) 152–62.
Iosifidis, P. (2002) 'Digital Convergence: Challenges for European Regulation', *Javnost/The Public* 9 (3) 27–47.
Iosifidis, P. (2005a) 'The Application of EC Competition Policy to the Media Industry', *International Journal of Media Management* 7 (3&4) 103–11.
Iosifidis, P. (2005b) 'Digital Switchover and the Role of BBC Services in Digital TV Take-up', *Convergence – The International Journal of Research into New Media Technologies* 11 (3) 57–74.
Iosifidis, P. (2006a) 'Digital Switchover in Europe' *Gazette – The International Journal for Communication Studies* 68 (3) 249–67.
Iosifidis, P. (2006b) 'The Role of Public Service Broadcasting in Achieving Digital Switchover' RIPE@2006 conference, Amsterdam and Hilversum, 16–18 November.
Iosifidis, P., J. Steemers and M. Wheeler (2005) *European Television Industries* (London: British Film Institute).
Ishikawa, S. (1996) *Quality Assessment in Television* (Luton: John Libbey Media).
IsICult (2004) (Instituto italiano per l'Industria Culturale)/Screen Digest Report *Observatory of Public Service Broadcasting in Europe* (May).
Jakubowicz, K. (2006) Keynote speech, RIPE@2006 conference, Amsterdam and Hilversum, 16–18 November.
James, A. (2005) 'Adieu? Non! Topper Hangs On – Tessier Hustles for New Term at Gaul's Powerful Pub-caster' *Variety* (19 January). Available at: http://www.variety.com/article/VR1117924658?categoryId=14&cs=1 (accessed May 2006).

Johnson, B. (2006) 'Britain Turns off – and Log's on', *Guardian*, 8 March. Available at http://business.guardian.co.uk/story/o,,1726126,00.html (accessed March 2007).
Jupiter Research (2004a) *Evolution of Media Use in Europe – Web Impacting Consumption*, (Jupiter Research Press Release, 2 December). Available at:http://www.theregister.co.uk/2004/12/02/europeans_ditch_tv (accessed January 2006).
Jupiter Research (2004b) *Europeans Ditch TV for PC* (Jupiter Research Press Release). Available athttp://www.theregister.co.uk/2004/12/02/europeans_ditch_tv/ (accessed February 2006).
Kagan World Media (1999) *Annual Report*.
Kathimerini (2005) 'Oi 5 Axones gia Isxyri ERT' (5 Axes for a Strong ERT) (Athens: 31 March).
Kean, J. (1991) *The Media and Democracy* (Cambridge: Polity Press).
Kevin, D. et al. (2004) *The Information of the Citizen in the EU: Obligations for the Media and the Institutions Concerning the Citizen's Right to be Fully and Objectively Informed*, Final Report prepared on behalf of the European Parliament (Dusseldorf: European Institute for the Media, 31 August).
Kirsch, T. (2004) *Television 2004 – International Key Facts*, IP Germany. Available at: http://www.ip-deutschland.de/ipdeutschland/download-data/TV2004-TV-Viewing.pdf (accessed June 2006).
KPMG (2003) *ERT's Strategic and Operational Plan 2003–08* (Athens: KPMG, June.
Kuhn, R. (2006) 'The Third Age of Public Television in France', paper submitted to PIRE@2006 conference, Amsterdam and Hilversum, 16–18 November.
Kuhn, R. and J. Stanyer (2001) 'Television and the State' eds. Scriven, M. and M. Lecomte *Television Broadcasting in Contemporary France and Britain* (London: Sage) 2–15.
Leiner, B. M. (2000) *A Brief History of the Internet*. Available at: http://www.isoc.org/internet-history/brief.html (accessed June 2006).
Leon, B. (2004) *Prime-time Programming in European Public Television: Information, Entertainment and Diversity*. GLOBAPLUR Project (Spain: University of Navarra).
Leon, B. (2006) University of Navarra, communication via e-mail (September).
Levy, D. (2006) Head of Public Affairs, BBC, Interview (London: 28 January).
L'Express, 11 March 2002.
Loebbecke, C. and R. G. Picard (2005) *The Impact of Regulatory Issues and Market Structure on the Digital Television Industry: A Comparison of the German and Swedish Markets* Working paper Series No. 2005-2 (Jonkoping, Sweden: Jonkoping International Business School).
Lovegrove, N. and L. Enriquez (2002) 'Promoting Investment and Quality'. *Television and Beyond: The Next Ten Years* (London: Independent Television Commission).
Lundberg, P. (2006) 'Scandinavia: Games Goose Nordic Ratings' *Variety*, 2 April. Available at: (accessed November).
McGonagle, M. (2005) 'Country Report – Ireland', *EU Commission Report on Co-regulation Measures in the Media Sector*. Available at http://co-reg.hans-bredow-institut.de and http://europa.eu.int/comm/avpolicy (accessed November 2006).

McKinsey & Company (1999) *Public Service Broadcasters Around the World* McKinsey Report for the BBC (London: January).
McKinsey & Company (2004) *Review of Public Service Broadcasting Around the World*, (London: September). Available at: http://www.ofcom.org.uk/consult/condocs/psb2/psb2/psbwp/wp3mck.pdf (accessed August 2006).
McLaughlin, C. (2005) Regulator ComReg, Interview (Dublin: 13 April).
McQuail, D. (1992) *Media Performance: Mass Communication and the Public Interest* (London: Sage).
McQuail, D. (1998) 'Commercialisation and Beyond' *Media Policy: Convergence, Concentration and Commerce*, eds D. McQuail and K. Sinue (London: Sage) 107–27.
Media 2007: Programme of Support for the European Audiovisual Sector. Available at http://europa.eu/scadplus/leg/en/lrb/l24224a.htm (accessed March 2007).
Médiamétric (2006) Année TV 2006.
Meijer, I. C. (2005) 'Impact or Content? – Ratings vs. Quality in Public Broadcasting', *European Journal of Communication*, 20 (1): 27–53.
MORI (2005) *Research on BBC New Services* (London: March). Available at: http://www.bbc.co.uk/thefuture/pdfs/bbc_licence_information3.pdf (accessed October 2006).
Mungiu-Pippidi, A. (1999) *State into Public: The Failed Reform of State TV in East Central Europe* (The Joan Shorenstein Centre on the Press, Politics and Public Policy, Working Paper Series). Available at: http://www.ksg.harvard.edu/presspol/Research_Publications/Papers/Working_Papers/2000_6.PDF (accessed December 2005).
Murdock, G. (2000) 'Digital Futures in the Age of Convergence' *Television Across Europe: A Comparative Introduction*, eds J. Wieten, G. Murdock and P. Dahlgren (London: Sage) 35–57.
Murphy, R. (2005) Managing Editor RTE e-publishing, Interview (Dublin: 13 April).
Murray, Ann-Marie (2006) 'Rationalisation of Public Service Broadcasting: Scheduling as a Tool of Management in RTE Television' Paper submitted to PIRE@2006 conference, Amsterdam and Hilversum, 16–8 November.
Nasopoulos, D. (2006) 'Terata Disekatommyrion stin ERT' (ERT's Multi-million Deals), *To VIMA*, 27 May.
Nicholls, D. (2004) 'Diabolical RTVE' *National, TV Radio, Barcelona Business* (1 June). Available at: http://www.spainmedia.com/index.php?p=31 (accessed August 2006).
Nissen, C. S. (2006) *Public Service Media in the Information Society*, Report prepared for the Council of Europe's Group of Specialists on Public Service Broadcasting in the Information Society (MC-S-PSB) (Media Division, Directorate General of Human Rights, Council of Europe, February). Available at: http://www.coe.int/t/e/human_rights/media/1_Intergovernmental_Co-operation/MC-S-PSB/H-Info(2006)003_en.pdf (accessed July 2006).
Nordic PSB Public Service broadcasting in the Nordic Countries (2004). Available at: http://www.dr.dk/omdr/pdf/NordiskPSB.pdf (accessed November 2006).

O'Connor, A. (2005) Special Advisor to the Director General RTE, Interview (Dublin: 13 April).
Odell, M. and A. Edgecliffe-Johnson (2005) 'Convergence: The Dirty Buzzword from the Nineties is Back with a Vengeance' *Financial Times* (11 November) 23.
O'Doherty, M. (2005) Manager of Publishing, RTE, Interview (Dublin: 13 April).
Ofcom (2004) *Public Consultation on Quality* (London: Ofcom, 21 April 2004). Available at: http://www.ofcom.org.uk/consult/condocs/psb/psb/volume2/quality (accessed September).
Ofcom (2005) *Review of Public Service Television Broadcasting: Phase 3 – Competition for Quality* (London: Ofcom, 8 February). Available at:http://www.ofcom.org.uk/consult/condocs/psb3/psb3.pdf (accessed October 2006).
Ofcom (2006) *The Communications Market* Interim Report (London: Ofcom, February). Available at:http://www.ofcom.org.uk/accessibility/rtfs/research/feb2006_report.rtf (accessed July 2006).
Oliver & Ohlbaum (2004) *An Assessment of the Market Impact of the BBC's Digital TV Services*, Report for the BBC's submission to the DCMS Review (London: Oliver & Ohlbaum Associates Ltd, March).
Opinion Leader Research (2006) *BBC Governors' Licence Fee Bid Forum – Findings from a One-day Citizens' Forum*, Prepared for BBC Governance Unit (March). Available at:http://www.bbcgovernors.co.uk/docs/reviews/olr_citizensforum.pdf (accessed October 2006).
Padovani, C. and M. Tracey (2003) 'Report on the Conditions of Public Service Broadcasting', *Television and New Media*, 4 (2) 131–53.
Panagiotou, P. (2000) 'To Programma tis Prooris Syntaxiodotisis tis ERT' (ERT's Early Retirement Programme) *To Ethnos tis Kyriakis* (Athens: 30 January).
Panhellenic Confederation of Trades Unions of ERT (POSP/ERT) (1997) Organotiki Anasigkrotisi tis ERT (ERT's Restructuring), (Athens: May).
Papathanassopoulos, S. (2002) *European Television in the Digital Age* (Oxford: Polity Press).
Papatheodorou, F. and D. Machin (2003) 'The Umbilical Cord That Was Never Cut – the Post-Dictatorial Intimacy Between the Political Elite and the Mass Media in Greece and Spain', *European Journal of Communication* 18 (1) 31–54.
Peacock Report (1986) *Report of the Committee on Financing the BBC*, Cmnd 9824 (London: July).
PWC (Price-Waterhouse-Coopers) (2004) *RTE Licence Fee Adjustment Review* (Dublin: PWC, 30 November. Available at: http://www.dcmnr.gov.ie/NR/rdonlyres/5A9E6C09-EB10-4DDA-B419-42AA0A9D43DF/0/041213RTEFOI Report.pdf (accessed October 2006).
Raboy, M. (1996) 'Public Service broadcasting in the context of Globalization', Introduction to M. Raboy, ed. *Public Broadcasting in the 21st Century* (Luton: John Libbey Media/University of Luton Press).
Radio and Television Act 1988, Number 20 of 1988. Available at: http://www.bci.ie/documents/88act.pdf (accessed November 2006).
Reding, V. (2004) EC Commissioner for Information Society and Media, Sport and Television: Ready to Face New Challenges? Speech (Monaco: 11 October).

Reding, V. (2005) EC Commissioner for Information Society and Media, 'Convergence is Here'! Speech, 4th Bienne Comdfays (Switzerland 31 October). Available at: http://www.followthemedia.com/mediarules/comdays311 02005.htm (accessed November 2005).

The Register (2006) *RTE Trials Mobile TV in Dublin* (12 June). Available at: http://www.theregister.co.uk/2006/06/12/bt_rte_movio (accessed November 2006).

RTÉ (Radio Telefis Eireann) (2002) *Application for Licence Fee Increase to the Minister for Communications, Marine and Natural Resources* (Dublin: RTE, November). Available at: http://www.rte.ie/about/2002finalapp.pdf (accessed November 2006).

RTÉ (Radio Telefis Eireann) (2004) *RTE's Commitment to Our Audience*. Available at: http://www.rte.ie/about/organisation/2004_commitments_english.pdf (accessed November 2006).

RTÉ (Radio Telefis Eireann) (2005) *RTE Annual Report*. Available at: http://www.rte.ie/about/ar2005/english/note1.html (accessed November 2006).

RTE (Radio Telefis Eireann) (2006) *Corporate Responsibility*. Available at: http://www.rte.ie/about/cr_report_english.pdf (accessed November 2006).

RTVE (2004) Annual Report. Available at: http://www.rtve.es/institucional/Documentos/Informe_RTVE2004.pdf (accessed October 2006)

Sanchez-Tabernero, A. (1999) Universidad de Navarra, Communication via e-mail (11 December).

Schwartz, P. (2005) 'Privatise Public Television', *The Spain Herald* (14 March). Available at: http://www.spainherald.com/403.html (accessed June 2006).

Screen Digest (1996) *Level of Advertising Revenue for Public and Private Channels in Europe* (April).

Skelly, B. (2006) 'TV Market Heats Up' *Irish Marketing and Advertising Journal* (6 June). Available at: http://www.adworld.ie/features/?guid=11a4a722-83bf-4ac5-bfec-36258a5fbf46 (accessed November 2006).

Starr, J. M. (2004) *An Alternative View of the Future of Public Television*, (Chicago: University of Chicago Cultural Policy Centre, 1 December). Available at: http://www.cipbonline.org/JerrysAlternateView.htm (accessed July 2006).

Stromqvist, D. (2005). Programme Policy and Scheduling, SVT, Interview (Stockholm: 3 May).

SVT Annual Reports 2002, 2005.

Television Business International, *TV in the World*.

Terzis, G. and M. Kontochristou (2004) 'Greek Media Landscape', *European Media Landscape* (December). Available at:http://www.ejc.nl/jr/emland/greece.html (accessed November 2006).

Timms, D. 'BBC Presses for £150 Licence Fee' *Media Guardian* (11 October 2005). Available at: http://media.guardian.co.uk/site/story/0,14173,1589563,00.html (accessed December 2005).

Tracey, M. (1998) *The Decline and Fall of Public Service Broadcasting* (Oxford: Oxford University Press).

Tsakiris, K. (2000) Head of Technical Services – ERT, Interview (Athens: 23 April).

Tsourvakas, G. (2004) 'Public Television Programming Strategy Before and After Competition: The Greek Case', *Journal of Media Economics*, 17 (3) 193–205.

Tunstall, J. (2003) 'The United Kingdom', *Euromedia Book* (London: Sage, 2003).

Variety (2006) *Local Giant Shapes Spanish Daily Life* 2 April.

Veljanovski, C. (1990) *The Media in Britain Today* (London: News International plc, 1990).

Wells, M. (2003) 'Digital TV at Turning Point as Converts Top 50%', *Guardian* (17 December).

Wieten, J., G. Murdock and P. Dahlgren (2000) *Television Across Europe* (London: Sage).

Winslow, G. (2005a) 'The Road to the New BBC', *World Screen* (April). Available at: http://www.worldscreen.com/featuresarchive.php?filename=0404bbc.htm (accessed November 2006).

Winslow, G. (2005b) 'The Pubcasters' *World Screen* (April 2005b). Available at: http://www.worldscreen.com/featurescurrent.php?filename=0405pub.htm (accessed July 2006).

World Screen (2006) *TV Europe*. Available at: http://www.worldscreen.com/europe.php (accessed August 2006).

Yankee Group (2004) *3G Forecasts in Europe*. Available at: https://333.3gnewsroom.com/3g_news/mar_04/news_4268.shtml (accessed May 2005).

Zenith Media (1999) *Television in Europe* (9 September).

Zenith/Optimedia (2005) 'TV Ad Spending Set to Peak in 2006' available at: http://money.cnn.com/2005/04/18/news/fortune500/tv_advertising (accessed November 2005).

Index

accountability, 183
advertising
  expenditure, 4
  growth, 60
  revenues, 60–1, 66–7
advertising companies, 48
American Online (AOL), 38, 39
Amsterdam Treaty, Protocol, 43, 57, 181
analogue television, 3
analogue terrestrial switch-off, 30, 45
  European Commission communications, 30
'Anglo Saxon' model of broadcasting, 59
anti-trust powers, 40
Application Program Interface (API), 32
Arpanet, 23–4
Association of Public Television Stations, USA, 6
Asymmetrical Digital Subscriber Lines, 24
A.T. Kearney, 77
audience shares
  Britain, 53, 89
  France, 109
  Greece, 166–7
  Ireland, 140
  Spain, 124–5
  Sweden, 156, 157
audiovisual industry
  competitiveness, 4
  Europe, 3
  USA, 35

Bagdikian, B., 35
BARB (Broadcasters' Audience Research Board), 53
Barnett, S., 103
Barwise, P., 103

BBC, 88
  allocation of cost of services, 95
  BBC One, 83, 90
  BBC One and BBC Two, hours of output, 91
  BBC Two, 83, 90
  bias, 93
  children's programmes, 94–5
  commercial activities, 98–100
  competition, 101–2
  coverage of Falklands war, 8
  coverage of Iraq war, 93, 102
  criticism of new services, 95–6
  digital technology, 94–5, 95–6
  governance reform, 93–4
  interactive television, 72
  internal restructuring, 78–9
  investment in new media, 94–5
  news coverage, 91–2
  new services and the licence fee, 96–8
  and Ofcom, 87
  portfolio of businesses, 76
  'Producer Choice', 78, 100
  prospects, 101–4
  public funding, 103
  public support for, 103
  restructuring, 100–1
  revenues, 88
  Royal Charter, 90, 96, 101
  take up of digital services, 72–3
  weaknesses in programming, 92–3
  websites, 94
  'window of creative competition' (WOCC), 101
BBC and Human Capital, 104
BBCi, 94
BBC Trust, 183
BBC Ventures Group, 99
BBC World, 99
BBC Worldwide, 99, 100

Belgium, digital television adoption, 28
Berners-Lee, Tim, 24
Bjorkman, P., 155, 157, 158
BMRB Omnibus Survey, 104
Born, G., 69, 72
Brands, K., 185n3
Britain, 7
  audience shares, 89
  Broadcasting Act, 78
  cable channels, 48–9, 52, 84
  Channel Five, 48
  Channel Four, 20–1, 48, 49, 83
  Communications Act, 10–11, 84, 85–7
  content regulation, 86
  digital television, 28, 49
  Five, 83
  funding model, 57
  general characteristics of the television market, 83–5
  impact of new channels on Audience share, 53
  Internet use, 26
  ITV1, 48
  ITV, 83, 189n5
  ITV digital, 30, 84
  licence fee, 58, 88, 96–8, 102
  media ownership, 86
  More4, 85
  multi-channel development, 89–90
  multi-channel penetration, 52
  plurality, 87
  programming, 90–3
  programming genres of public channels, 65
  public service obligation, 48, 84
  public television, 88–9
    funding, 88
  regulatory framework, 85–7
  satellite, 52, 84
  satellite companies, merger, 31
  statistics, 83
  television liberalisation, 52
  television viewing time, 54
  'universal minimum standards', 86
  Welsh Fourth Channel S4C, 83–4
  see also BBC
broadband, 25–6
BSkyB, 39, 45, 49, 84

cable and satellite transmission systems, 9, 22–3
  and proliferation of channels, 23
cable television
  Britain, 48–9, 52, 84
  in Europe, 23
  France, 52, 107
  Greece, 52, 164
  Spain, 52, 121, 122
Carnegie Commission, 5
Channel Four, 48
Chazal, P., 114
citizens, and the state, 41, 187n7
CLT-UFA, 37
CMT, 121
commercial revenues, 60–1
  of public television companies, 179
Communication Act, UK, 10–11, 84, 85–7
competition, 6–9, 34, 179, 184
  effects on public channels, 51–4
  and programming strategies, 12–13
  in public television, 47–54
  unfair, 43
competition policy, 39–40
concentrated ownership, 36
consumer choice, 34–5
consumer-citizens, 48
consumer habits, 25–6
content, 179
  Ireland, 143–4
content regulation, 86
  France, 108
Coppens, T., 15
Corcoran, F., 74, 148
Corporation for Public Broadcasting, USA, 6
Council of Europe, 7, 16, 20, 59, 62

Index 203

Council of the European Union, 43, 57
'country of origin principle', 4
Cowie, C., 100
Cox, B., 93, 97
CSA (Conseil Superieure d'Audiovisuel), 59
cultural differentiation, 41

Dahlgren, P., 41, 153, 161, 180
data collection techniques, 21
Dataxis, 3, 28
DCMNR (Department of Communication, Marine and Natural Resources), 139
DCMS (Department of Culture, Media and Sport), 93, 94, 99, 101
De Bens, E., 63, 185n3
decoders, 32
De Espana, R., 128
Deloitte & Touche, 26
De Pablos, E., 128, 129
deregulation, 10
  France, 49
  and liberalisation, 33–6
  and sources of information, 43
Derieux, E., 108
de Smaele, H., 63
Digital Strategy Group, European Broadcasting Union, 32
digital technologies, 14
  BBC, 94–5
digital television, 27–8, 182
  regulation of services, 31–3
digital television adoption, 28–30
  Britain, 28, 49
  Europe, 3
digital television consortia, strategic alliances, 30–1
digital terrestrial television, 29
  France, 73–4, 107, 115–16
  Greece, 28, 175–6
  household adoption in Europe, 29
  Spain, 28, 121, 129–30
  Sweden, 28, 153, 158, 161–2

Digital Video Broadcasting Project, 32, 70
diversity, 184
DSG (Design Strategy Group), 62, 70
Duignan, C., 142

EAO (European Audiovisual Observatory), 3, 4, 10
economies of scope, 36
The Economist, 96, 101
Edgecliffe-Johnson, A., 25
EIAA (European Interactive Advertising Association) European Media Consumption Study II, 25, 55
electronic communications, regulatory framework, 40–1
Electronic Programme Guides (EPGs), 32–3
El Pais, 128
EMI, 38
Enders Analysis, 116
Enriquez, L., 108
EPC, 60, 71
Ernst & Young, 169
EUMAP (EU Monitoring and Advocacy Program), 70, 106, 108, 110, 112, 113, 117, 119
Europe
  audiovisual market, 3
  cable in, 23
  digital television adoption, 28–30
  Internet use, 24
  public television model, 6–7
European Commission competition authorities, 43
European Publishers Council, 59, 60, 181
European Union
  competition policy framework, 39
  support programmes for audiovisual production, 4
external pluralism, 35

feature films, 31
Feeney, P., 146

204   Index

Finland, digital television adoption, 28
Flextech, 75
Fontaine, G., 114, 115
France
  advertising, 110-11, 117
  annual output of national
    terrestrial TV channels, 111,
    112
  Arte, 111, 112
  audience shares, 109
  broadcast quotas, 108
  cable television, 52, 107
  Canal Plus, 106
  Canal Satellite, 106
  commercial state television, 106
  content regulation, 108
  cultural programming, 112-13
  deregulation, 49
  digital consortia, 75
  digital television adoption, 28
  digital terrestrial television, 73-4,
    107, 115-16
  France 2, 113
  France 5, 69, 69-70
  reduction of operating costs,
    77-8
  France Télévisions, 73-4, 77-8,
    109, 111
  funding, 110
  prospects, 116-19
  public support for, 119
  restructuring, 118
  funding model, 57
  general characteristics of the
    television market, 105-7
  government control of television,
    49, 117
  High Council of Broadcasting
    (CSA), 59, 106
  interactive services, 74
  Lagardere media, 12
  Law 86-1067 on Freedom of
    Communication, 107
  Law on Audiovisual
    Communication (Fillioud
    law), 49
  Law on Electronic
    Communications, 107
  Law on Freedom of
    Communication, 77, 109
  licence fee, 58, 110, 111, 116-17,
    118
  M6, 106, 107
  multi-channel penetration, 52
  news, 113
  Objectives and Means contracts,
    110
  Office of Fair Trading (DGCCRF),
    116
  ownership regulation, 108
  programming genres of public
    channels, 65
  programming policy, 111-13
  protection of culture and
    language, 108-9
  public television, 109-10
    funding, 110-11
  regulatory framework, 107-9
  satellite television, 52, 74, 107, 108
  statistics, 105
  talk shows, 113
  television liberalisation, 52
  television and politics, 105-6
  television viewing time, 54
  TF-1, 106
  thematic channels, 73, 105,
    114-15
Franco-German Treaty, 70
free market, and programme
  diversity, 36
Freeview, 30, 84, 186n1
free viewing, 181
funding methods, 13-14
funding model, 56-8, 179
  commercial revenue, 60-1
  mixed funding, 57
  state funding, 61-2
  see also licence fee

Galvin, P., 145
Garnham, N., 35, 36
General Electric, 38

general interest channels, 42
Germany, 68-9
  Bertelsmann, 12
  digital television adoption, 28
  Gilligan affair, 93
  Giudicelli, L., 108
  globalisation, and media concentration, 36-9
  GLOBAPLUR, 63
Greece, 7, 17
  advertising expenditure, 168
  ANT1, 164
  audience shares, 166-7
  cable television, 52, 164
  competition, 172
  digital initiatives, 175-6
  digital television adoption, 28
  ERT (Elliniki Radiofonia Tileorasi), 51, 67-8, 163, 188$n1$
    early retirement programme, 170-1
    five year strategic management plan, 171-2
    football broadcasting rights, 174-5
    income, 167-8
    modernisation, 168-70
    political influence, 177
    programming objectives, 177
    prospects, 176-7
  ET-1, 165
  ET-3, 165
  funding model, 57
  general characteristics of the television market, 163-5
  Hellenic Broadcasting Corporation, 165
  Law 170/1987, 165
  Law 1866/1989, 165
  Law 2173, 165
  Law 2328, 165, 166
  Law 2644, 165
  Law 2747, 171
  liberalisation, 34, 164, 166
  licence fee, 58
  media ownership rules, 166
  MEGA, 164
  Ministry of the Press and the Mass media, 165
  Multichoice Hellas, 165
  National Council of Radio and Television, 165
  NET, 68, 165
  private channels, 51, 164, 165
  programming convergence, 180
  programming genres of public channels, 65
  programming mix by genre, 173-4
  programming strategy, 172-4
  public television, 164, 166-8
  regulation, 164
  regulatory framework, 165-6
  restructuring efforts, 168-70
  satellite and multi-channel penetration, 52, 164
  statistics, 163
  television liberalisation, 52
  television viewing time, 54
  top ten television programmes, 174

Habermas, J., 35
Heilemann, J., 96, 103
Hopewell, J., 129
Hoynes, W., 6
Human Capital Study, 92
Humphreys, P., 7
Hunt, J., 139, 145, 146, 148, 149, 150

IDATE, 23
independence, of public channels, 183
individualism, 41
industry consolidation, 'light touch', 11
information society, 134
infrastructure, 82
innovation, 180
Integrated Services Digital Networks, 24
Interactive Media Player, 94
interactive services, France, 74

interactive television, 27
  BBC, 72
interactive web sites, 17
internal pluralism, 35
Internet, 23–4, 37, 70–1
  negative impact on TV
    consumption, 25–6
  and television viewing, 55–6
Internet World Stats, 24
investment in new technologies,
  14–15
Iosifidis, P., 3, 11, 30, 40, 72, 181
Iosifidis, P. *et al.*, 7, 11, 25, 28, 87,
  106, 108, 130, 153, 165
Iraq war, BBC coverage, 93, 102
Ireland
  audience shares, 140
  British TV channels, 137–8
  Broadcasting Act, 138
  Broadcasting Authority Act, 138
  Broadcasting Commission of
    Ireland, 138
  Broadcasting (Funding) Act, 138
  cable television, 52, 96, 137
  CanWest, 138
  Commission for Communications
    Regulation, 138
  Communications Act, 138
  competition, 50, 136–7, 150
  digital television, 28, 137, 148–9
  funding model, 57
  general characteristics of the TV
    market, 136–8
  Independent Radio and
    Television Commission
    (IRTC), 138
  licence fee, 58, 141–2, 150
  multimedia services, 149
  private television channels, 137
  programming genres of public
    channels, 65
  programming policy, 142–5
  Public Service Broadcasting
    Charter, 139
  public television, 139–40
  Radio and Television Act, 138

Radio Telifís Éireann (RTE), 50, 74,
  136, 137, 138, 139
  accountability, 183
  commercial revenues, 142
  content commitment, 143–4
  funding, 141–2
  hours of content by genre, 144
  independent production, 145
  Integrated Business divisions,
    145, 146–7
  organisational development,
    145–7
  prospects, 149–51
  RTE Two, 144
  Transformation Plan, 145
regulatory framework, 138–9
satellite and multi-channels, 52,
  96, 137
statistics, 136
television liberalisation, 52
television viewing time, 54
thematic channels, 149
top ten television programmes, 143
Ishikawa, S., 36, 185*n*3
IsICult, 110, 111, 125
IsICult/*Screen Digest* Report, 65, 69
Italy, 68–9
  digital television adoption, 28
  Fininvest, 12
  liberalisation, 34
  programming genres of public
    channels, 65

Jakubowicz, K., 179, 180
James, A., 110
joint ventures, 75
Jupiter Research, 25, 26, 55

Kathimerini, 176
Kirsch, T., 54
Kontochristou, M., 166
KPMG, 171, 172
Kuhn, R., 49, 105

language and culture, 82
'Latin' model of broadcasting, 59

Leiner, B.M., 24
Leon, B., 63, 93, 112, 127, 129, 133, 160, 161
Levy, D., 79, 101
liberalisation
  and deregulation, 33–6
  and mergers and acquisitions, 44
Liberty Media, 12
licence fee, 13, 14, 58–60, 76, 179
  Britain, 88, 96–8, 102, 103
  drawbacks, 59
  France, 110
  Greece, 58
  Ireland, 58, 141–2, 150
  Sweden, 8
'light touch', in industry consolidation, 11, 87
Locksley, G., 36
Loebbecke, C., 154
Lovegrove, N., 108
Lundberg, P., 159
Luxembourg, SBS Broadcasting, 12

McGonagle, M., 138, 139
McKinsey & Company, 6, 56, 58, 63, 64, 66, 161
McQuail, D., 63, 185$n3$
management-oriented approach, 16
market concentration, 11–12
market forces, 36
market mechanisms, 33–4
market size, 81–2
mass appeal, 62
Media 2007, 4
media, role in society, 5
media concentration
  and globalisation, 36–9
  and regulation, 39–41
Media II, 4
media ownership, Britain, 86
Media Plus, 4, 185$n1$
media value chain, 11–12
Meijer, I.C., 64, 187$n7$
Merger Regulation (Council Regulation (EEC) No. 4064/89), 40

mergers and acquisitions, 37–40, 187$n10$
  and liberalisation, 44
minority programmes, 61, 69–70
Mitterrand, Francois, 49
mobile phones, 26–7
mobile platforms, 85
monopolies, 7, 32
MORI, 104
multi-channel development, Britain, 89–90
'multi-channel flow', 70
multi-channel technologies, 41–2
Multimedia Home Platform (MHP), 32
multimedia services, Ireland, 149
Multipoint Microwave Distribution System (MMDS), 137
Murdoch, Rupert, 39, 49
Murdock, G., 186$n5$
Murphy, R., 148, 149
Murray, A.-M., 183

national strategies, public television, 16–17
NBC-Universal, 12
Near Video on Demand (NVOD), 28
neo-liberal ideology, 34
Netherlands, 7
  digital television adoption, 28, 30
News Corporation, 12, 31
new technologies, investment in, 14–15
'niche' channels, 17, 42, 180
Nicholls, D., 126, 127, 132, 134
Nissen, C.S., 5, 10, 12, 41

O'Connor, A., 139, 145, 148, 149, 150
Odell, M., 25
O'Doherty, M., 146
Ofcom, 54, 84, 86, 93
  and the BBC, 87
Oliver & Ohlbaum, 92
Olympic Games, 46
online services, 17

Opinion Leader Research, 104
organisational reform, public television, 15–16
organisational restructuring, public television, 76

Padovani, C., 13, 96
Papathanassopoulos, S., 28
partnerships, 75
pay-TV, 27, 28, 29–30
Peacock Report, 97
Picard, R.G., 154
pluralisation, 180
plurality, Britain, 87
'political clientalism', 7
political climate, 81
PricewaterhouseCoopers, 142, 146, 150–1
private television channels, 48
production companies, 48
production costs, 36
programme diversity, and the free market, 36
programming
  Britain, 90–3
  of broadcasters that depend on advertising revenues, 66–7
  and dependence on commercial revenues, 63–4
programming convergence, 63–4, 180
programming policy
  France, 111–13
  Ireland, 142–5
programming strategy, 62
  Greece, 172–4
  Spain, 126–8
  Sweden, 158–60
public, use of term, 185n2
Public Broadcasting Service, USA, 6
public channels
  cost of digitalising, 44
  effects of competition, 51–4
  independence, 183
public interest, 12, 186n6
public service
content, 180–1
objectives, 56
obligations, Britain, 84, 102
public sphere, 35
public television
  accountability of broadcasters, 183
  Britain, 88–9
  commercial revenues, 179
  competition in, 8–9, 47–54
  consequences of social changes, 42–6
  European model, 6–7
  France, 109–10
  funding and structure in Europe, 7–8
  Greece, 166–8
  investment in new technologies, 14–15, 70
  Ireland, 139–40
  mission, 8
  national strategies, 16–17
  organisational reform, 15–16
  organisational restructuring, 76
  political and economic developments, 9
  programming, of broadcasters that depend on advertising revenues, 66–7
  publicly funded broadcasters' output, 64–5
  regulatory changes, 10–11
  replication of commercial services, 180
  socio-cultural shifts, 10
  Spain, 124–6
  and strategic alliances, 74–6
  Sweden, 155–8
  technological changes, 9–10
  US model, 5–6

quality, 8
definition of, 185n3

Raboy, M., 179
Reding, V., 3, 27
The Register, 149

regulation, 9
  of digital television, 31–3
  and media concentration, 39–41
Regulation on the Control of
  Concentrations between
  Undertakings, Council of the
  European Economic
  Community, 49
regulations, abolition of, 33
regulatory changes, public
  television, 10–11
regulatory climate, 81
regulatory framework
  Britain, 85–7
  for electronic communications,
    40–1
  France, 107–9
  Greece, 165–6
  Ireland, 138–9
  Spain, 122–3
  Sweden, 154
RLT Group S.A., 37

Saeys, F., 15
Sanchez-Tabernero, A., 124
satellite television
  adoption, 53
  Britain, 84
  France, 52, 74, 107, 108
Schwartz, P., 131
'simulcasting', 44
Skelly, B., 150
Sky Italia, 39
social change, 41–2, 180
  consequences for public
    television, 42–6
socio-cultural shifts, public
  television, 10
Spain, 7
  advertising, 124
  Antena 3, 124
  audience shares, 124–5
  audiovisual market regulation,
    122–3
  cable industry regulation, 122
  cable television, 52, 121

competition, 49
Council for the Reform of the
  Communication Media,
  report, 123
Department of Development and
  Thematic channels, 129
digital initiatives, 129–30, 134
digital satellite consortia, 125
digital terrestrial television, 28,
  121, 129–30
draft legislation on broadcasting,
  131–2
Federation of Autonomous Radio
  and Television (FORTA), 124
'Frankism', 120
funding model, 57
funding of public television,
  49–50
general characteristics of the TV
  market, 120–1
Marco plan, 130, 133
merger of satellite companies, 31
news coverage, 126–7
private channels, 49, 121
Private Television Act 10/1988,
  122
programming convergence, 180
programming genres of public
  channels, 65
programming quality, 127–8
programming strategy, 126–9,
  133–4
pubic channels, share of
  transmissions by genre, 127
public television, 124–6
  funding, 125–6
  regulation, 123
Radio Television Council of
  Catalonia, 122
regulatory framework, 122–3
restructuring attempts, 130–3
revenues for free-to-air TV, 126
satellite and multi-channel
  penetration, 52, 121
state funding, 61–2
statistics, 120

Spain – *continued*
  Tele 5, 124
  Telecommunication Committee of CMT, 122
  Television Espanola (TVE), 68, 121, 124, 125–6
    funding, 130–1, 133
    prospects for, 133–5
  television liberalisation, 52
  television viewing time, 54
  TVE Tematica, 129
spectrum scarcity, 42
sport, 27, 31–2
  cost of broadcast rights, 45–6
Stanyer, J., 49, 105
Starr, J.M., 5
state, relationship with the citizen, 41
state funding, 61–2
'state paternalism', 7
strategic alliances, 40, 74–6
  digital television consortia, 30–1
  and public television, 74–6
Stromqvist, D., 157, 158, 159, 160, 161
Sweden, 7
  advertising, 153
  audience shares, 156, 157
  Bonnier group, 154
  Broadcasting Commission, 154
  cable and satellite, 50, 52, 153, 160–1
  commercial broadcasting, 153
  competition, 50
  Council for Pluralism in the Media, 154
  digital switchover, 153, 158, 161–2
  digital television adoption, 28
  Fundamental Law on Freedom of Expression, 154
  funding model, 57, 66
  general characteristics of the television market, 152–3
  Kanal 1 (STV1), 156
  Kanal 5, 152, 153
  licence fee, 58
  multi-channel penetration, 52
  programming genres of public channels, 65
  programming strategy, 158–60
  public support, 161
  public television, 155–8
    funding, 155–6
    new services, 158
    reorganisation, 156–8
  Radio and Television Act, 154
  regulatory framework, 154
  SR(public radio), 155
  statistics, 152
  Sveriges Television (SVT), 66, 152
    charter, 154
    income, 155–6
    programming genres, 160
    prospects, 160–2
    regulation, 154
    staff reductions, 157–8
  television liberalisation, 52
  television viewing time, 54
  TV3, 152, 153
  TV4, 153
  UR (educational broadcasting company), 155

technological convergence, 25
television channels, number, 9–10
television organisations, revenue, 3–4
television viewing time, 54
'Television Without Frontiers' (TWF) Directive (89/552/EEC), 4–5, 46
Terzis, G., 166
thematic channels, 42, 44, 71
  digital, 55
  France, 73, 105, 115
  Ireland, 149
Third Generation (3G) mobile telephony, 26–7, 42, 85
Thompson, Mark, 101
time-shift technologies, 41–2
Time Warner, 38, 39
Timms, D., 97
Tracey, M., 13, 96

trans-national arena, 23
Transparency directive (EC), 71
Tsakiris, K., 175
Tsouvakas, G., 172
Tunstall, J., 53

universality of content, 62
'universal minimum standards', 86
USA
    Association of Public Television Stations, 6
    audiovisual sector, 35
    commercial broadcasting industry, 6
    Public Broadcasting Service, 6
    public television model, 5–6

vertical integration, 39
video on demand (VOD), 27
viewing shifts, 179
viewing time, 54
Vivendi, 38, 189$n1$
Vivendi Universal, 106

Wells, M., 98
'window of creative competition' (WOCC), 101
Winslow, G., 103, 132
World Wide Web, 24

Yankee Group, 27

Zenith/Optimedia, 4

The manufacturer's authorised representative in the EU is Springer Nature Customer Service Centre GmbH, Europaplatz 3, 69115 Heidelberg, Germany. If you have any concerns regarding our products, please contact ProductSafety@springernature.com

Printed and bound by CPI Group (UK) Ltd, Croydon, CR0 4YY

23/03/2026

02076459-0014